rockschool®

Hot Rock
Guitar Grade 4

8 classic rock tracks specially edited for Grade 4, plus full transcriptions and backing tracks on CD

Harlequin House, Ground Floor, 7 High Street, Teddington, Middlesex TW11 8EE
www.rockschool.co.uk

Acknowledgements

Rockschool would like to thank all the people who worked on this book. We would particularly like to thank our colleagues at Music Sales Ltd who granted us licences to print the music and who did such a great job on the audio.

Published by:	Rockschool Ltd. © Rockschool Ltd 2013 – *www.rockschool.co.uk* under license from Music Sales Ltd
Compiled and edited by:	James Uings, Stephen Lawson, Simon Pitt, Simon Troup and Jeremy Ward
Full transcriptions provided by:	Music Sales Ltd
Music engraving:	Simon and Jennie Troup – *www.digitalmusicart.com*
Cover design:	Philip Millard – *www.philipmillarddesign.com*
Layout and internal design:	Simon Troup – *www.digitalmusicart.com*
Cover photography:	© Chad Batka/Corbis – *www.corbis.com*
Printed in the UK:	Caligraving Ltd, Brunel Way, Thetford, Norfolk, IP24 1HP
CD manufacturing:	Brandedmedia – *www.brandedmedia.co.uk*
Exclusive distributors:	Music Sales Ltd, Newmarket Road, Bury St Edmunds, Suffolk, IP33 3YB – *www.musicroom.com*
Audio Producer:	Tom Farncombe, Music Sales Ltd *(except 'Ice 9' and 'Edge Of Darkness')*
Audio Engineer:	Jonas Persson, Music Sales Ltd *(except 'Ice 9' and 'Edge Of Darkness')*
Mixing:	Jonas Persson, Music Sales Ltd *(except 'Ice 9' and 'Edge Of Darkness')*
Mixing:	Duncan Jordan *('Ice 9' and 'Edge Of Darkness' and all exam versions)*
Mastering:	Duncan Jordan
Musicians:	Arthur Dick *(guitar on all tracks except 'Ice 9' and 'Edge Of Darkness')*
	Steve Allsworth *(guitar and bass on 'Ice 9' and 'Edge Of Darkness')*
	Charlie Griffiths *(guitar on all exam versions)*
	Paul Townsend *(bass on 'Don't Look Back In Anger', 'The Boys Are Back In Town', 'For Whom The Bell Tolls' and 'Iron Man')*
	Tom Farncombe *(bass on 'Whole Lotta Rosie' and 'Before I Fall To Pieces')*
	Noam Lederman *(drums on all tracks except 'Ice 9' and 'Edge Of Darkness')*
	Jason Bowld *(drums on 'Ice 9' and 'Edge Of Darkness')*
Legal information:	*Rockschool, the Rockschool logo and all other Rockschool product or service names are trademarks of Rockschool Ltd*

Table of Contents

Introductions, Information & Appendices

Page

- 4   Guitar Notation Explained
- 5   Welcome to Hot Rock Guitar Grade 4
- 6   Introduction To Tone

Sections

Page		CD	Tracks
	Exam Versions		
9	Razorlight – 'Before I Fall To Pieces'	CD 1	1–2
15	Thin Lizzy – 'The Boys Are Back In Town'	CD 1	3–4
21	Oasis – 'Don't Look Back In Anger'	CD 1	5–6
25	Eric Clapton – 'Edge Of Darkness'	CD 1	7–8
29	Metallica – 'For Whom The Bell Tolls'	CD 1	9–10
33	Joe Satriani – 'Ice 9'	CD 1	11–12
39	Black Sabbath – 'Iron Man'	CD 1	13–14
45	AC/DC – 'Whole Lotta Rosie'	CD 1	15–16
	Full Transcriptions		
52	Razorlight – 'Before I Fall To Pieces'	CD 2	1–2
60	Thin Lizzy – 'The Boys Are Back In Town'	CD 2	3–4
74	Oasis – 'Don't Look Back In Anger'	CD 2	5–6
84	Eric Clapton – 'Edge Of Darkness'	CD 2	7–8
90	Metallica – 'For Whom The Bell Tolls'	CD 2	9–10
98	Joe Satriani – 'Ice 9'	CD 2	11–12
106	Black Sabbath – 'Iron Man'	CD 2	13–14
114	AC/DC – 'Whole Lotta Rosie'	CD 2	15–16

Guitar Notation Explained

THE MUSICAL STAVE shows pitches and rhythms and is divided by lines into bars. Pitches are named after the first seven letters of the alphabet.

TABLATURE graphically represents the guitar fingerboard. Each horizontal line represents a string and each number represents a fret.

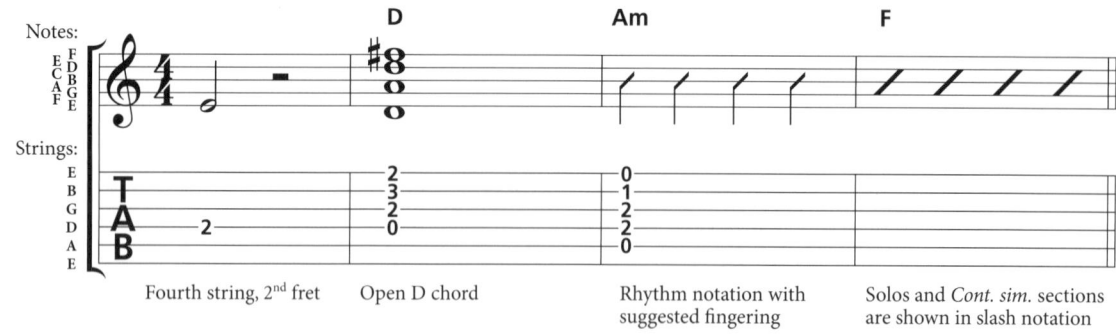

Fourth string, 2nd fret • Open D chord • Rhythm notation with suggested fingering • Solos and *Cont. sim.* sections are shown in slash notation

Definitions For Special Guitar Notation

HAMMER-ON: Pick the lower note, then sound the higher note by fretting it without picking.

PULL-OFF: Pick the higher note then sound the lower note by lifting the finger without picking.

SLIDE: Pick the first note and slide to the next. If the line connects (as below) the second note is *not* repicked.

GLISSANDO: Slide off of a note at the end of its rhythmic value. The note that follows *is* repicked.

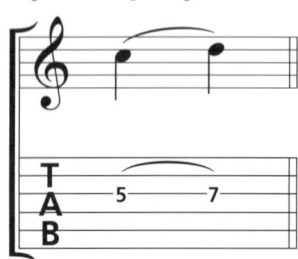  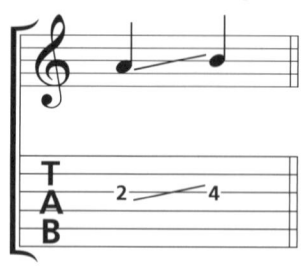 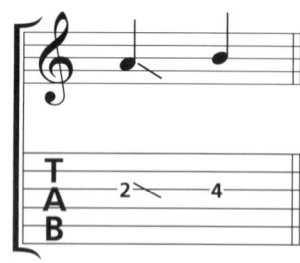

STRING BENDS: Pick the first note then bend (or release the bend) to the pitch indicated in brackets.

VIBRATO: Vibrate the note by bending and releasing the string smoothly and continuously.

TRILL: Rapidly alternate between the two bracketed notes by hammering on and pulling off.

NATURAL HARMONICS: Lightly touch the string above the indicated fret then pick to sound a harmonic.

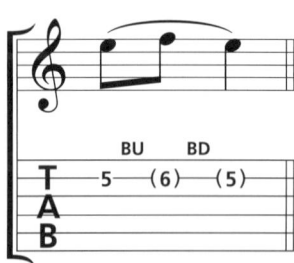 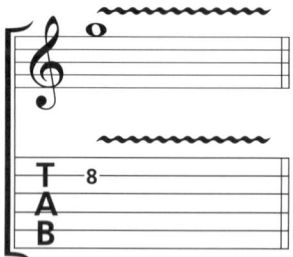  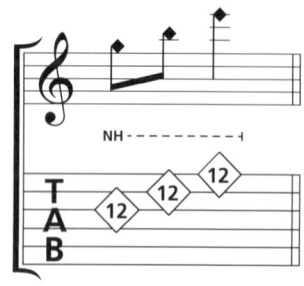

PINCHED HARMONICS: Bring the thumb of the picking hand into contact with the string immediately after the pick.

PICK-HAND TAP: Strike the indicated note with a finger from the picking hand. Usually followed by a pull-off.

FRET-HAND TAP: As pick-hand tap, but use fretting hand. Usually followed by a pull-off or hammer-on.

QUARTER-TONE BEND: Pick the note indicated and bend the string up by a quarter tone.

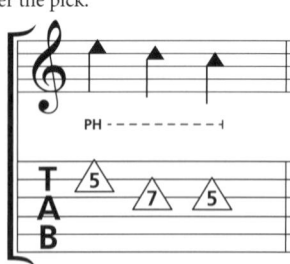 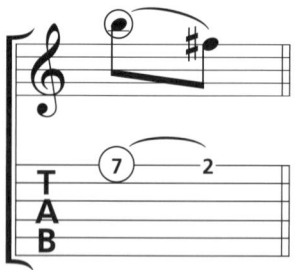 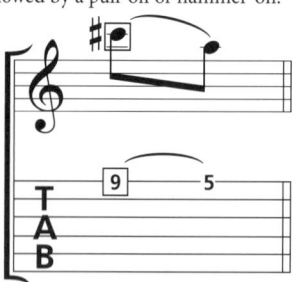 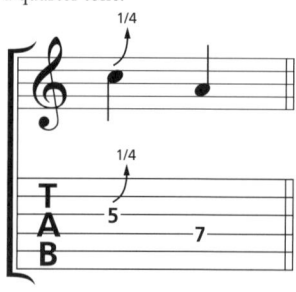

PRE-BENDS: Before picking the note, bend the string from the fret indicated between the staves, to the equivalent pitch indicated in brackets in the TAB.

WHAMMY BAR BEND: Use the whammy bar to bend notes to the pitches indicated in brackets in the TAB.

D.%. al Coda

D.C. al Fine

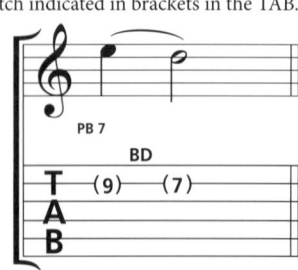 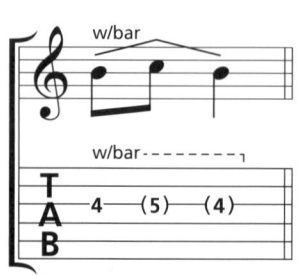

- Go back to the sign (%), then play until the bar marked **To Coda** ✚ then skip to the section marked ✚ **Coda**.

- Go back to the beginning of the song and play until the bar marked **Fine** (end).

- Repeat the bars between the repeat signs.

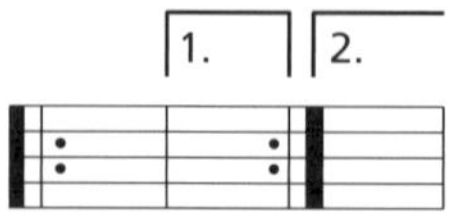

- When a repeated section has different endings, play the first ending only the first time and the second ending only the second time.

Welcome to Hot Rock Guitar Grade 4

Welcome to Hot Rock Grade 4 for Guitar. This book of classic and contemporary rock tracks has been compiled to give you a resource to help you develop your guitar skills and performance chops.

The songs in their edited forms can be used as Free Choice Pieces in the Rockschool Guitar Grade 4 exam. Alternatively, you can use either the edited or the full versions in the performance units in public exams such as GCSEs or A Levels. You can, of course, enjoy playing the tracks for their own sake.

Hot Rock Guitar Grade 4 contains eight classic songs that cover a wide range of styles and artists of the last 40 years. It is divided into two sections. The first section is made up of eight chapters. Each chapter is based on a version of a well-known track that has been specially edited to make it Grade 4 standard. The full transcription of each song is printed in the second half of the book.

Accompanying the book are two CDs of specially recorded backing tracks featuring all live instruments. The first CD contains performances of the edited pieces along with a backing track.

The second CD contains performances of the fully transcribed pieces, along with backing tracks for you to practise along to. Both CDs have count-ins on the backing tracks and the full mixes.

A word about musical notation: we refer throughout the book to quarter notes, eighth notes, 16th notes etc rather than crotchets, quavers and semiquavers.

We hope that you enjoy playing these pieces. You can find further details about Rockschool's guitar and other instrumental syllabuses by visiting our website at *www.rockschool.co.uk*.

Introduction To Tone

A large part of an effective guitar performance is selecting the right tone. The electric guitar's sound is subject to a wide range of variables. This guide outlines the basic controls present on most amplifiers as well as the common variations between models. There is also a basic overview of pickups and the effect their location on the guitar has on the guitar's tone. Finally, it covers the differences between the distortion types – crucial to getting your basic sound right.

At Grade 4 the tone may change within the course of a piece. You should aim to use a tone that is stylistically appropriate and you may bring your own equipment to the exam room for this purpose. There is a tone guide at the start of each Walkthrough to help you.

Basic amplifier controls
Most amplifiers come with a standard set of controls that are the same as, or very similar to, the diagram below. It's important to understand what each control is and the effect it has on your guitar's tone.

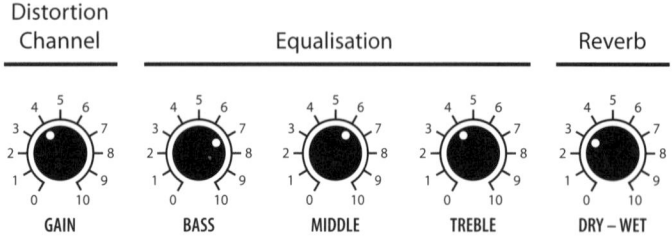

- **Channel (Clean/Distortion)**
  Most amplifiers have two channels, which can be selected by either a switch on the amp or a footswitch. One channel is usually clean while the other can be driven harder to create a distorted (or 'dirty') tone. If your amp doesn't have two channels, read 'Variations of basic controls' below to see how to get clean and dirty tones from a single-channel amp.

- **Gain**
  In simple terms the gain determines how hard you drive the amp. This governs how distorted the dirty (also called 'drive', 'overdrive' or 'distortion') channel is and acts as a second volume control on the clean channel (though a high gain setting will distort even the clean channel).

- **Bass**
  This adjusts the lowest frequencies. Boost it to add warmth and reduce or cut it if your sound is muddy or woolly.

- **Middle**
  This is the most important equalisation (often shortened to just 'EQ') control. Most of the guitar's tonal character is found in the midrange, so adjusting this control has a lot of impact on your tone. Boosting it with a dirty sound will give a more classic rock sound, while cutting it will produce a more metal tone.

- **Treble**
  This adjusts the high frequencies. Boost it to add brightness and cut it if the sound is too harsh or brittle.

- **Reverb**
  Short for 'reverberation'. This artificially recreates the ambience of your guitar in a large room, usually a hall. This dial controls the balance between the dry sound (without reverb) and wet sound (with reverb).

Variations of basic controls
The diagram above shows the most common amp controls. There are many variations of this basic setup, which can be confusing. The following is a breakdown of some of the other amp controls you may encounter.

- **Presence control**
  Sometimes this dial replaces the middle control and sometimes it appears in addition to it. It adjusts the higher midrange frequencies (those found between the middle and treble dials).

- **No reverb control**
  Reverb can be a nice addition to your guitar tone, but it is not essential. Don't be concerned if your amp does not have a reverb control.

- **Volume, gain, master setup**
  Single-channel amplifiers often have an extra volume control (in addition to the master volume) located next to the gain control. For clean sounds keep the gain set low, the volume similarly low and use the master control for overall volume. If the master control is on 10 and you require more level, turn the volume control up (though you may find this starts to distort as you reach the higher numbers).

  To get a distorted tone turn the volume down low and the gain up till you get the amount of distortion you require. Regulate the overall level with the master volume. As before, if the master control is on 10 and you require more level, turn the volume up. In this case, however, you may find you lose clarity before you reach maximum.

Pickups

Entire books have been devoted to the intricacies of pickups. However, three basic pieces of information will help you understand a lot about your guitar tone:

- **Singlecoils**
  Singlecoils are narrow pickups that you'll see fitted to many guitars. The Fender Stratocaster is the most famous guitar fitted with singlecoils. They produce a bright, cutting sound that can sound thin in some situations, especially in heavier styles of rock music.

- **Humbuckers**
  Humbuckers were originally designed to remove or 'buck' the hum produced by singlecoil pickups, hence the name 'humbuckers'. They produce a warm, mellow sound compared to singlecoil pickups, but have a tendency to sound muddy in some situations. They are easily identified because they are usually twice the width of a singlecoil pickup. The Gibson Les Paul is a well-known guitar that is fitted with humbucking pickups.

- **Pickup location**
  Pickups located near the guitar's neck will have the warmest sound, while pickups located near the bridge will have the brightest sound.

Different types of 'dirty' tones

There are lots of different words to describe the dirty guitar sounds. In fact, all the sounds are 'distortions' of the clean tone, which can be confusing when you consider there's a type of distortion called 'distortion'! Below is a simplified breakdown of the three main types of dirty sounds and some listening material to help you through this tonal minefield.

- **Overdrive**
  This is the mildest form of distortion. It can be quite subtle and only evident when the guitar is played strongly. It can also be full-on and aggressive.
  Hear it on: Cream – 'Sunshine Of Your Love', AC/DC – 'Back In Black', Oasis – 'Cigarettes And Alcohol'

- **Distortion**
  Distortion is usually associated with heavy metal and hard rock music. It is dense and heavy sounding, and the most extreme of the dirty tones.
  Hear it on: Metallica – 'Enter Sandman', Avenged Sevenfold – 'Bat Country', Bon Jovi – 'You Give Love A Bad Name'

- **Fuzz**
  As the name implies, fuzz is a broken, 'fuzzy' sound. It was very popular in the 1960s, but, while still popular, is less common now.
  Hear it on: Jimi Hendrix Experience – 'Purple Haze', The Kinks – 'You Really Got Me'

Examination Versions

These examination versions are arranged from the original songs. While adjustments have been made to the arrangements to make the pieces playable at Grade 4 and make them appropriate as examination pieces, we have worked hard to maintain the integrity and spirit of the original music.

The accompanying audio for these arrangements can be found on CD 1. There are two tracks for each song. The first is the full performance including the guitar part, while the second is the backing track without the guitar part. The backing tracks should be used in examinations.

The edited part is printed over two to four pages and is preceded by a Fact File detailing information about the song, the band and the guitarist who played on it and some recommended listening if you wish to research the artist further. At the end of each chapter there is a Walkthrough which gives you tips on how to play the piece and any technical challenges to look out for as you practise the song.

We have also included some general advice on getting an authentic tone for each track, including suggested amp settings. Treat these as a guide to point you in the right direction rather than a strict set of instructions that must be followed slavishly: guitar and amplifier sounds differ significantly, so the right setup for one guitar may not be the correct setup for another. Your ears should always be the final judge about whether something sounds good or not. If you require more information on amplifiers and their controls, pickups and guitar tones in general, please refer to our Introduction To Tone on pages 4 and 5.

© Neal Preston/Corbis

Razorlight

SONG TITLE: BEFORE I FALL TO PIECES
ALBUM: RAZORLIGHT
RELEASED: 2006
LABEL: VERTIGO
GENRE: INDIE ROCK

PERSONNEL: JOHNNY BORRELL (VOX+GTR)
BJÖRN ÅGREN (GUITAR)
CARL DALEMO (BASS)
ANDY BURROWS (DRUMS)

UK CHART PEAK: 17
US CHART PEAK: N/A

© Andreas Pessenlehner/epa/Corbis

BACKGROUND INFO

'Before I Fall To Pieces' was the third single from Razorlight's second album, the self-titled *Razorlight*. The song features the interplay between the guitars of frontman Johnny Borrell and guitarist Björn Ågren that was a trademark of the band's early material.

THE BIGGER PICTURE

Razorlight formed in 2002 after Johnny Borrell placed an advert for a guitarist in NME, stating 'Guitarist wanted. No pentatonics.' Borrell was inspired by groups like Television and Velvet Underground who shunned typical minor pentatonic leads in favour of more original guitar parts. In Björn Ågren Johnny got his wish: a player who used his musical intuition rather than familiar finger patterns. This pair was soon joined by Ågren's fellow Swede Carl Dalemo on bass and Christian Smith-Pancorvo on drums (replaced in 2004 by Andy Burrows). Razorlight's debut album *Up All Night* was acclaimed by the media and fans of stripped-down indie rock on its release in 2004. *Razorlight* followed in 2006, an album written and recorded with hopes of mainstream success. It debuted at the top of the British charts and was described by Q magazine as "the best guitar album since Oasis's *Definitely Maybe*."

NOTES

Since Razorlight's early years it had been known that the relationship between Johnny Borrell and his bandmates was a strained one. The band made no secret of it. So it came as no surprise when in 2009 Andy Burrows quit the group and was followed in January 2011 by Ågren and Dalemo. Their last album as a unit, 2009's *Slipway Fires*, lacked the spark of their first two full-length releases and the single 'Wire to Wire' failed to chart. However, the band continues to operate with replacements playing alongside Borrell, the only remaining original member.

RECOMMENDED LISTENING

Razorlight's debut album *Up All Night* featured an irresistible mix of The Strokes and The Libertines. 'Rip It Up' shows Borrell and Ågren's guitar chemistry and betrays the influence of The Strokes. The highlight, though, is 'Golden Touch': an indie pop anthem that demonstrated Borrell's knack for crafting songs so effective you swear you've heard them before. On their next, self-titled, album 'Kirby's House' could have come from the same mould, while tracks like 'America' with its Edge-like delayed guitar effect betrayed Razorlight's ambition to be as big as U2 and the other stadium-filling rock giants.

Before I Fall To Pieces

CD 1 Tracks 1 & 2

Razorlight
Words & Music by Johnny Borrell & Andy Burrows

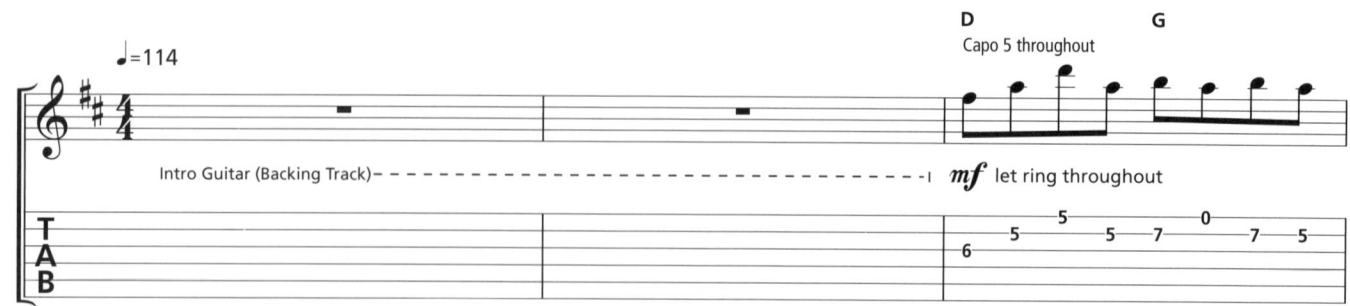
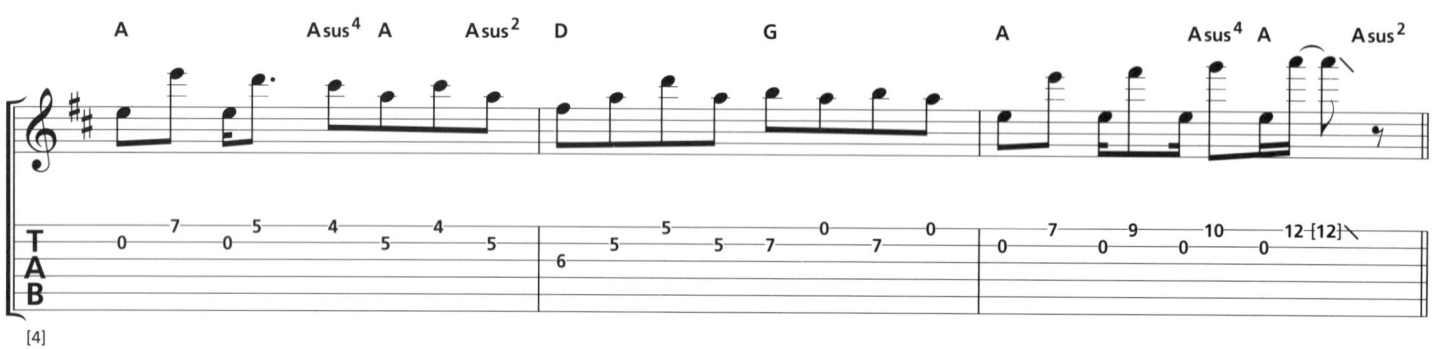
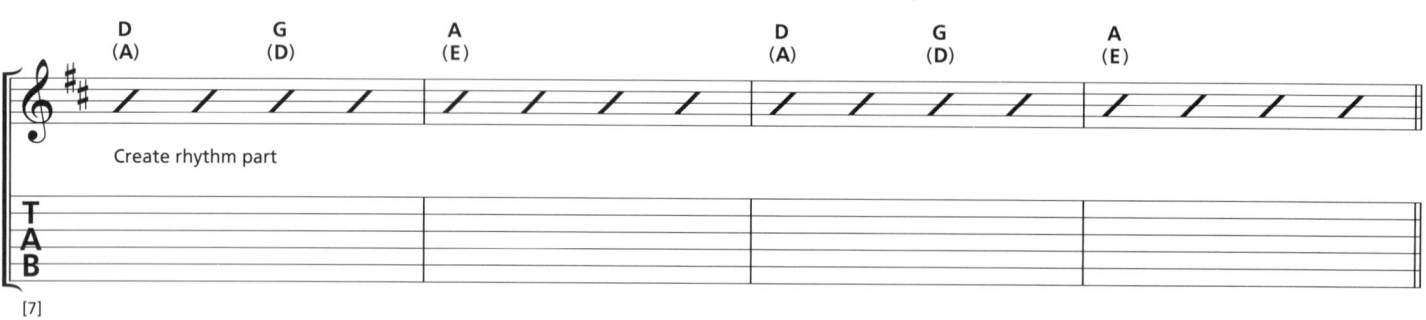
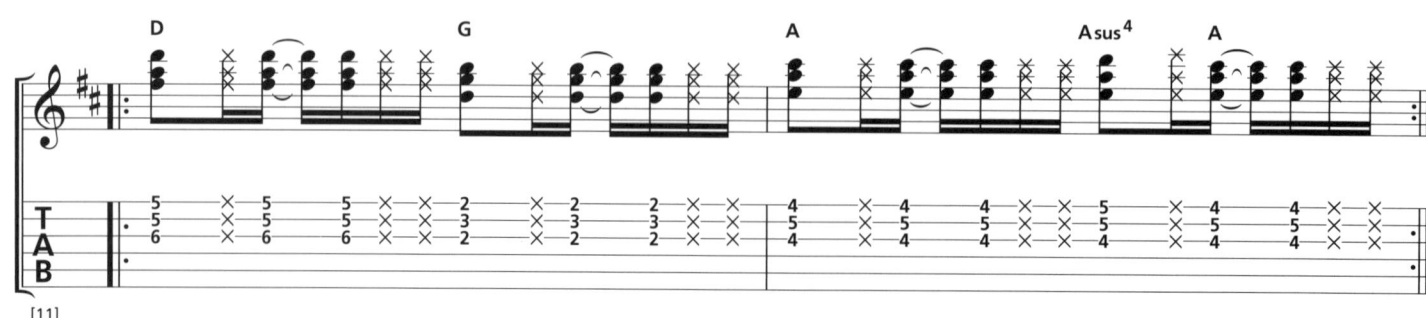

© Copyright 2006 Sony/ATV Music Publishing.
All Rights Reserved. International Copyright Secured.

D G A Asus4 A
TAB
[13]
D G A
TAB
[15]
D G A Asus4 A Asus2
TAB
[17]
D G A Asus4 A Asus2
TAB
[19]
D G A Asus4 A Asus2
TAB
[21]

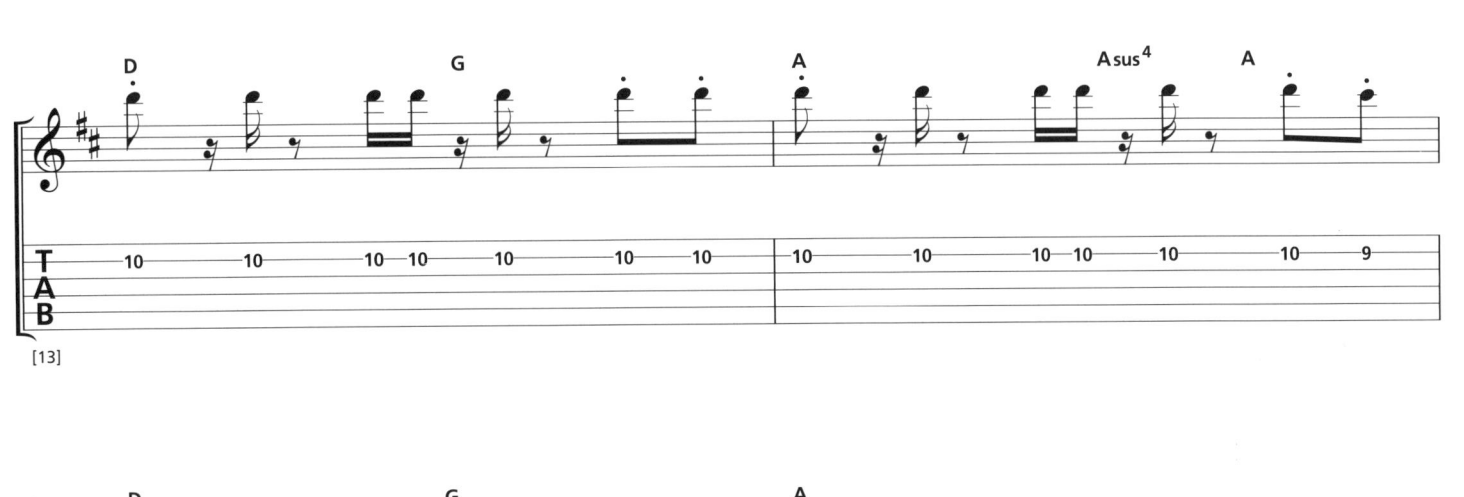

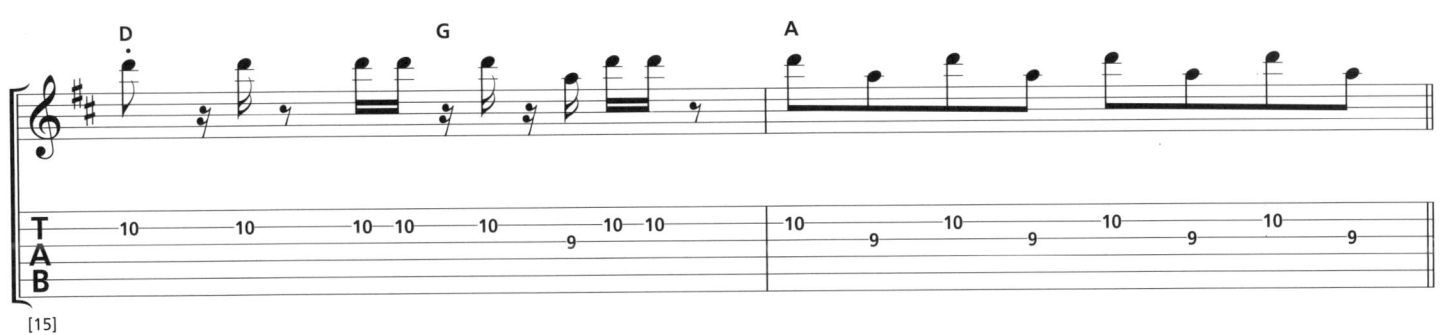

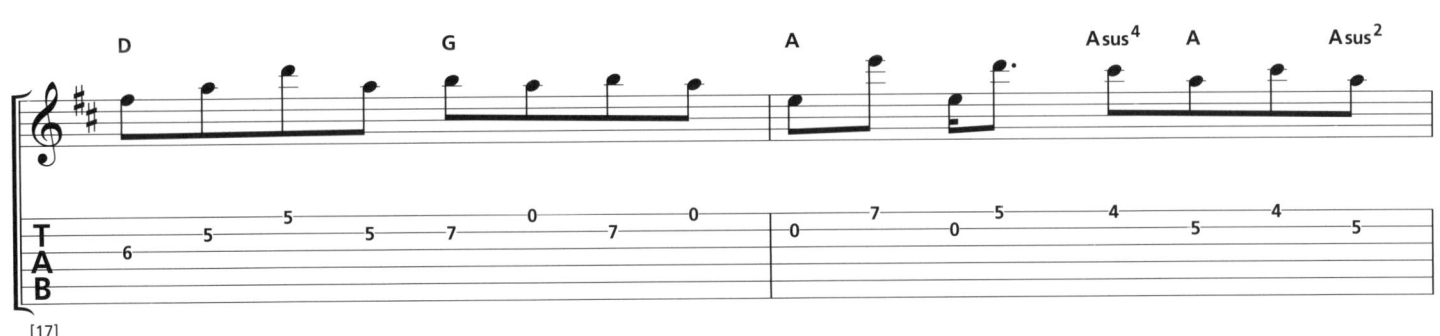

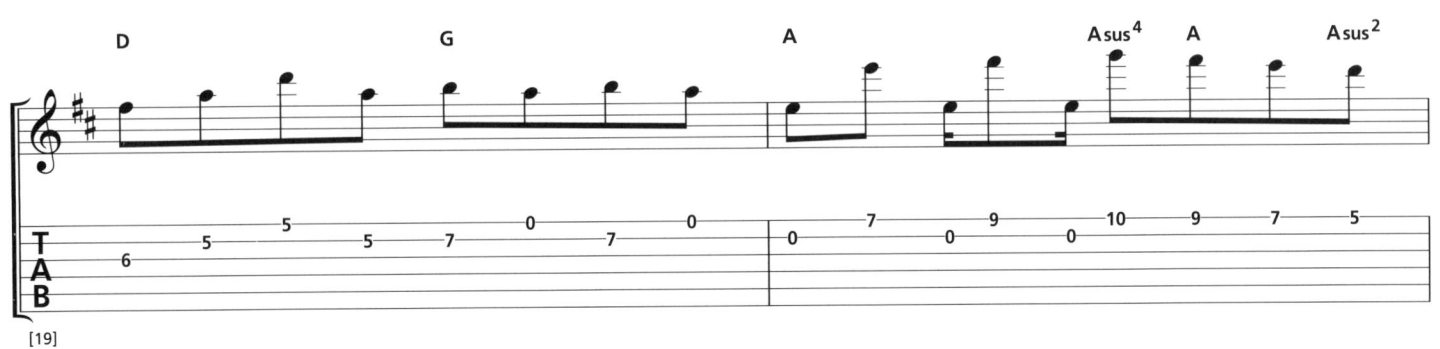

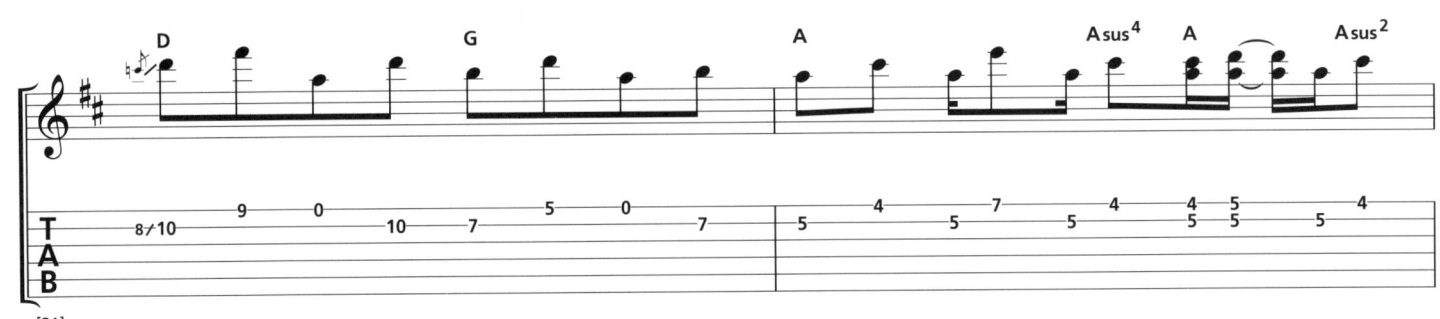

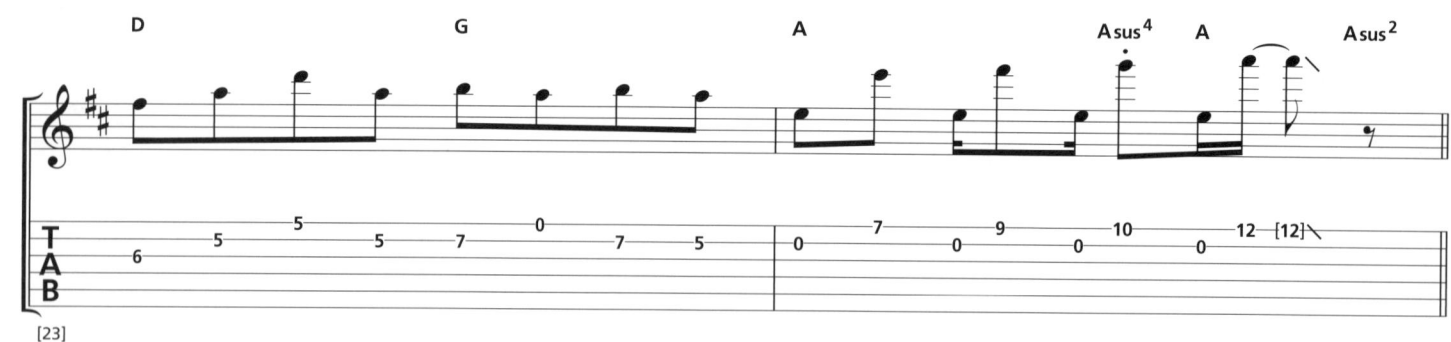
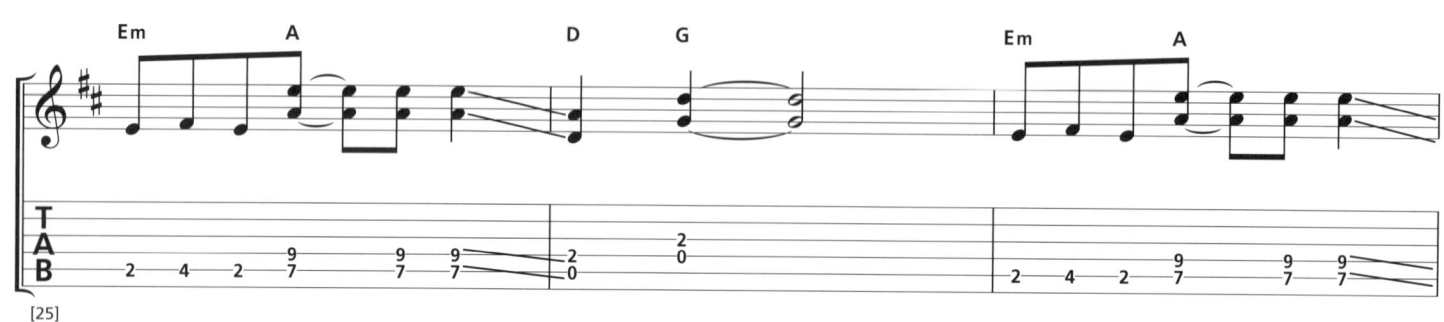
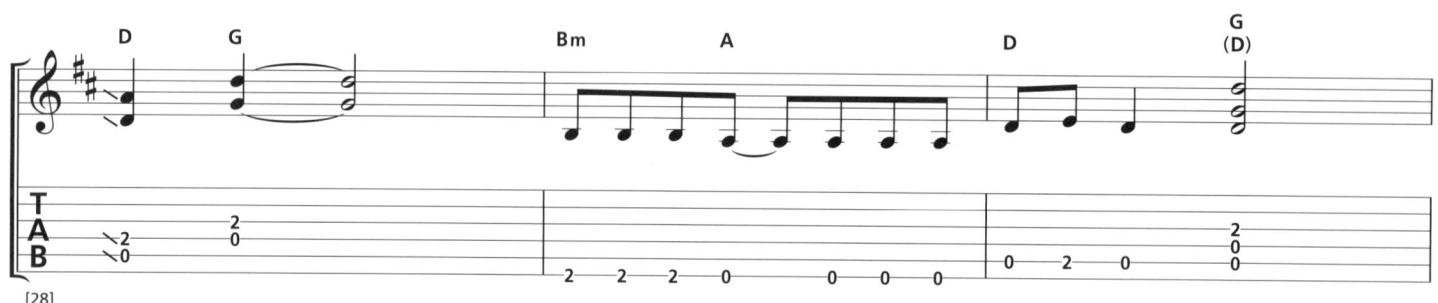
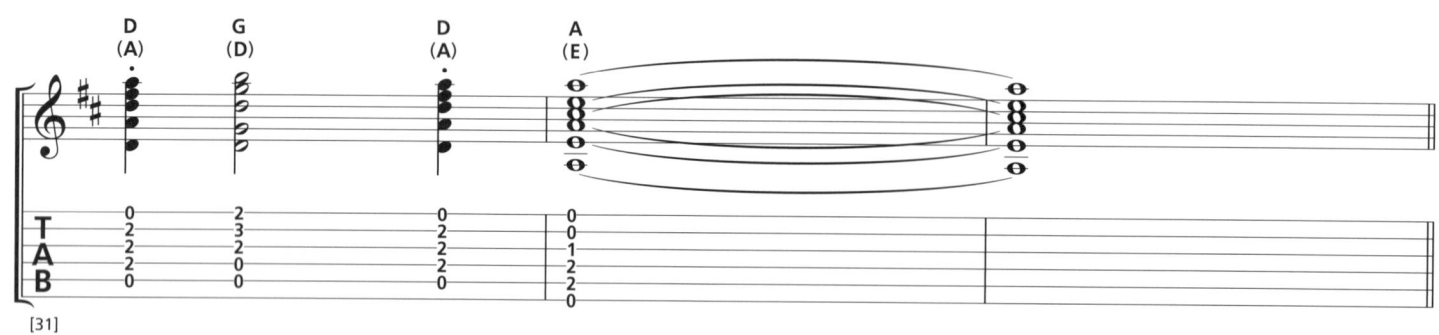
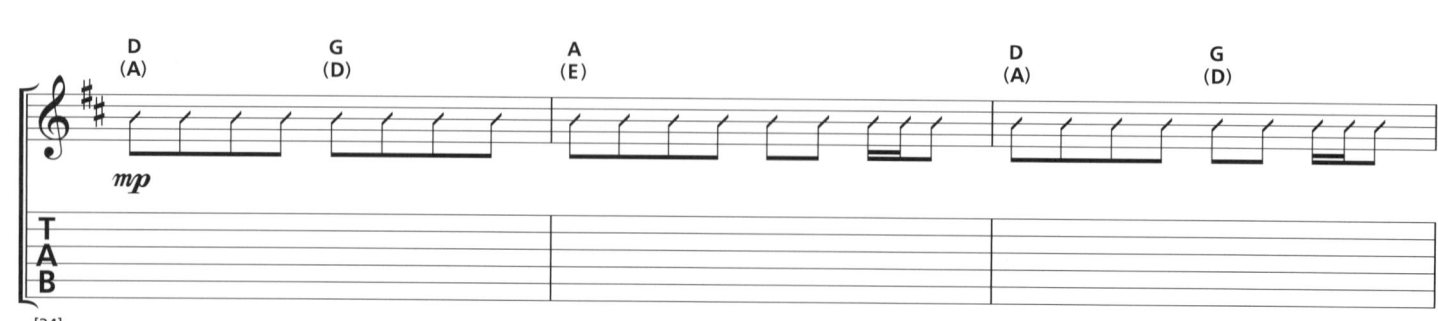

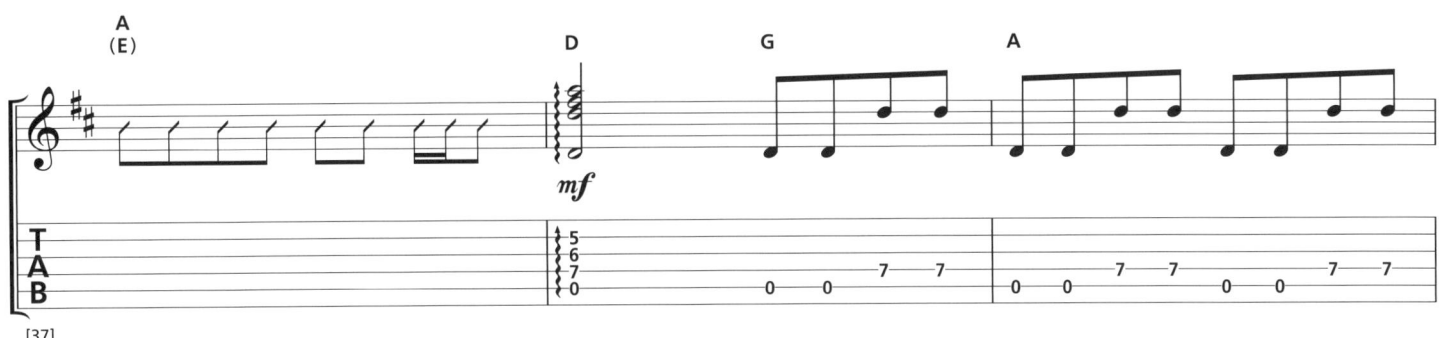

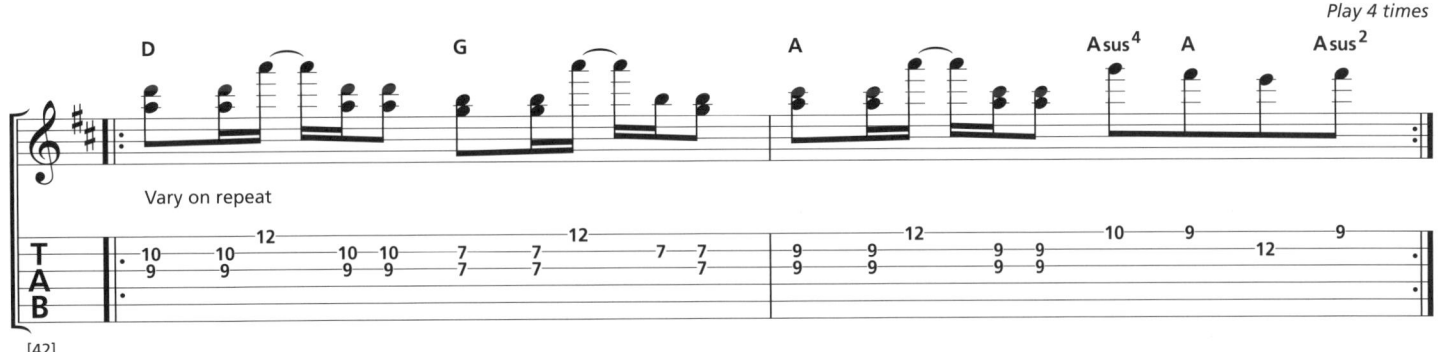
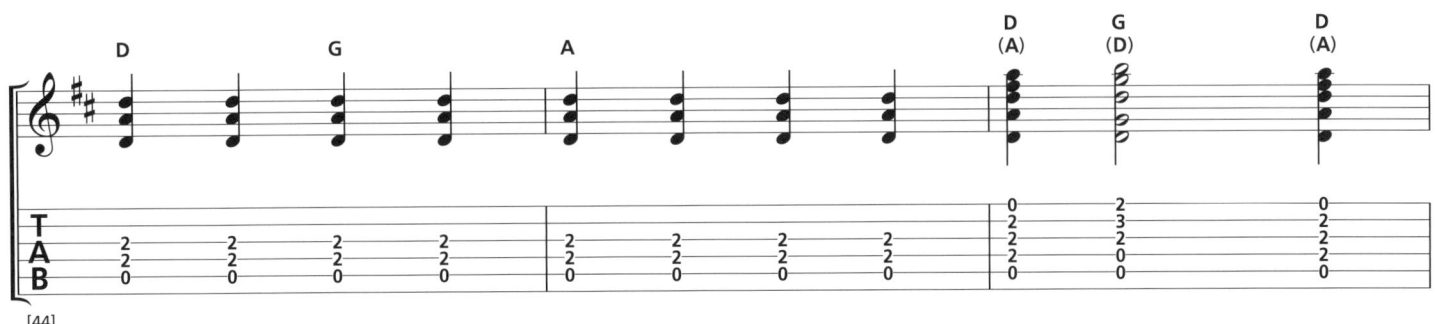
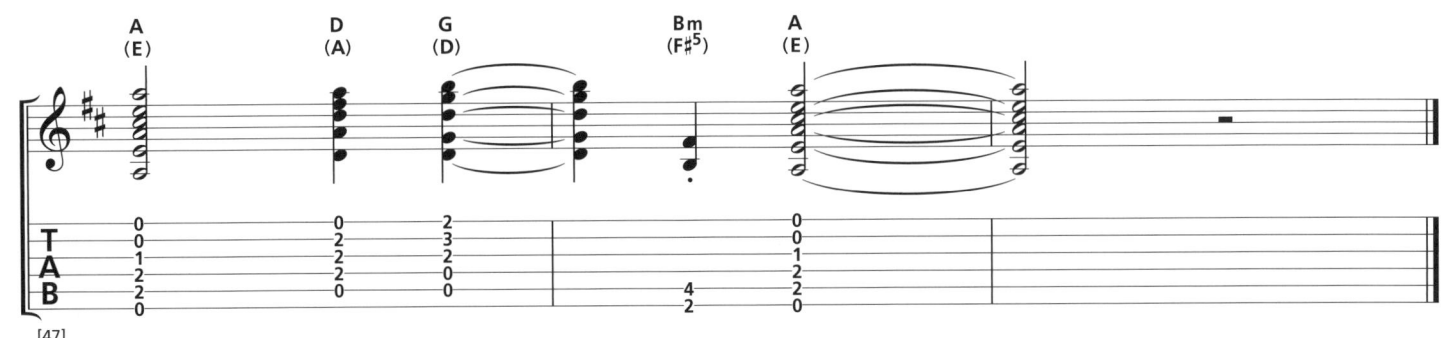

Walkthrough

Tone
Aim for a bright, clean sound. Selecting a pickup nearer the bridge will give you the brightest tone. Add some reverb, but make sure you don't add too much otherwise the guitar's sound will lose its clarity.

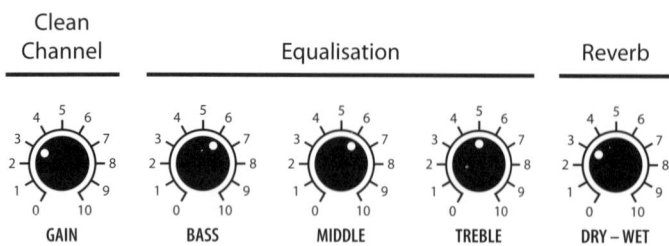

Using a capo
The capo should be placed close to but not on top of the fret in a position parallel to the fret. Set it up so there is just enough (i.e. not too much) pressure on the strings as this could put them out of tune. Make sure that you place the capo directly on top of the strings as you clamp it down (in the position you intend it to be in once it's clamped) so that the strings aren't bent out of tune.

Intro (Bars 1–6)
The intro comprises the melodic guitar part that features later in the song's chorus.

Bars 7–10 | *Capo notation*
The numbers in the TAB notation are relative to the position of the capo. This means a note marked as '6' should be played six frets higher than the capo.

Verse (Bars 7–10)
You are required to create your own rhythm part in the verse, based on the chords above the TAB.

Bars 7–10 | *Selecting chord voicings*
The chords above the notation show the actual pitches of the chords. However, because of the capo, playing the regular open chord shapes that match these symbols will produce the wrong chord. The chords in brackets are suggestions for the open chord shapes that will produce the correct sound while using the capo (Fig. 1).

Pre-chorus 1 (Bars 11–16)
The pre-chorus features quickly strummed chords followed by a rhythmic, single-note riff.

Bars 11–12 | *16th-note strumming*
It can be difficult to play these two bars fluently because your hand has to move four times per beat at a high tempo. Aim to strum only the three strings indicated in the TAB. This will reduce both the distance your hand has to travel and the effort you have to make to strum the part (Fig. 2).

Chorus 1 (Bars 17–24)
The chorus features a variation of the intro riff in which the melody is varied and double-stop chords are introduced.

Bridge & Pre-chorus 2 (Bars 25–41)
The bridge introduces a change of feel with powerchords and open chords sustained over several beats. The pre-chorus uses dynamics to increase the musical intensity gradually for the last chorus.

Bars 34–37 | *Choosing chord voicings*
You can use whichever chord voicings you feel work best, but remember to account for the capo if using open chords.

Chorus 2 & Outro (Bars 42–49)
The second chorus features a part that mixes rhythm and lead. The outro uses open chords for a powerful ending.

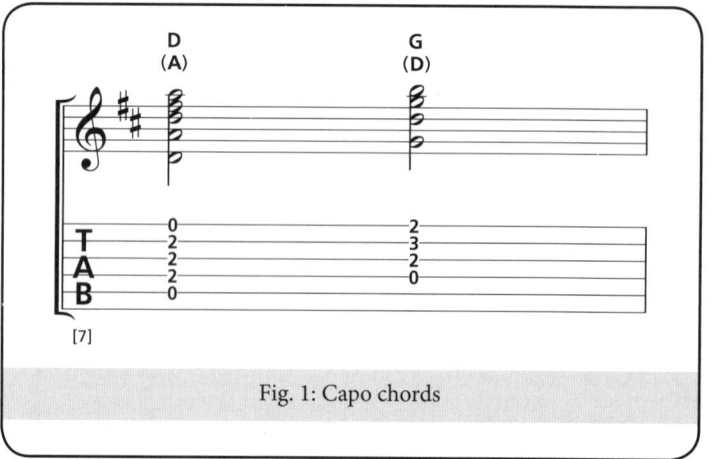

Fig. 1: Capo chords

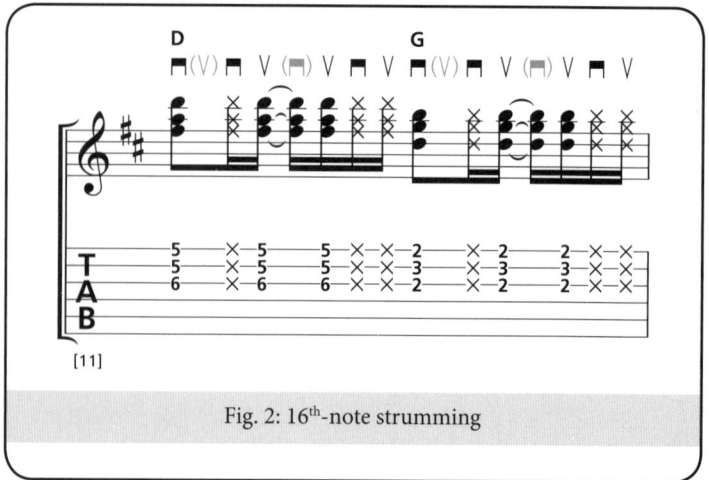

Fig. 2: 16th-note strumming

Thin Lizzy

SONG TITLE: THE BOYS ARE BACK IN TOWN
ALBUM: JAILBREAK
RELEASED: 1976
LABEL: UNIVERSAL
GENRE: CLASSIC ROCK

PERSONNEL: PHIL LYNOTT (VOX+BASS)
SCOTT GORHAM (GUITAR)
BRIAN ROBERTSON (GUITAR)
PHIL DOWNEY (DRUMS)
TIM HINKLEY (KEYS)

UK CHART PEAK: 8
US CHART PEAK: 12

© Gene Ambo/Retna Ltd/Corbis

BACKGROUND INFO

'The Boys Are Back In Town' was the first single released from Thin Lizzy's sixth studio album, *Jailbreak*. It features the distinctive twin lead guitars of Scott Gorham and Brian Robertson.

THE BIGGER PICTURE

Jailbreak was the third album by the classic Thin Lizzy line-up of Phil Lynott, Scott Gorham, Brian Robertson and Brian Downey. On their previous release, 1975's *Fighting*, Gorham and Robertson had introduced their twin lead guitar sound that became the group's trademark. However, *Fighting* failed to make the charts, just as all of Thin Lizzy's albums had done. *Jailbreak* then was the band's breakthrough, reaching number 10 in Britain and number 18 in the American album charts. 'The Boys Are Back In Town' continued the success when it was released as a single by climbing to number 8 in the British singles chart, just two places behind the group's most successful release, 'Whiskey In The Jar', which had gone to number 6 in 1972.

Although Thin Lizzy is often credited with developing the twin lead guitar sound, the group was not the first to use it, as Scott Gorham admitted:

"Wishbone Ash had done the twin guitar thing before us, but we took the idea and put it into a hard rock context with more aggression."

NOTES

Thin Lizzy's frontman and main songwriter Phil Lynott would often come into the studio with a basic idea for a song and expect the other band members to come up with complementary parts. At the start of the writing sessions for 'The Boys Are Back In Town' Lynott had the song's bassline worked out and asked his guitarists to write their own parts – specifically, to produce a part that would join the verse and chorus. Gorham and Robertson then came up with the famous harmonised line that is the song's signature.

RECOMMENDED LISTENING

Jailbreak is a great example of Thin Lizzy's classic line-up in the studio. As well as 'The Boys Are Back In Town' the album features the menacing, Celtic-sounding 'Emerald' and the excellent title track with its tight powerchord-based riff. Gary Moore played for Thin Lizzy at various stages and his lead playing can be heard on the album 'Black Rose' (1979), especially on the medley that closes the album.

The Boys Are Back In Town

Thin Lizzy
Words & Music by Phil Lynott

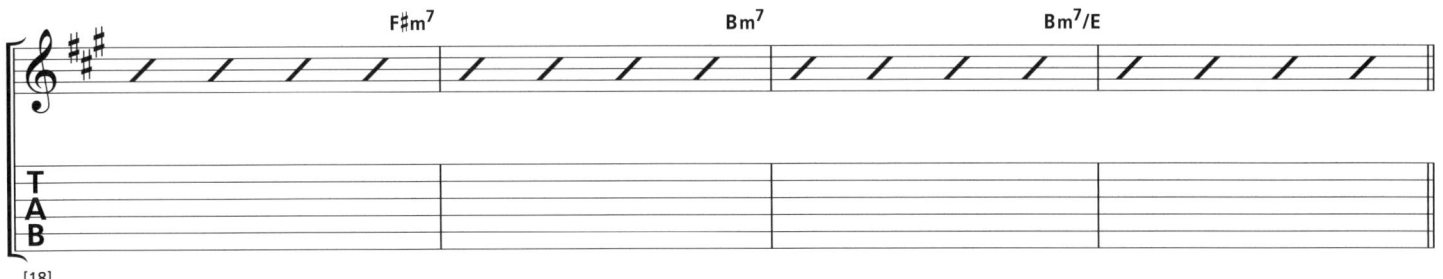
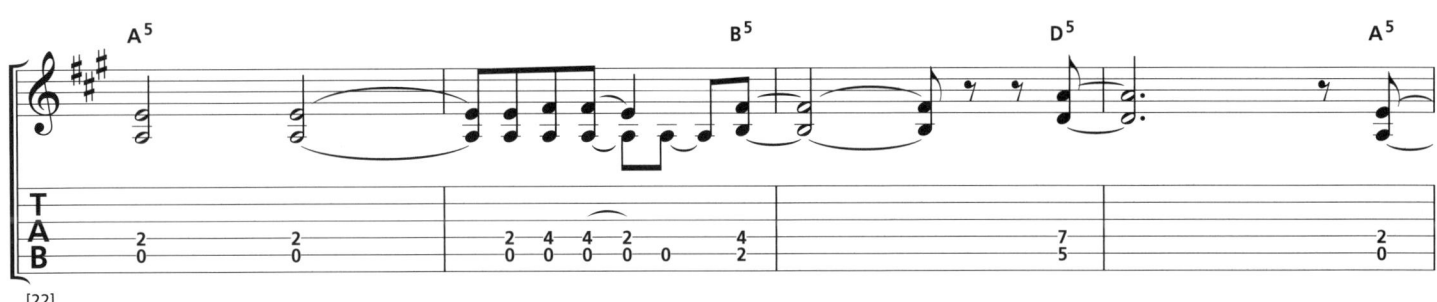
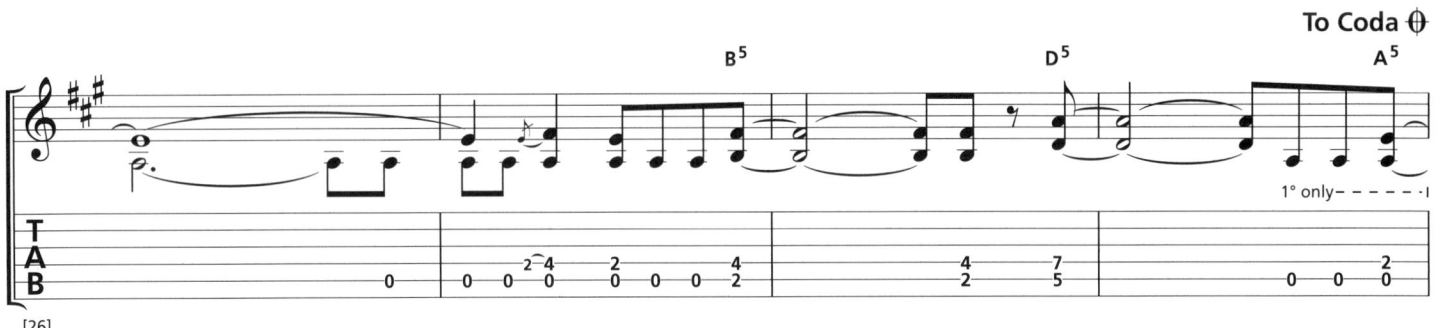
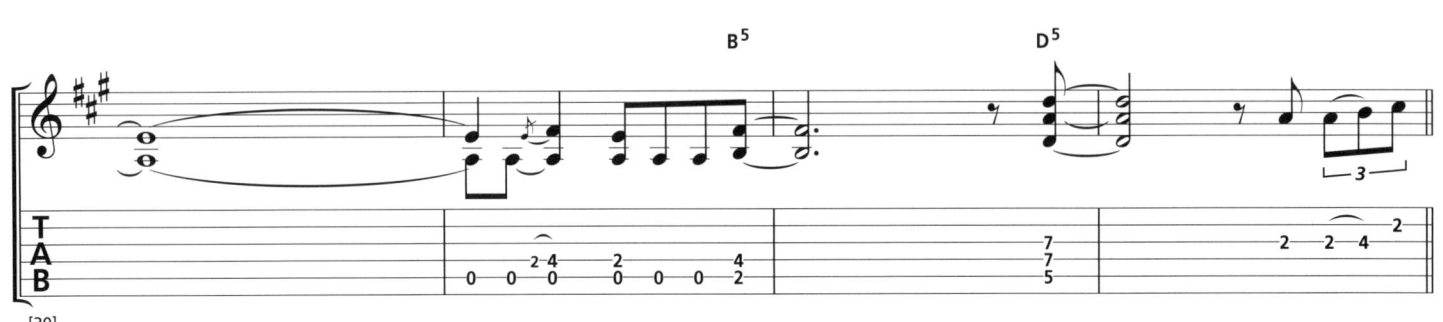

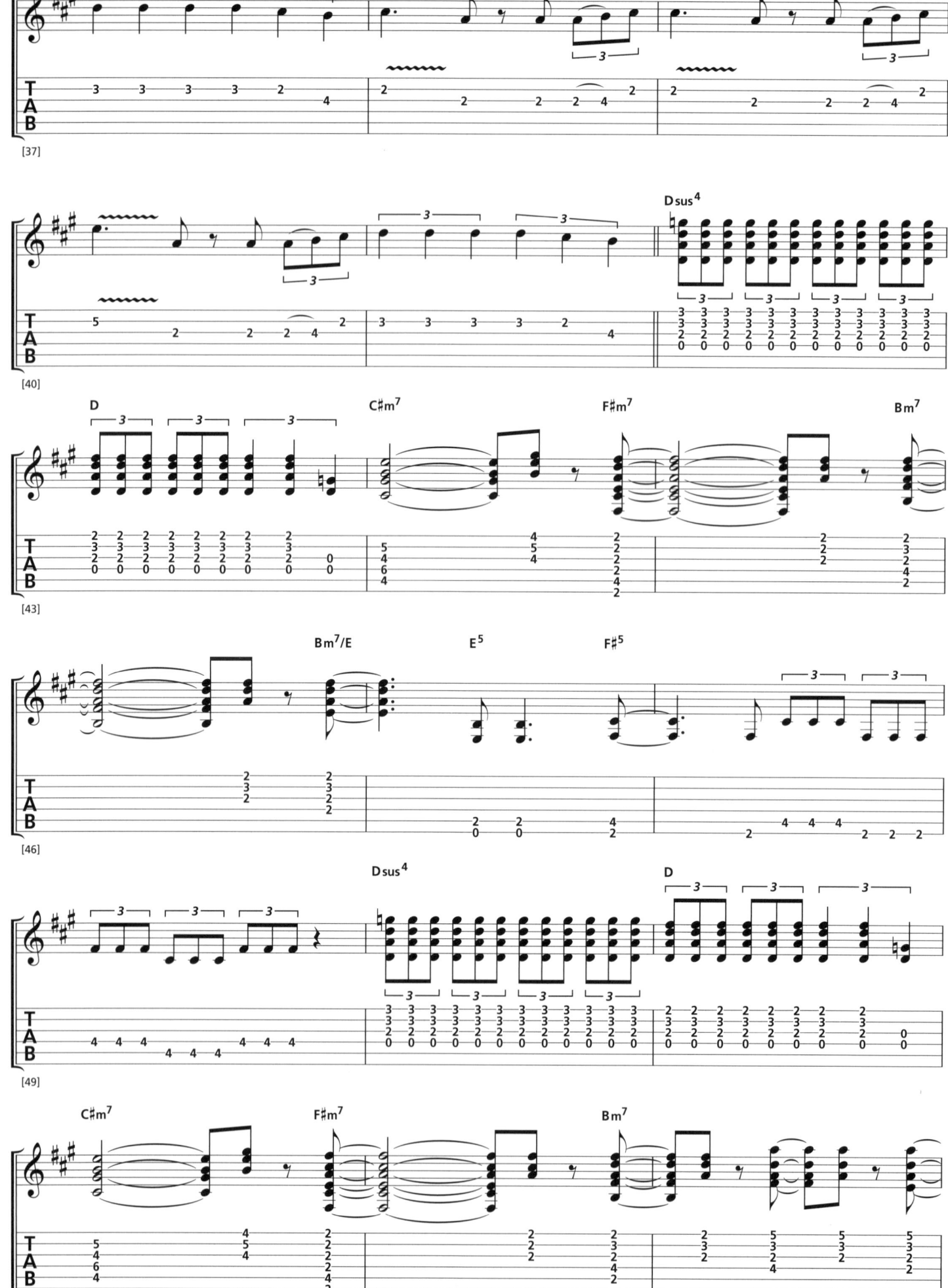

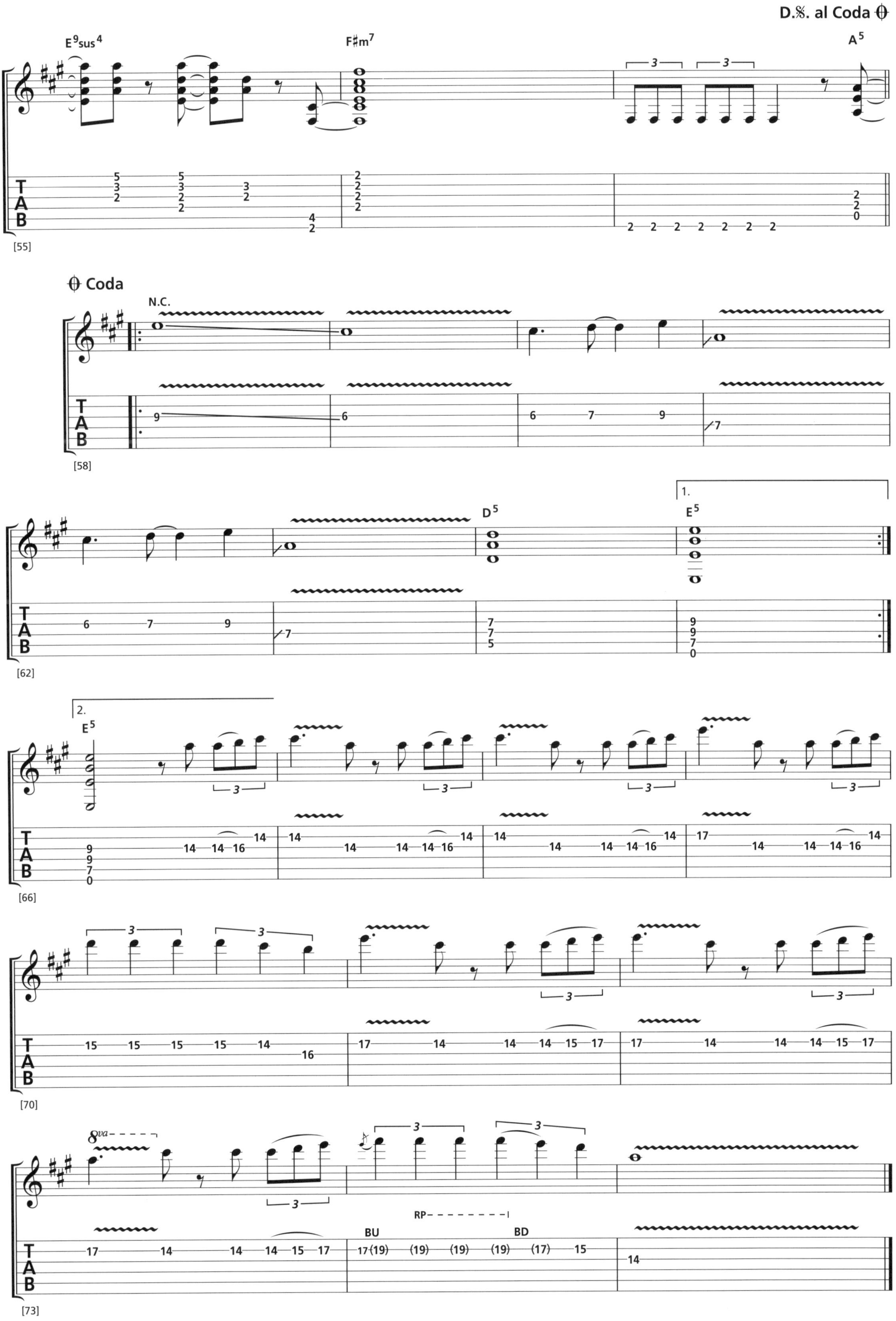
D.%. al Coda
E9sus4
F♯m7
A5
[55]
Coda
N.C.
[58]
D5
1.
E5
[62]
2.
E5
[66]
[70]
8va
RP
BU
BD
[73]

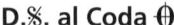

Walkthrough

Tone
In classic rock the mid is usually boosted to give the guitar an aggressive sound that cuts through the rest of the band. You should use an overdrive with the gain set to around 7. Don't add too much gain: you need clarity as well as grit.

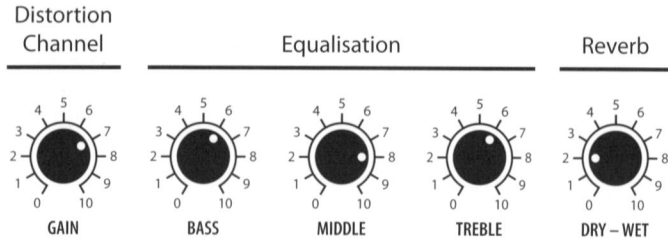

Intro & Verse (Bars 1–21)
The intro combines sustained chords with a single-note phrase. The verse uses barre chords that aren't often seen in this style of music.

Bars 5–12 | *Swing rhythm strumming*
Your eighth-note strumming pattern should be uneven to reflect the song's swing feel. The downstrokes should last slightly longer than the upstrokes to produce the distinctive lopsided feel.

Bars 13–21 | *Cont. sim.*
Cont. sim. means you should continue in a similar way but vary the part slightly. Some ways in which you might do this are to change the rhythm or alter the chord voicings.

Chorus & Harmony Solo (Bars 22–41)
The chorus is based on powerchords with embellishments added to the A^5 chords. The harmony solo is an interlude with a catchy melody that uses hammer-ons, vibrato and some unusual triplet rhythms.

Bar 37 | *Quarter-note triplet*
A quarter-note triplet places three notes evenly across a half note. This can be tricky to play correctly at first, so listen to the recording and practise counting, saying 'ev-en-ly' as you play the three notes (Fig. 1).

Bridge (Bars 42–57)
The bridge features fast triplet strumming, choppy barre chord rhythms and single-note phrases.

Bars 42–43 | *Triplet strumming*
The fast pattern should be played with alternate strumming. Because the notes are grouped in threes rather than the more common groupings of two or four, the second and fourth beats of the bar will start with upstrokes not downstrokes. This may feel unusual at first.

Bar 43 | *Position shifts*
The open D and G strings are played between the fast chord change from the D to the $C\sharp m^7$ chord. As you play these open strings, move your hand quickly from the D to the $C\sharp m^7$ so that your hand is in position to play the $C\sharp m^7$ slightly before it is actually due to be played.

Interlude & Outro (Bars 58–75)
The instrumental interlude is another harmony melody that leads into the outro, which is a variation of the harmony melody featured earlier.

Bar 71 | *Triplet hammer-ons*
Make sure all three notes in beat four are of the same length. It is common, especially when using hammer-ons, to play two 16th notes followed by an eighth note rather than three triplets (Fig. 2).

Bar 74 | *Harmony bends*
Pay close attention to the timing and pitch of the bends. Normally, a player would have some room for interpretation, but the fact that this is a harmony part means the bends must synchronise *exactly* with the other guitar part. Practise this unaccompanied but also make sure you devote time to playing with the backing track so that you lock in with the harmony guitar part.

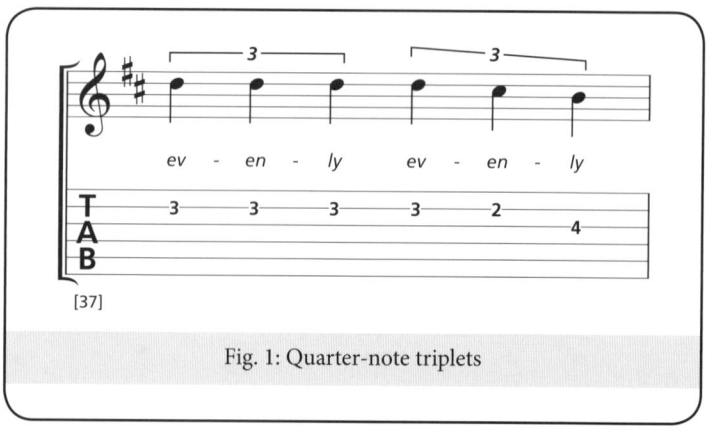

Fig. 1: Quarter-note triplets

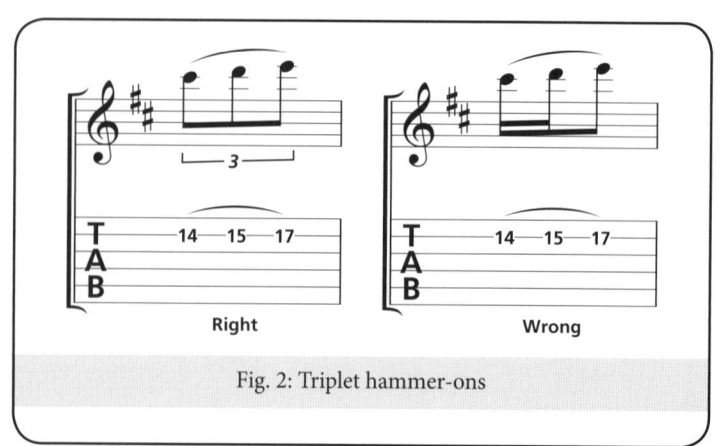

Fig. 2: Triplet hammer-ons

Oasis

SONG TITLE: DON'T LOOK BACK IN ANGER
ALBUM: (WHAT'S THE STORY) MORNING GLORY?
RELEASED: 1996
LABEL: CREATION
GENRE: INDIE ROCK

PERSONNEL: NOEL GALLAGHER (GTR)
LIAM GALLAGHER (VOX)
PAUL MCGUIGAN (BASS)
ALAN WHITE (DRUMS)

UK CHART PEAK: 1
US CHART PEAK: 55

© Tim Mosenfelder/Corbis

BACKGROUND INFO

'Don't Look Back In Anger' was the fifth single from Oasis's *(What's The Story) Morning Glory?*, the group's classic second album.

THE BIGGER PICTURE

When Oasis went into the studio in 1995 to record the follow-up to their first album *Definitely Maybe*, the band was all over the national media, thanks to the rock and roll lifestyles and outspokenness of brothers Liam and Noel Gallagher. *Definitely Maybe* had become the fastest-selling British debut album in history – Oasis had conquered the UK music scene in just a year since the release of their first single. Noel, undaunted by the group's success, focused on writing huge singalong choruses for the album that became *(What's The Story) Morning Glory?*.

'Don't Look Back In Anger' was written while Oasis was on tour. Noel would strum the song's chords on an acoustic guitar and sing nonsense words that fit the melody. One night before a gig at Sheffield Arena Liam mistook some of Noel's gibberish for 'So Sally can wait', which Noel liked, so it stuck. That same night Noel played the new song unaccompanied on acoustic guitar in front of a stadium full of Oasis fans.

NOTES

Much of Oasis's fame – or infamy – was built on the sibling rivalry of Noel and Liam Gallagher. The band formed properly when the more experienced Noel joined Liam's group on the condition that he write all the songs and plot the band's route to success. After years of public arguments and fallouts, the group split just before a gig in Paris in 2009 when Liam swung a guitar and threw a plum at his brother, prompting Noel to quit the band immediately. Noel launched a successful solo career and the rest of the band regrouped as Beady Eye.

RECOMMENDED LISTENING

Oasis's debut *Definitely Maybe* (1994) is the band at its rawest, before bigger recording budgets gave them a more polished sound. It produced four singles: 'Supersonic', 'Shakermaker', 'Live Forever' and 'Cigarettes And Alcohol'. Its follow-up, *(What's The Story) Morning Glory?* (1995), was a more mature sounding album bearing extra instrumentation and the influence of The Beatles. 'Wonderwall', 'Some Might Say' and 'She's Electric' were highlights. For an overview of Oasis's career, try the compilation *Stop The Clocks* (2006), which features most of the band's hits from the 1990s to the mid 2000s.

Don't Look Back In Anger

Oasis

Words & Music by Noel Gallagher

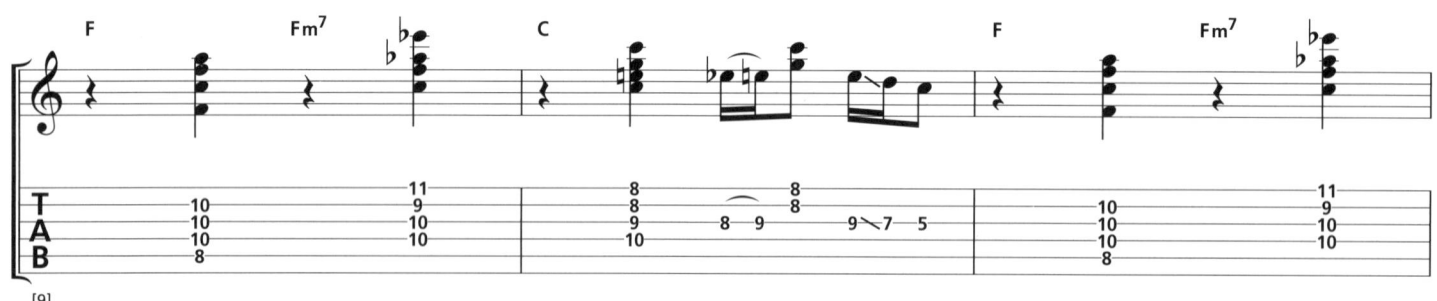
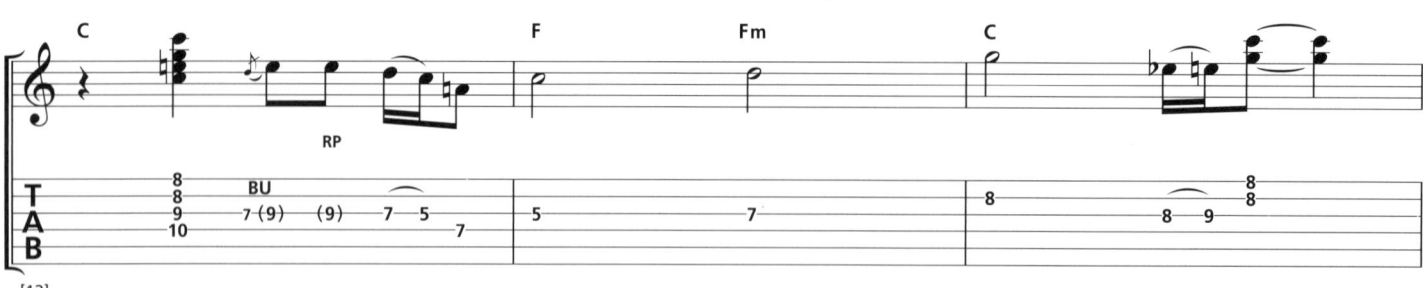
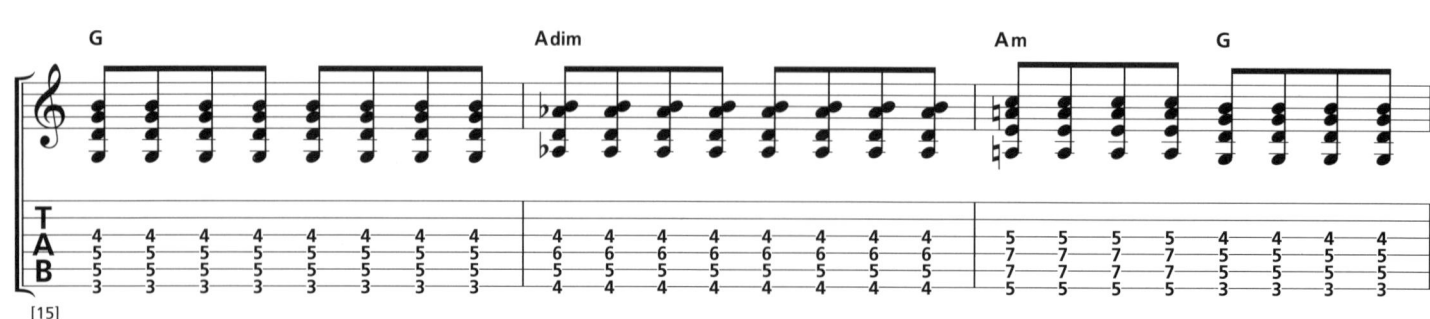

© Copyright 1995 Creation Songs Limited/Oasis Music (GB).
Sony/ATV Music Publishing.
All Rights Reserved. International Copyright Secured.

Walkthrough

Tone

Aim for quite a lot of overdrive, but be careful not to turn the gain up too high as this will affect the clarity of your sound, especially while playing the rhythmic parts.

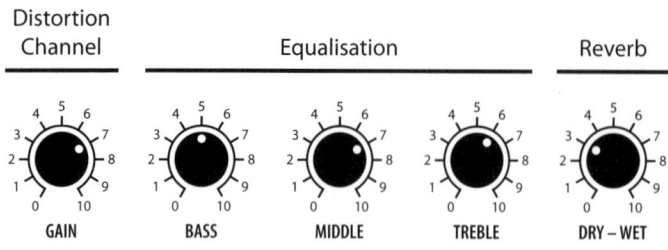

Verse (Bars 1–8)

The verse is based mostly on single-note, minor pentatonic phrases that use string bends, hammer-ons and pull-offs.

Bars 3–8 | *Rhythmic accuracy*

The phrases in this section use lots of fast hammer-ons. A common error is to rush hammer-ons so that the first note is too short and the second too long. Aim to make both notes the same length (Fig. 1).

Pre-chorus (Bars 9–20)

The first half of the pre-chorus combines syncopated chord stabs with lead guitar fills. The second half uses low chords followed by a single-note phrase that leads to the chorus.

Bars 9–12 | *Playing tightly*

These bars may look simple, but their difficulty lies in playing them to a high standard. The relatively slow tempo means it is easy to rush the offbeat chords and the fills that follow them. Be aware of the backing track and aim to lock in with the rest of the band so the notes you play coincide exactly with the other instruments, particularly the drums.

Bars 15–17 | *16th-note strumming*

These bars could be played with eighth-note strumming; however, to play *all* the strumming sections of this piece fluently you will need to use 16th-note strumming. This is where the picking hand strums four times for every beat of the bar. The pick doesn't actually strike the string four times per beat: some of these will be 'ghost strums'. (Fig. 2)

Chorus 1 (Bars 21–24)

In the chorus you are required to choose your own chord voicings, which you should play in the notated rhythm.

Bars 21–24 | *Choosing chord voicings*

While you can use whichever voicings you feel work best, you may find voicings that are too far away from each other are difficult to move between and may sound disjointed.

Solo (Bars 25–32)

In this section you have the opportunity to create your own solo over the song's pre-chorus chords.

Bars 25–32 | *Scale choice*

The first chord of the solo section is an F; however, the solo itself is actually in the key of C major. The C major pentatonic is therefore the most obvious scale choice for the whole of the solo. While you could make adjustments in your scale choice to account for the non-diatonic (not in the key) F minor and A diminished chords, it may be best to treat these as passing chords that create a temporarily discordant but still pleasing sound.

Chorus 2 (Bars 21–41)

This is a reprise of the chorus with a variation involving spread chords and single-note melodies.

Bars 34–37 | *Spread chords*

The wavy vertical lines next to the chords in bars 34–36 indicate that although the notes of the chords are to be played simultaneously, you should spread them out slightly. Rather than strumming the chords, brush your pick across the strings to produce a sound that is midway between a strummed chord and one that is arpeggiated.

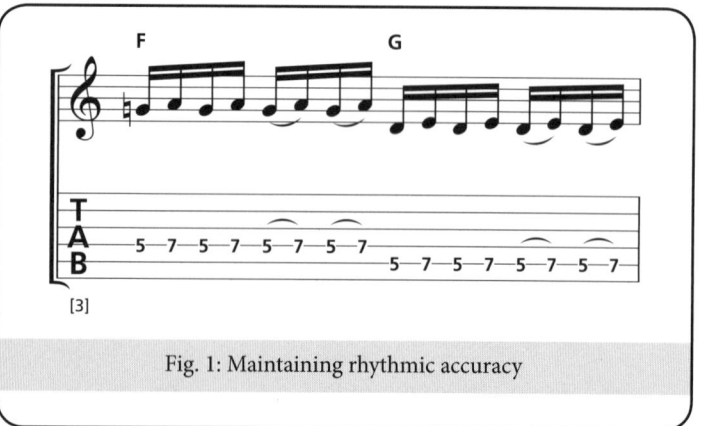

Fig. 1: Maintaining rhythmic accuracy

Fig. 2: Ghost strums

Eric Clapton

SONG TITLE: EDGE OF DARKNESS
ALBUM: EDGE OF DARKNESS SOUNDTRACK
RELEASED: 1985
LABEL: BBC RECORDS & TAPES
GENRE: INSTRUMENTAL ROCK

PERSONNEL: ERIC CLAPTON (GUITAR)
MICHAEL KAMEN (ARGMT)

UK CHART PEAK: 65
US CHART PEAK: N/A

© Neal Preston/Corbis

BACKGROUND INFO

'Edge Of Darkness' was the title theme of a BBC political thriller broadcast in 1985. It was written by Eric Clapton with the help of his composer friend Michael Kamen.

THE BIGGER PICTURE

Eric Clapton is one of the most important players in the history of guitar music. Clapton was regarded as the finest guitarist of the British Blues Boom, a wave of young British bands inspired by American blues and R&B in the 1960s. The movement was focused on London, where the slogan 'Clapton is God' could be seen sprayed on walls – proof of Eric's esteem among fans of the style (although Clapton wasn't the only great player to emerge from the scene: Jeff Beck, Jimmy Page and Peter Green were his contemporaries). Clapton's greatest contribution to rock music was his teaming of agile blues licks with a Gibson Les Paul and Marshall amp on the album *Bluesbreakers* by John Mayall. This became the sound of hard rock, adopted by groups such as Thin Lizzy, Free and Guns N' Roses. Clapton also played with the Yardbirds, Cream and Blind Faith before embarking on his own successful solo career, which shows no sign of ending any time soon.

NOTES

Nowadays Eric Clapton is usually associated with the Fender Stratocaster. However, in his formative years as a professional musician – while playing with John Mayall and Cream – Clapton relied on Gibson guitars for his sound. As one of John Mayall's band of 'Bluesbreakers', Clapton laid the foundations of hard rock tone with his Les Paul; while with Cream he added an SG and cherry red ES-335 to his arsenal. It was with the SG (painted in psychedelic livery by a London art collective known as The Fool) that Clapton developed his famous 'woman tone'. This smooth sound can be heard on the lead guitar parts of Cream's 'Sunshine Of Your Love'. Clapton produced it by selecting the neck pickup of his SG and turning the tone control back to zero.

RECOMMENDED LISTENING

Original copies of the *Edge Of Darkness* soundtrack album are now hard to find. Instead you could buy a copy of Clapton's *24 Nights*, a live album recorded at the Royal Albert Hall in London during 1990 and 1991 which features an excellent version of the track. To hear more of Clapton's melodic style, try 'Badge' (Cream, 1969), 'While My Guitar Gently Weeps' (The Beatles, 1968) and 'Wonderful Tonight' (1977).

Edge Of Darkness

CD 1 Tracks 7 & 8

Eric Clapton
Music by Eric Clapton & Michael Kamen

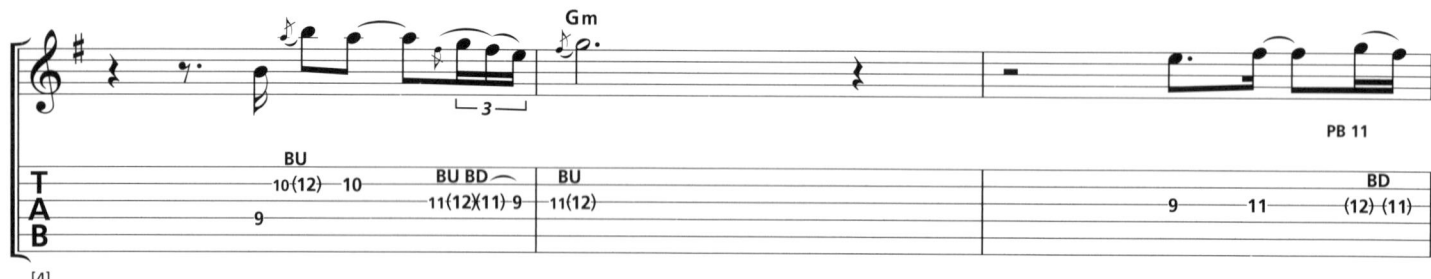

[4]

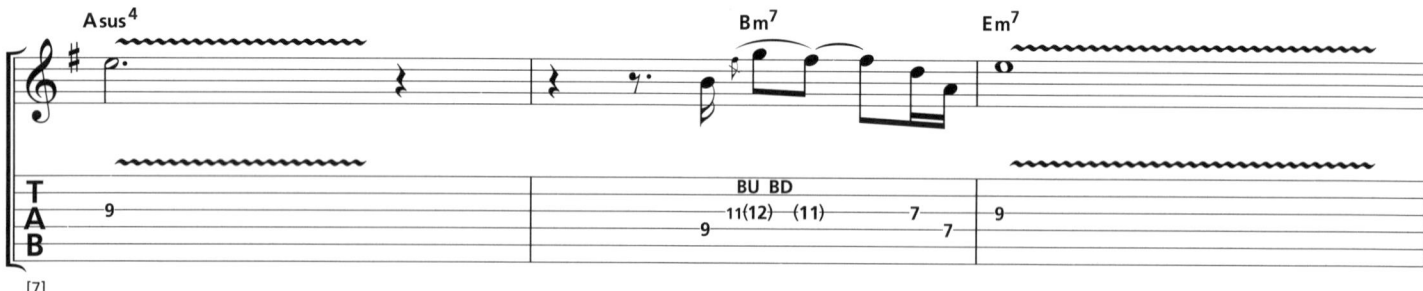

[7]

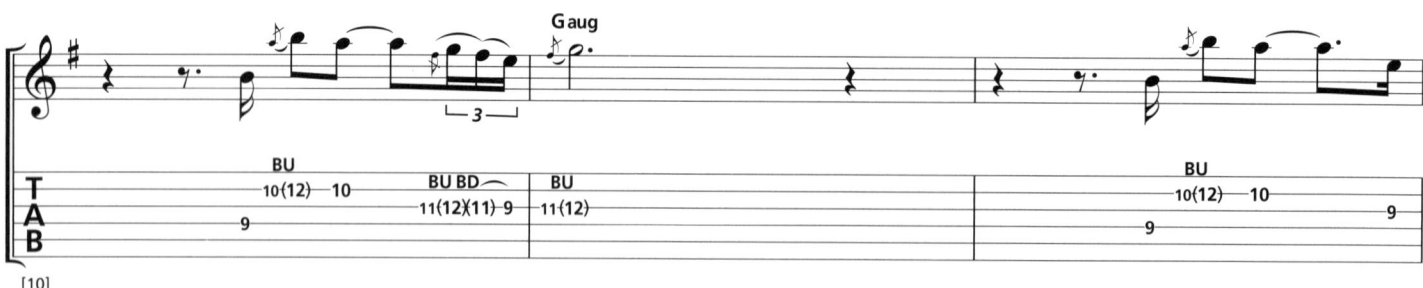

[10]

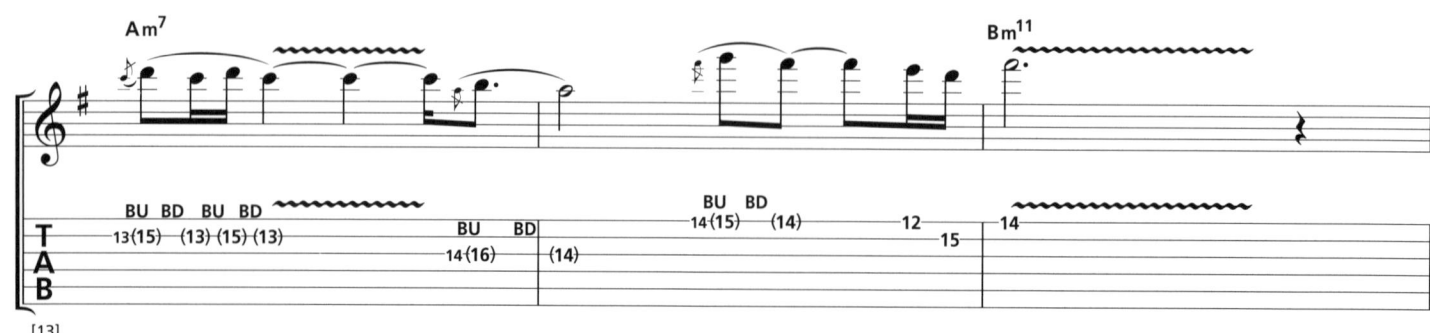

[13]

© Copyright 1985 & 1991 E.C. Music Limited/Mother Fortune Inc.
E.C. Music Limited/Intersong Music Ltd.
All Rights Reserved. International Copyright Secured.

Walkthrough

Tone

Aim for a fairly overdriven tone, but resist the temptation to make the sound too distorted as this will mask the subtleties of this delicate piece. Boost the middle to add a little bite to the tone and add a generous amount of reverb.

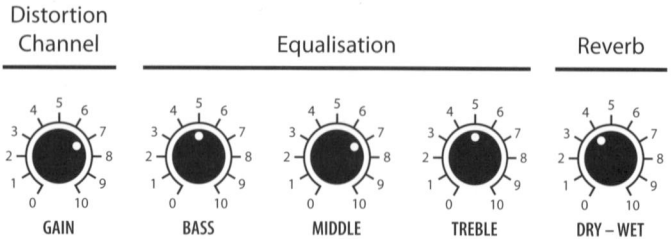

Bars 1–35 | Edge Of Darkness

This instrumental piece doesn't follow a traditional song structure and cannot be divided into obvious sections. The melody contains one distinctive phrase that opens the piece and is repeated with variations throughout.

Bars 1–35 | *Bending accuracy*

'Edge Of Darkness' features many string bends of both a tone and semi-tone. These use lots of different articulations, which are explored below. Whatever the interval or technique, your main concern should always be to ensure your bends are in tune. Practise each phrase slowly, making sure the bends reach the target notes (the notes in brackets). It can be helpful to play the target note before you play the bend so the correct pitch is fresh in your mind (Fig. 1).

Bars 1–35 | *Complex notation*

The slow tempo of this piece means that phrases that are simple to re-create by ear can look quite intimidating when written down. Be sure to listen to the track several times before attempting to play it so you are familiar with the melody. It may also help you to play along with the audio track with the guitar melody.

Bars 1–2 | *Fast bends*

Fast bends are difficult to play in tune because your ear has less time to register the changes in pitch and recognise when the bend is in tune. Muscle memory plays a big part in fast bends. Play these types of bends slowly and repeatedly, paying close attention to the tuning. This will teach your fingers how far the string should be bent. Gradually increase the speed as you become more comfortable.

Bar 6 | *Pre-bends*

A pre-bend involves bending a note to the pitch indicated above the notation *without* playing it. The note is then played and (usually) released straight away (Fig. 2).

Bar 7 | *Vibrato*

Vibrato varies tremendously from one player to another: it is one of the most distinctive aspects of a guitarist's style. Whether your vibrato is fast and wide or slow and shallow, make sure that the movement is even and consistent or you will sound out of tune.

Bar 13 | *Multiple bend and releases*

This bar requires you to bend and release a tone bend twice. As well as reaching the correct pitch you will need to make sure the string continues to ring for the duration of the bend. Pressing into the fretboard to keep the string in contact with the fret throughout the bending action will help.

Bar 20 | *Playing a fill over complex chords*

There are several opportunities to create your own fills in this piece, most of which are to be played over quite complex chords. Try not to be intimidated by this: either the E blues, E natural minor or a combination of the two scales will work in all cases. In fact, Eric Clapton uses these scales in the original recording. Spend time experimenting with different phrases until you find some that you are happy with.

Bars 33–34 | *Ending the piece*

The main challenge with the fill in bar 33 is making sure that you play a phrase which gives you time to play – and lead musically into – the final note at the start of bar 34.

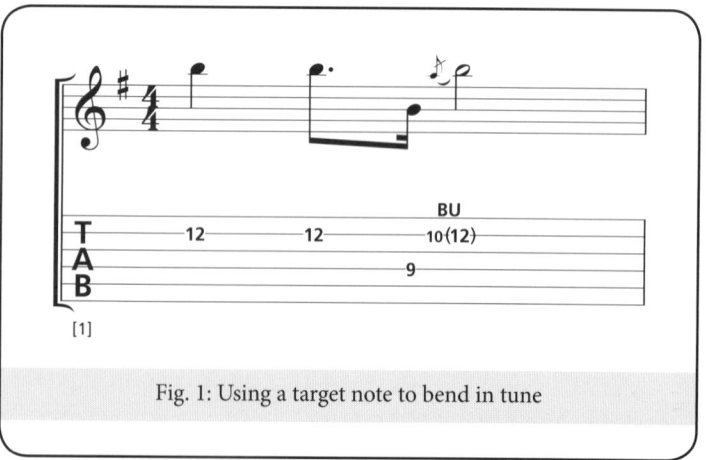

Fig. 1: Using a target note to bend in tune

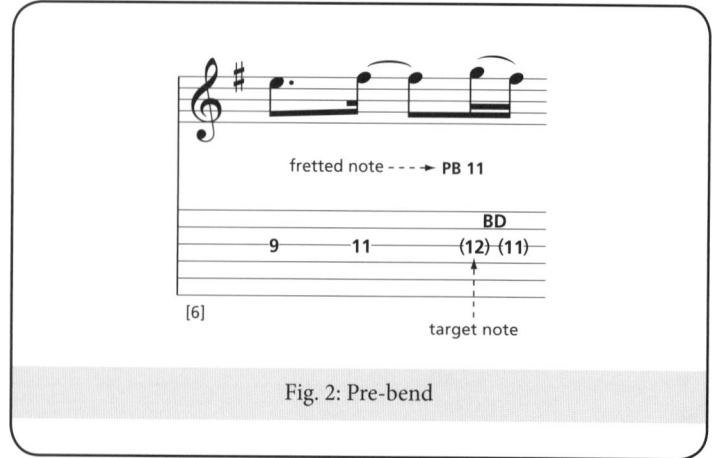

Fig. 2: Pre-bend

Metallica

SONG TITLE: FOR WHOM THE BELL TOLLS
ALBUM: RIDE THE LIGHTNING
RELEASED: 1984
LABEL: MERCURY
GENRE: METAL

PERSONNEL: JAMES HETFIELD (VOX+GTR)
KIRK HAMMETT (GTR)
CLIFF BURTON (BASS)
LARS ULRICH (DRUMS)

UK CHART PEAK: N/A
US CHART PEAK: N/A

© Georg Hochmuth/epa/Corbis

BACKGROUND INFO

'For Whom The Bell Tolls' is one of Metallica's most popular songs and can be found on their second album *Ride The Lightning*, released in 1984. It features an attention-grabbing chromatic intro riff that sounds like guitar but was actually played on bass…

THE BIGGER PICTURE

Metallica began as one of the major thrash metal bands of the 1980s. Like their fellow thrashers, Metallica were inspired by the New Wave Of British Heavy Metal (NWOBHM) and staple-gunned the riffs and motifs of this movement to the fast, aggressive drums of the hardcore punk scene.

This was the sound of Metallica's debut album *Kill 'Em All* (1983). However, by the time the group started to record their second album *Ride The Lightning* they had begun experimenting with slower tempos and a more melodic style of metal. This was evident on the power ballad 'Fade To Black' and also on 'For Whom The Bell Tolls', which clocks in at 120 BPM as opposed to thrash's more common 160+. It was the start of a progression from thrash to something bigger and broader, which led to Metallica's becoming the biggest metal band on the planet.

NOTES

The opening riff of 'For Whom The Bell Tolls' was written on bass guitar by Cliff Burton before he joined Metallica. Footage on YouTube of Metallica performing at the Day On The Green, Oakland in 1985 shows Burton playing the figure at the 16th fret of his bass while using a wah pedal. Burton was a hugely creative bass player and contributed much to the band before his death in a road accident during a tour of Europe in 1986. You can hear more of his bass playing on '(Anesthesia) Pulling Teeth' from the album *Kill 'Em All* – and listen out for his classical-sounding solo on *Master Of Puppets*'s 'Orion'.

RECOMMENDED LISTENING

'Whiplash' and 'Seek And Destroy' off *Kill 'Em All* epitomise Metallica's early thrash sound. *Master Of Puppets* signalled the beginning of a move away from thrash and was the peak of Metallica's musical accomplishments during the Cliff Burton era. The title track summed this up best in its fusing of classical guitars with fierce thrash riffing. 1991's 'Black Album' was controversial for its introduction of shorter, single-friendly arrangements but remains one of Metallica's finest records. 'Enter Sandman', 'Sad But True' and 'The Unforgiven' are just a few highlights.

For Whom The Bell Tolls

CD 1 Tracks 9 & 10

Metallica
Words & Music by James Hetfield, Lars Ulrich & Cliff Burton

© Copyright 1984 Creeping Death Music.
Universal Music Publishing Limited.
All Rights Reserved. International Copyright Secured.

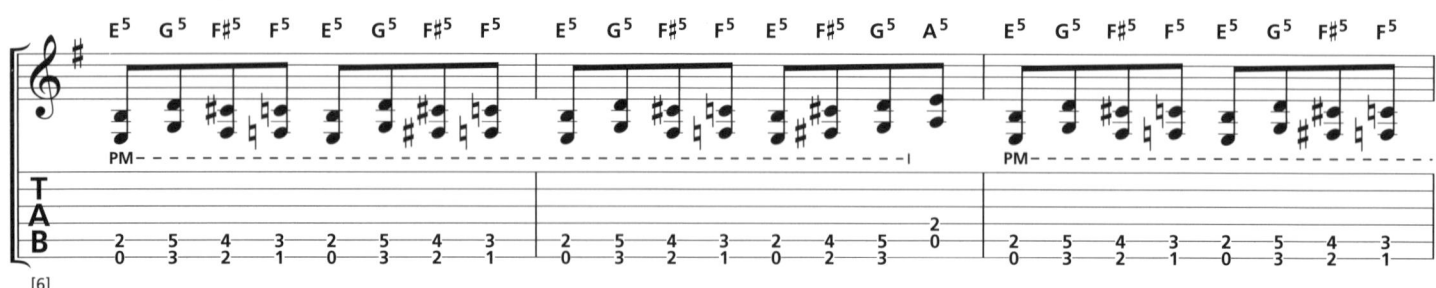
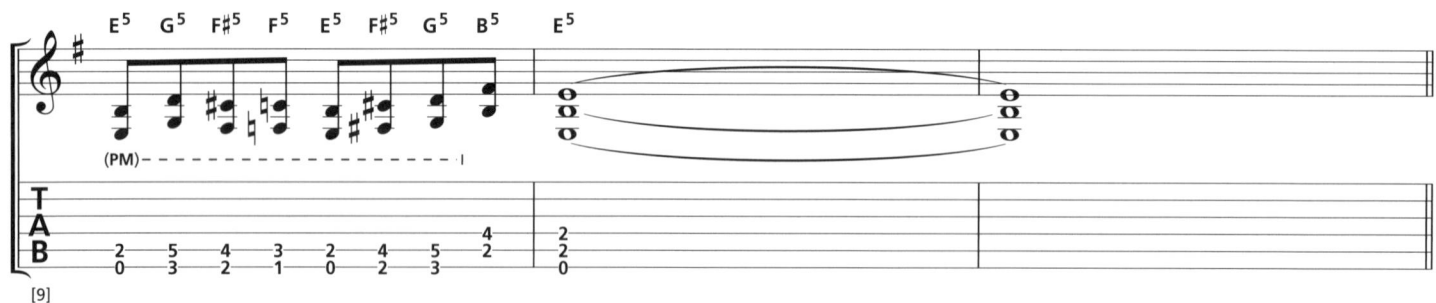
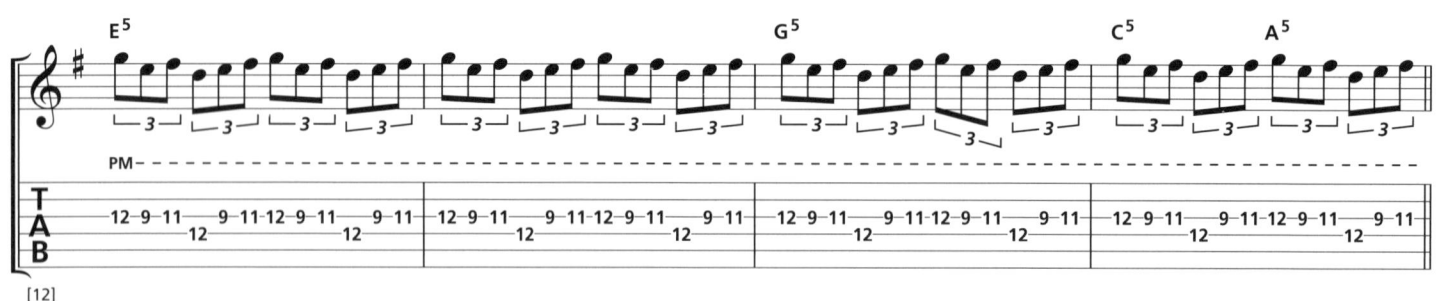
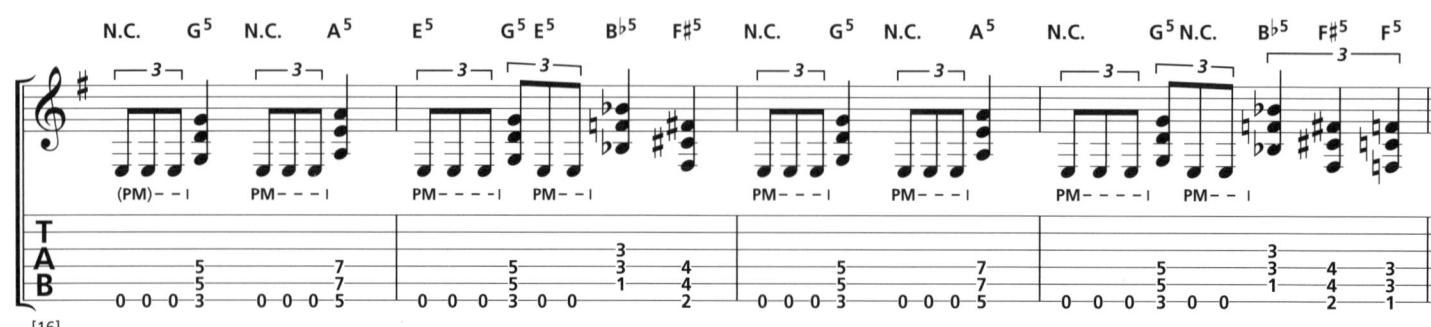

E5 G5
[20]
E5 G5 C5 A5
[24]
N.C. G5 N.C. A5 E5 G5 E5 B♭5 F♯5 N.C. G5 N.C. A5 N.C. G5 N.C. B♭5 F♯5 F5
PM
[28]
E5
PM
[32]
G5 E5 B5
PM
[35]
Solo (6 bars)
E5 F♯5 E5 F♯5 G5
[38]
E5 F♯5 E5 F♯5 G5 E5
[41]

Walkthrough

Tone
Aim for a thick, distorted tone with the tone controls set for a scooped sound (boost bass and treble, turn down mid).

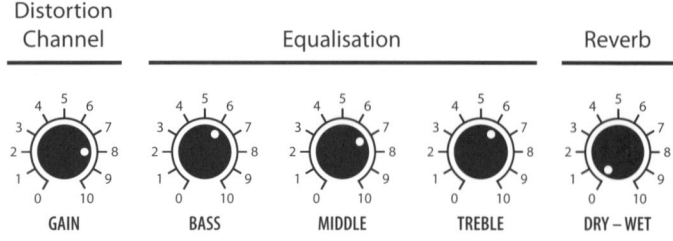

Intro (Bars 1–15)
The intro features a chromatic opening figure, some quick chord changes and a catchy riff played in triplets.

Bars 2–5 | *Chromatic riff*
Use one finger per fret to play this opening, chromatic riff. Make sure that you don't play on the first beat of bars 2 and 4 so that the riff starts on the correct beat (beat two). You can apply heavy vibrato to the F♯ at the end of the riff.

Bars 6–9 | *Quick fretting hand movement*
To play this riff you will have to change powerchords quickly. You can improve the fluency of these chord changes by focusing on keeping the same fretting hand shape throughout, then moving your hand as a unit (with your fingers in the exact same position) to change chord.

Bars 12–15 | *Alternate picking*
Alternate picking is the best way to approach this riff. Although it's technically possible to play using all downstrokes, you may struggle to maintain the speed throughout the whole four bars (Fig. 1).

Chorus 1 & 2 (Bars 16–19 & 28–31)
The chorus features more triplets and powerchords with the open low E string used as a pedal tone.

Bars 16–19 & 28–31 | *Minimising pick motion*
Using downstrokes on every note will produce an authentic metal sound. However, this can be tiring. You can avoid fatigue by using as little movement of the pick as possible. With each downstroke the pick should move only a small amount past the string. Likewise, when you return the pick to the other side of the string you should make sure it moves back only a small distance from the string, ready to perform another downstroke.

Verse & Interlude (Bars 20–37)
The verse features powerchords that are performed on every beat of the bar. The interlude has more lead playing based on triplet rhythms.

Solo & Outro (Bars 38–44)
You will solo over a set of chords here which you will then play as the outro.

Bars 38–40 | *Scale choice*
E minor pentatonic will work well here. A more advanced choice would be E dorian, which is used in the interlude.

Bars 38–40 | *2/4 bar*
Many people treat a 2/4 bar and the first half of the next bar as a bar of 4/4. However, this places the strong beat of the bar (usually beat one) in the wrong place and can be confusing. Count through the bars to help you feel where each new bar starts. You could try playing eighth notes here so it's easier to count through the bars.

Bars 41–43 | *Quarter-note triplets*
The F♯5 and G5 chords are grouped in quarter-note triplets, which means each triplet is spread across two beats. However, you play only the first two notes of each triplet here. Try counting out loud "ev-en-ly" (where each consonant relates to a different note of each triplet) as you play through this section. On the quarter-note triplets you should play only on the "ev-en" part of "ev-en-ly". Fig. 2 shows how the count relates to the TAB.

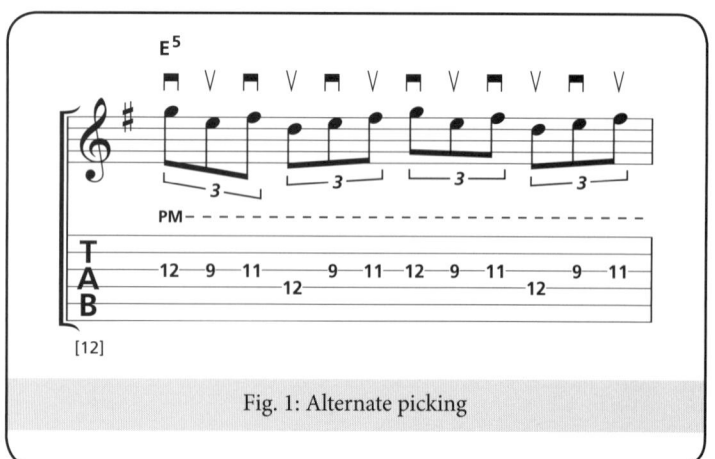

Fig. 1: Alternate picking

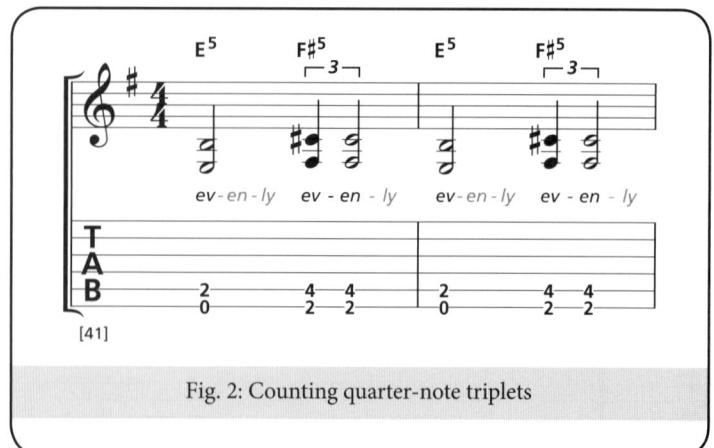

Fig. 2: Counting quarter-note triplets

Joe Satriani

SONG TITLE: ICE 9
ALBUM: SURFING WITH THE ALIEN
RELEASED: 1987
LABEL: EPIC
GENRE: INSTRUMENTAL ROCK

PERSONNEL: JOE SATRIANI (ALL)

UK CHART PEAK: N/A
US CHART PEAK: N/A

© Tim Mosenfelder/TJM/Corbis

BACKGROUND INFO

'Ice 9' was one of three singles released from Joe Satriani's second album, the groundbreaking *Surfing With The Alien*. It features some great, achievable lead work as well as some inspiring soloing from a player who combines virtuosity with musical taste.

THE BIGGER PICTURE

Joe Satriani is one of the best known players in the shred guitar scene. Shredders like Satriani, Steve Vai and Paul Gilbert have incredible technical ability and usually play distorted guitars in an instrumental setting. Satch (as he's known) paid for his first album using a credit card and played most of the instruments himself on it and *Surfing With The Alien*, his second full-length release. Satriani admitted he was worried that after *Surfing…* was released his record company would cancel his contract. When it was released as a single, 'Ice 9' didn't chart, but the album went to number 29 on the American album charts and the title track and 'Satch Boogie' were both played heavily on American rock radio stations. This was unusual for an instrumental guitar album and testimony to Satch's songwriting and arranging skills, which set him apart from many of his contemporaries in the shred scene. He needn't have worried after all.

NOTES

Satriani is a fan of science fiction and much of his work is littered with references to the genre. The song 'Ice 9' is named after a substance in the novel 'Cat's Cradle' by SF author Kurt Vonnegut. More obviously, there's the title of his second album 'Surfing With The Alien' and its cover featuring the Marvel Comics character, the Silver Surfer. The illustration comes from the first issue of the Marvel series 'Silver Surfer' (1982) and its creator, the comic book artist John Byrne, claims he was neither consulted nor paid for its use on Satch's album cover. However, Marvel is credited in the album's sleeve notes and Satriani has explained that a deal was struck between Marvel and the record company.

RECOMMENDED LISTENING

Also from the album *Surfing With The Alien*, 'Midnight' is played entirely by two-hand tapping (where the fingers of the fretting and picking hands are used to tap out chords and melodies). Satriani's third album *Flying In A Blue Dream* (1989) is also considered one of his best and the title track is one of his most popular tunes. The song 'Cool #9' from the album *Joe Satriani* (1995) features some impressive use of wah and whammy effects.

Ice 9

CD 1 Tracks 11 & 12

Joe Satriani
Music by Joe Satriani

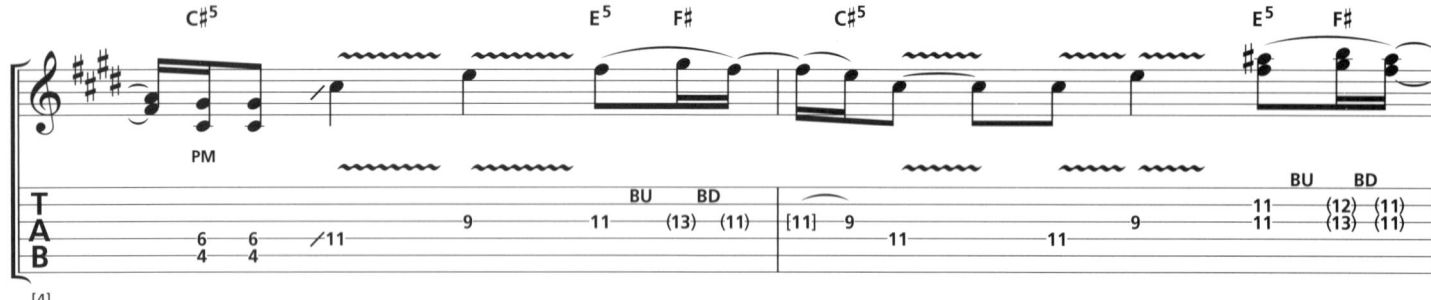
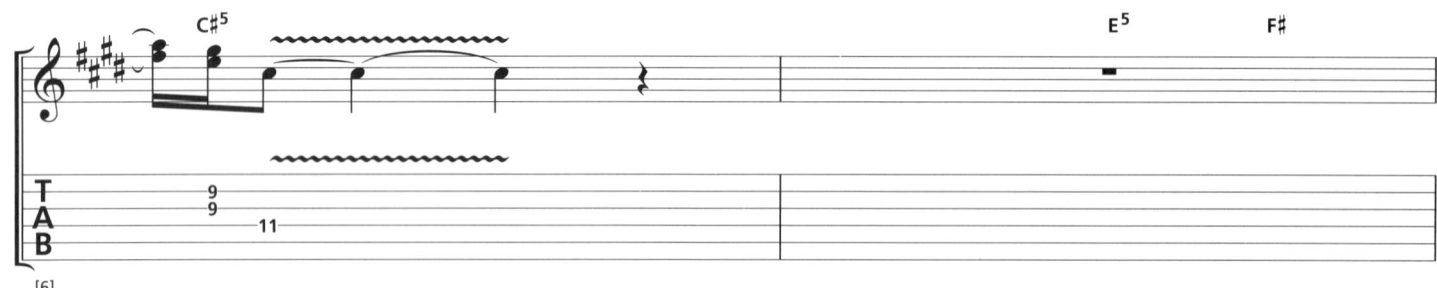
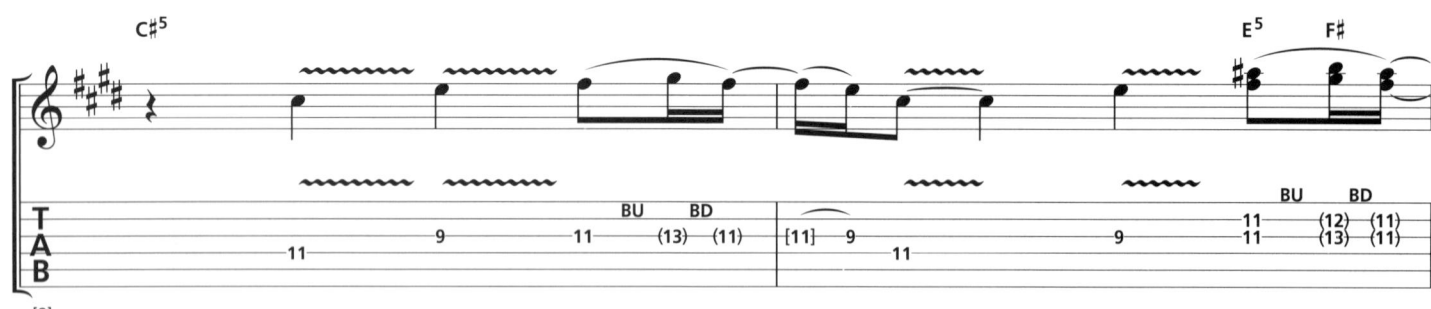
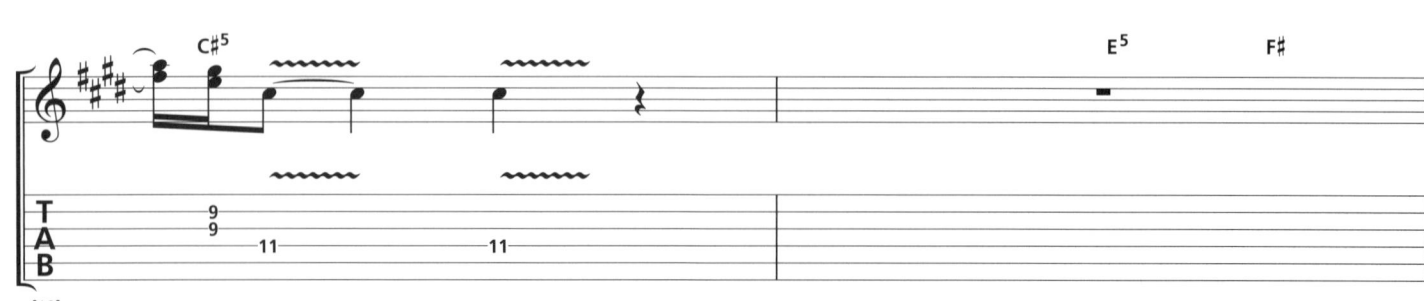

© Copyright Strange Beautiful Music.
Sony/ATV Music Publishing.
All Rights Reserved. International Copyright Secured.

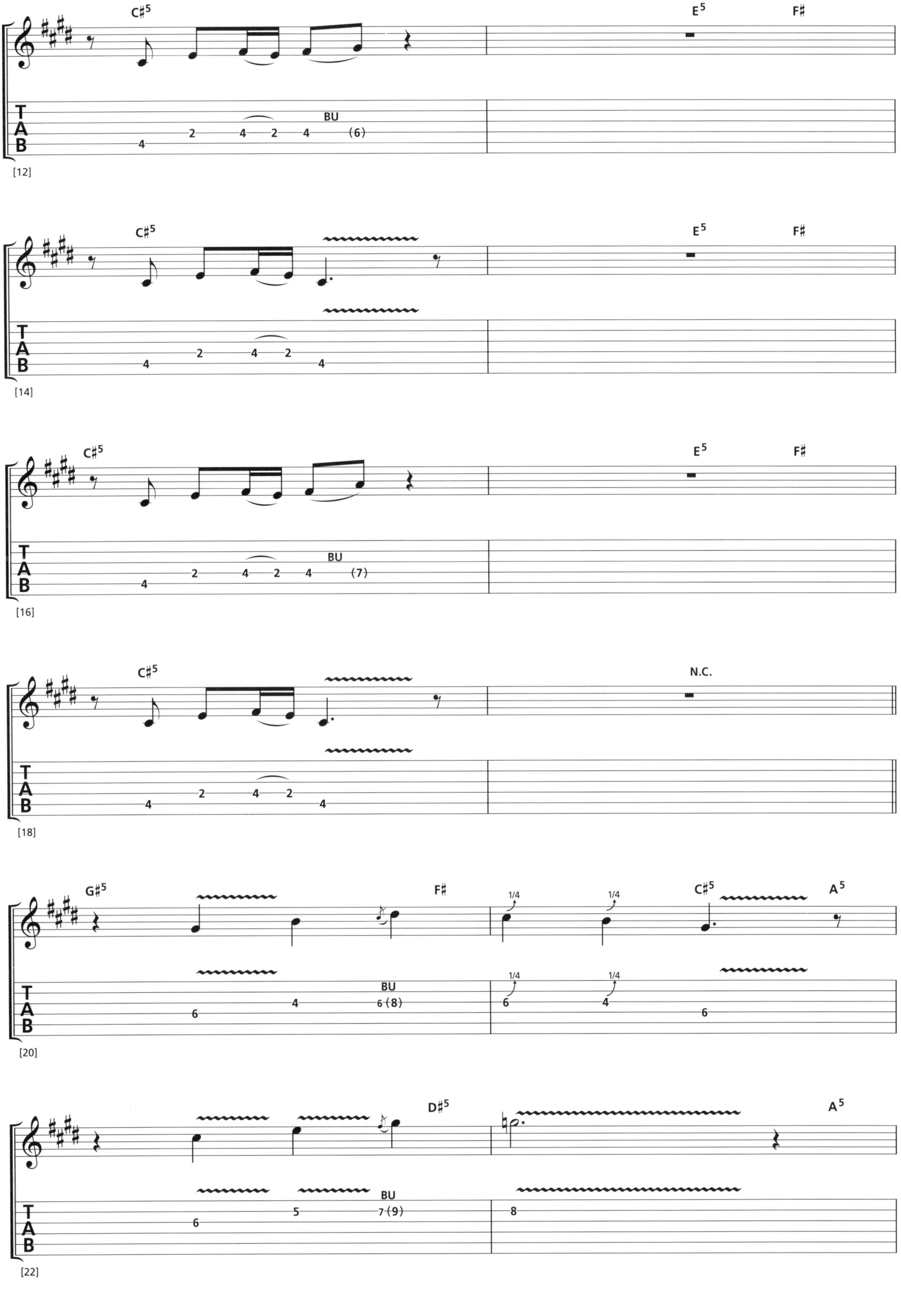
C♯5
E5
F♯
BU
[12]
C♯5
E5
F♯
[14]
C♯5
E5
F♯
BU
[16]
C♯5
N.C.
[18]
G♯5
F♯
1/4
C♯5
A5
BU
[20]
D♯5
A5
BU
[22]

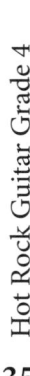

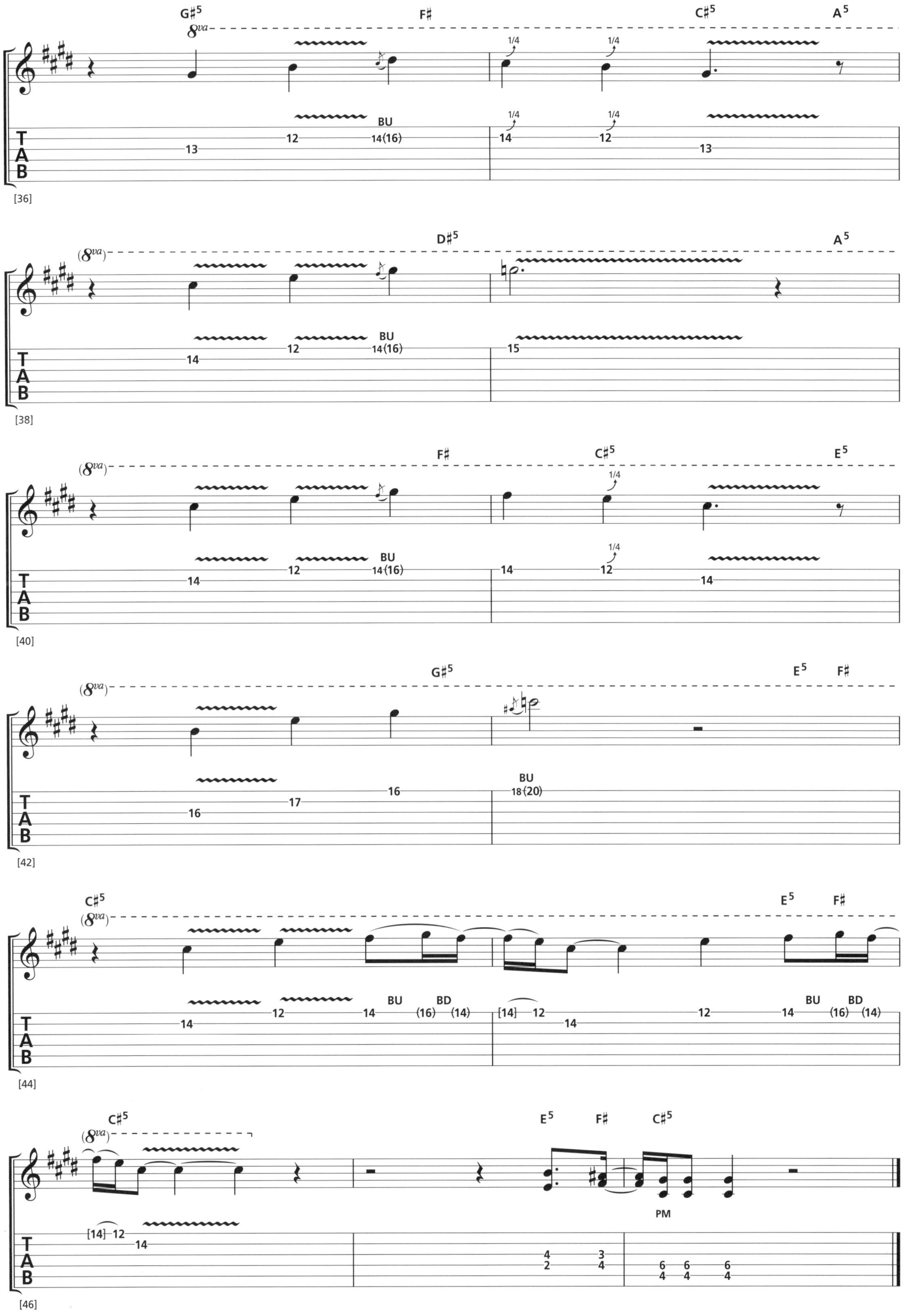

Walkthrough

Tone
Aim for a thick, distorted tone, but avoid the scooped sound where you boost the bass and treble and cut the middle; Satriani's tone on 'Ice 9' has plenty of mid.

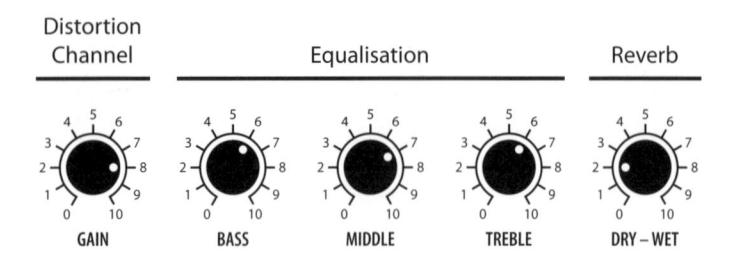

Distortion Channel	Equalisation			Reverb
GAIN	BASS	MIDDLE	TREBLE	DRY – WET

Intro & Verse (Bars 1–11)
The intro is a riff based on the C♯ powerchord at the 4th fret. The verse contains the main theme, based on the C♯ minor pentatonic shape at the 9th fret.

Bars 4–11 | *Rhythmic accuracy*
One of the biggest challenges of this piece is making sure the string bends are performed with the correct rhythms. Try practising the bends with a metronome set to a slower tempo. Once you are confident your bends are played with the correct rhythm, gradually increase the tempo until you are able to play along accurately with the track (Fig. 1).

Bars 4–11 | *Vibrato*
To make your vibrato consistent and more musical try moving your finger in time to a metronome. Play and hold a note while you apply vibrato. Try a shallow vibrato (the string moves only a small distance from its starting point) and a wide vibrato (shake the string more aggressively so it moves further). Aim at being able to move the string by the same amount each time you move it so that your vibrato is consistent in its pitch.

Bars 5–11 | *Double-stop bends*
Fret the double-stop bend with your third finger supported by your first and second fingers. Make sure you maintain pressure into the neck to help keep the notes ringing for the duration of the bend.

Pre-chorus (Bars 12–19)
A new melody is introduced here and performed over the same chord progression as the verse.

Bar 16 | *Minor third string bend*
Use your third finger supported by your first and second fingers to bend the string down towards the floor to achieve this challenging bend. The key to good string bends is making sure they reach the target note (the note in brackets in the TAB). A good exercise to help you develop your string bends is to play and hold the target note then play the bend.

Having the target note fresh in your memory will help you bend to the correct pitch (Fig. 2).

Chorus 1 (Bars 20–31)
The chorus features some more challenging string bends and opportunities to work on your vibrato.

Bars 20–27 | *Fast string bends*
Fast bends are difficult to play in tune because your ear has less time to register the changes in pitch and recognise when the bend is in tune. Muscle memory plays a big part in fast bends. Play the bends in this phrase slowly and repeatedly, paying close attention to the tuning. This will teach your fingers how far the string should be bent. Gradually increase the speed as you become more comfortable.

Solo & Chorus 2 (Bars 32–48)
This is an edited version of the original 'Ice 9' solo. It stays in one key rather than moving through four. Chorus 2 is a repeat of the first chorus.

Bars 32–35 | *Scale selection*
The C♯ minor pentatonic is the most obvious scale choice for the solo. Another, more advanced, scale choice would be the C♯ dorian mode.

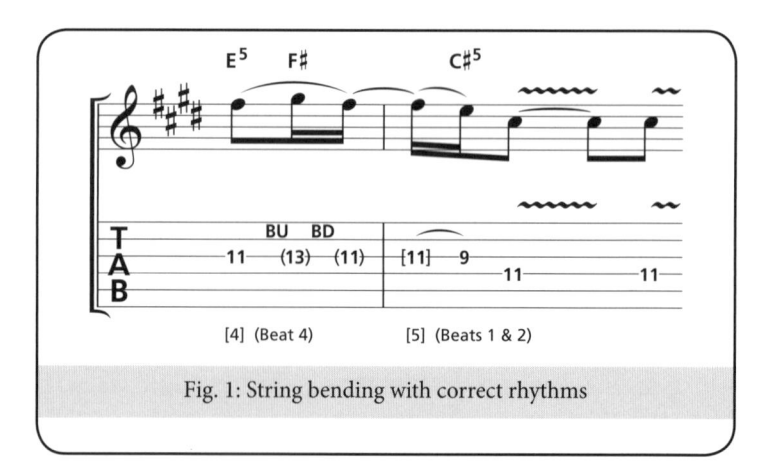

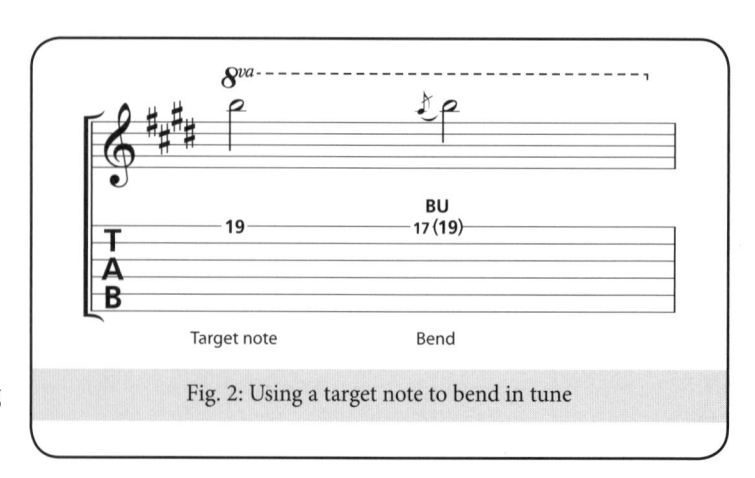

Fig. 1: String bending with correct rhythms

Fig. 2: Using a target note to bend in tune

Black Sabbath

SONG TITLE: IRON MAN
ALBUM: PARANOID
RELEASED: 1970
LABEL: SANCTUARY
GENRE: METAL

PERSONNEL: OZZY OSBOURNE (VOX)
TONY IOMMI (GUITAR)
GEEZER BUTLER (BASS)
BILL WARD (DRUMS)

UK CHART PEAK: N/A
US CHART PEAK: 52

© Scott D. Smith/Retna Ltd/Corbis

BACKGROUND INFO

'Iron Man' is one of several standout tracks from Black Sabbath's second album *Paranoid*. Guitarist Tony Iommi is a tireless creator of classic riffs and this song has plenty of those to offer…

THE BIGGER PICTURE

Black Sabbath was the first proper metal band. Groups like The Kinks, The Who and Led Zeppelin performed heavy, distorted guitar riffs throughout the late 1960s, but it was Black Sabbath who combined in one act so many elements of what is now considered metal: the lyrics that run from the sinister to the political; the bleak imagery; and Tony Iommi's drop-tuned (i.e. heavy) guitar sound. Iommi's drop tuning was a particularly impressive breakthrough: today you would struggle to name a single metal band formed in the past 20 years that doesn't use it.

The group formed in 1969 in Birmingham, an industrial city at the heart of England's Midlands. Musically, Sabbath was inspired by the kind of heavy blues pioneered by the band Cream, but by the end of 1970 Osbourne, Iommi, Butler and Ward had released a self-titled debut and a follow-up, *Paranoid*, which sounded shockingly new. Metal was born.

NOTES

Iommi lost the fingertips of his fretting hand in an accident while working in a factory that produced sheet metal. Incredibly, Iommi struggled on, playing his guitar with home-made replacement tips that eased the pain of pressing down on his guitar strings. He found that tuning his strings down helped too, as the slack strings were more forgiving on his fingertips. It was already common to tune down to E♭ if a singer felt more comfortable singing in a lower key, but Iommi dropped his low E string all the way down to C♯ (and the other strings by the same interval). The effect was welcome pain relief but also a mean, growling sound that has become metal's signature.

RECOMMENDED LISTENING

The title track of *Black Sabbath* is famous for its use of the tritone or 'Devil's interval' in its riff. It's a ♭5, which in the song's key of G is D♭. The sinister sound was influenced by Hammer Horror film soundtracks. 'War Pigs', like 'Iron Man', is a feast of guitar riffs off the album *Paranoid*. The third Black Sabbath album, *Master Of Reality* (1971), is notable for its use of down-tuning. 'Children Of The Grave', 'Lord Of This World' and 'Into The Void' were the first recorded instances of Tony Iommi tuned his guitar down to C♯.

Iron Man

CD 1 Tracks 13 & 14

Black Sabbath
Words & Music by Frank Iommi, Terence Butler, William Ward & John Osbourne

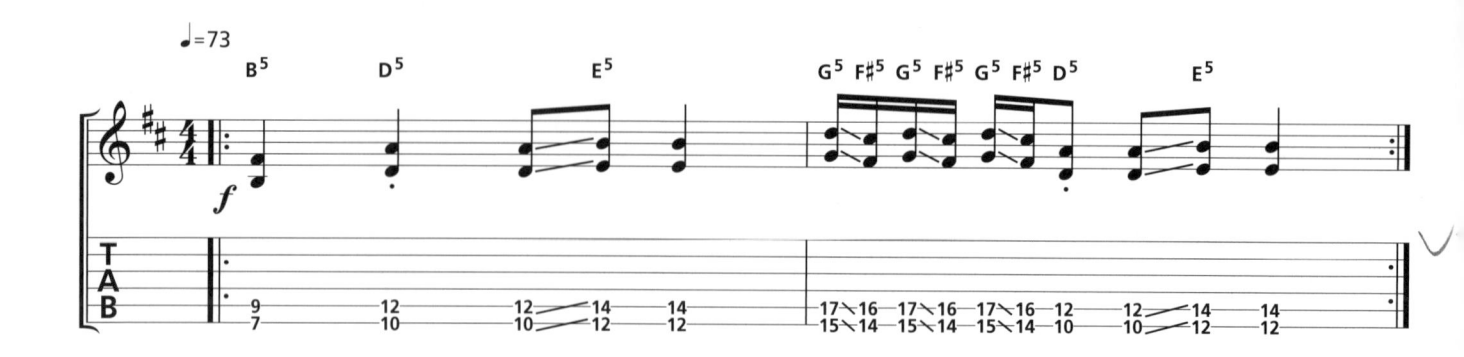

© Copyright 1971 Westminster Music Limited.
All Rights Reserved. International Copyright Secured.

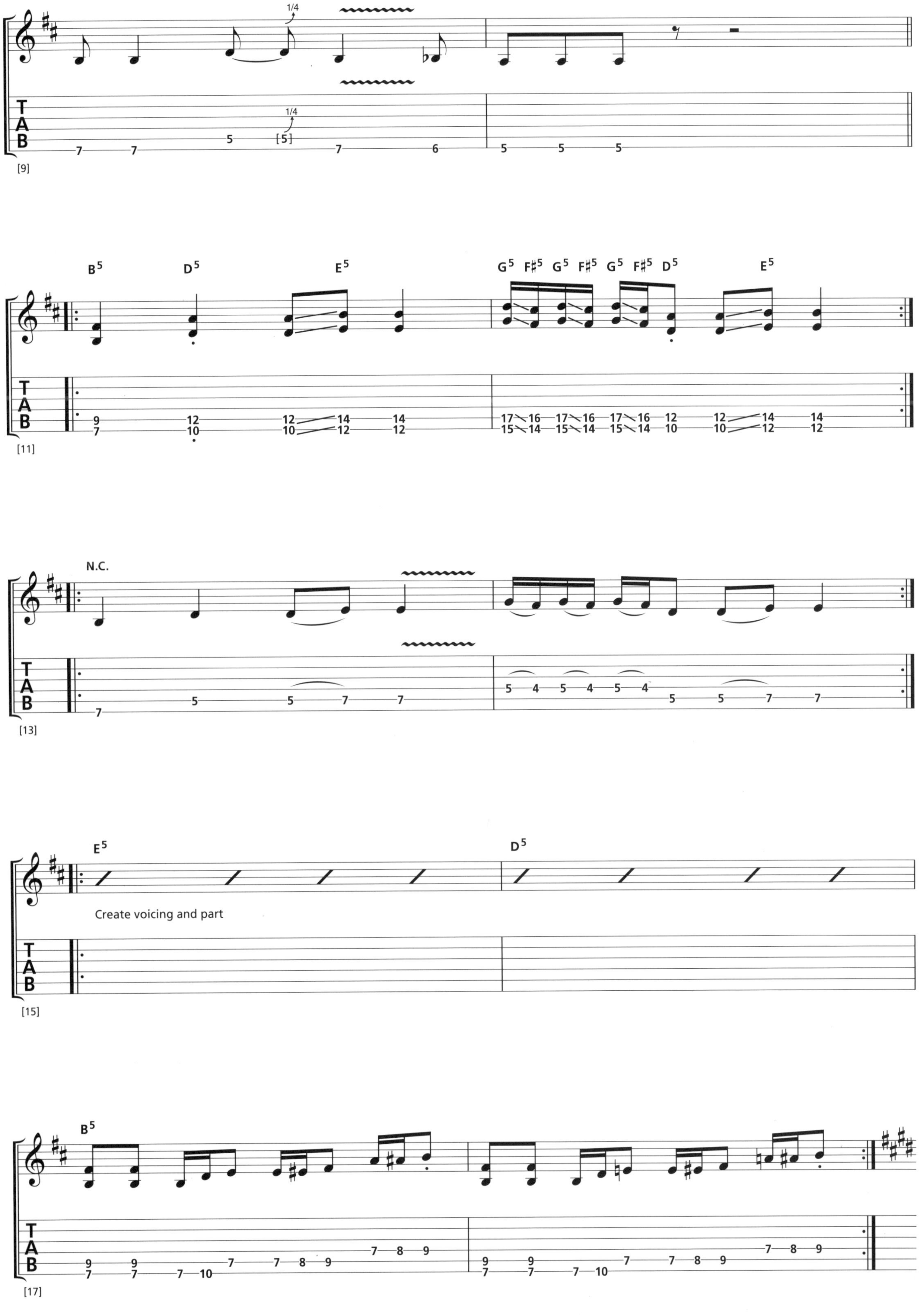
[9]
B5
D5
E5
G5 F♯5 G5 F♯5 G5 F♯5 D5
E5
[11]
N.C.
[13]
E5
D5
Create voicing and part
[15]
B5
[17]

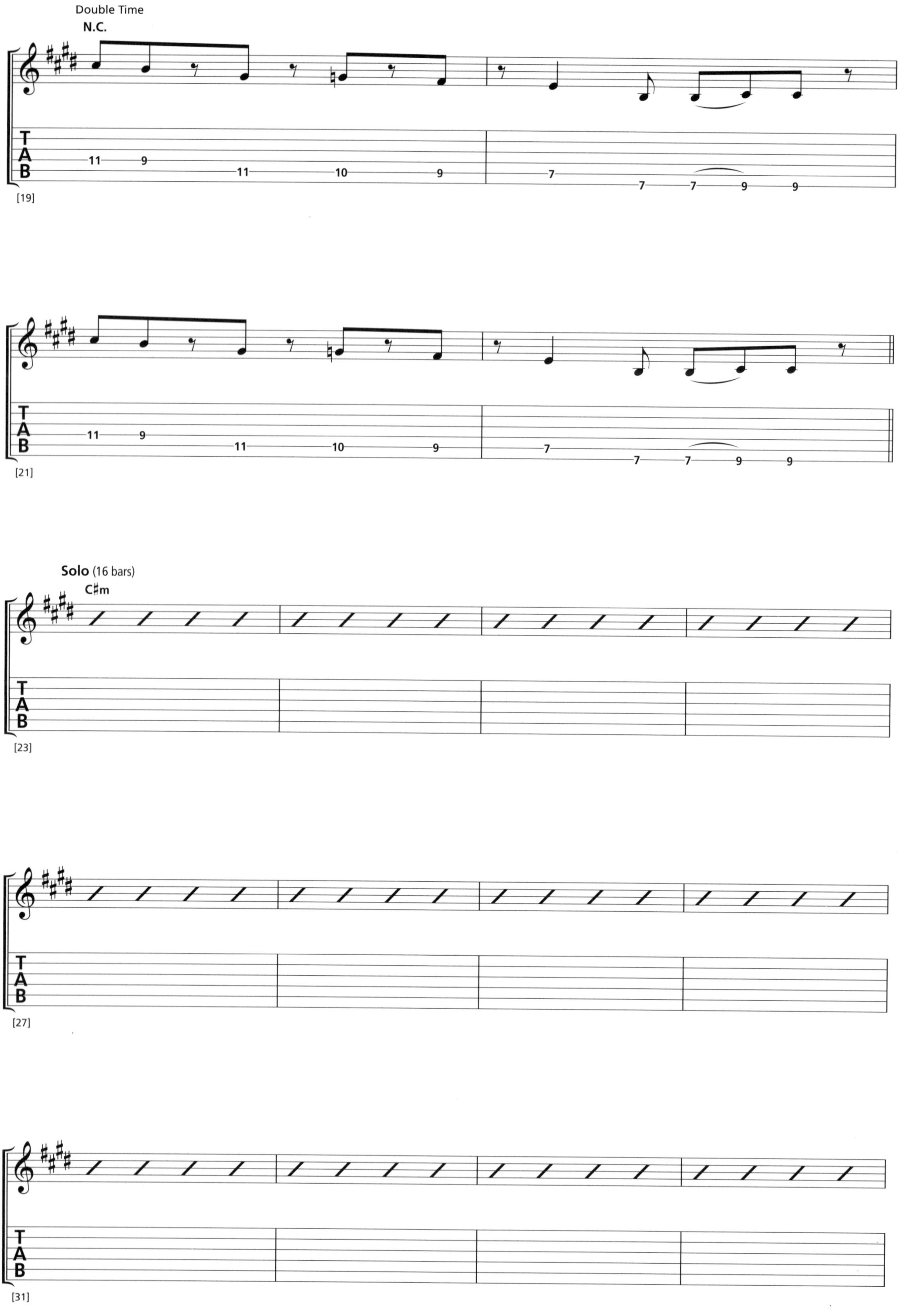
Double Time
N.C.
[19]
[21]
Solo (16 bars)
C♯m
[23]
[27]
[31]

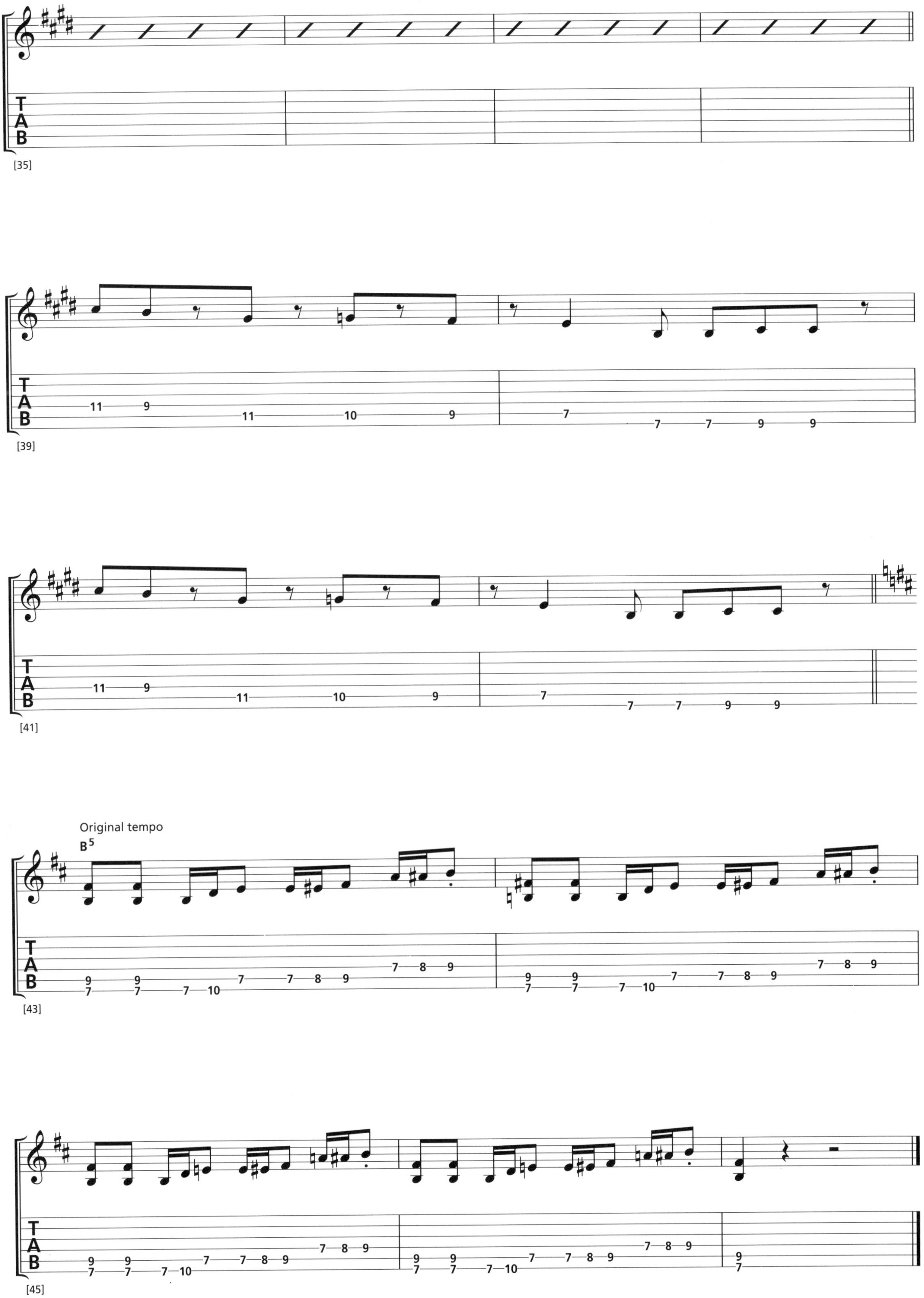
[35]
[39]
[41]
Original tempo
B5
[43]
[45]

Walkthrough

Tone
Aim for a heavily distorted tone with plenty of middle and treble. 'Iron Man' is surprisingly light on bass.

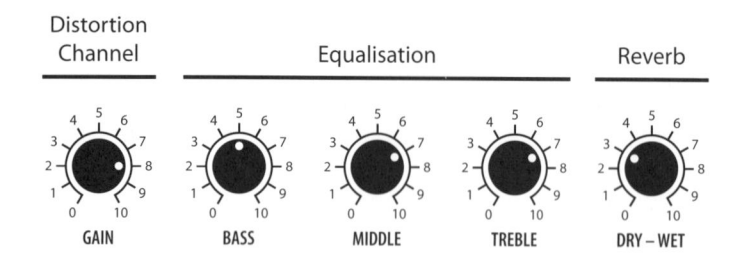

Verse 1 (Bars 1–4)
The song's signature powerchord riff is played in bars 1 and 2. A variation of this riff, played as single notes, follows.

Bars 1–2 | *Moving powerchords*
Think of the powerchords in this riff as a single shape moved around the fretboard. Lock your hand into the powerchord shape when you play the B^5 chord then think of moving your whole hand rather than individual fingers.

Bars 1–2 | *Sliding powerchords*
Maintain pressure into the neck throughout each slide so the strings ring out and there are no gaps. This is especially important for the 16th notes on the first beat of bar 2.

Bar 4 | *Playing evenly*
Guitarists tend to rush when playing 16th-note pull-offs like those at the start of bar 4. All these notes should be the same length. Practise playing along with a metronome, concentrating on playing the first note of each beat at the exact same time as the metronome click and ensuring that each 16th note is the same length as the others (Fig. 1).

Interlude (Bars 5–10)
Another single-note riff is introduced here with lots of vibrato and quarter-tone bends to deal with.

Bars 5–10 | *Quarter-tone bends*
A quarter-tone bend is usually quick and players should avoid trying to make their bends precisely a quarter tone. Use your instinct to guide you; the quarter-tone bend is a technique that relies heavily on feel for its sound.

Verse 2 (Bars 11–14)
Verse 2 is a reprise of the previous section. It uses both the powerchord and single-note versions of the riff, and leads the song into the chorus.

Chorus (Bars 15–18)
You should create your own chord voicings and part in the first two bars of the chorus. These are followed by a riff that repeats in the next two bars.

Bars 15–16 | *Create voicing and part*
In bars 15–16 you can use whichever voicings you feel work best, but you may find that voicings that are far away from each other will be difficult to move between and may sound disjointed. Use a rhythm you think fits the style of the piece.

Double Time Riff & Solo (Bars 19–42)
The double time blues scale riff precedes and follows the guitar solo.

Bars 23–38 | *Scale choice*
The C♯ minor pentatonic scale is the most obvious scale choice for the solo. Another good choice would be the C♯ blues scale (Fig. 2).

Bars 23–38 | *Guitar solo*
With a solo of this length over a bassline that implies a single chord it is easy to fall into playing collections of licks rather than creating a coherent musical idea. You will need to plan a basic structure (even if you improvise within it) to build an effective solo that has direction and complements the song.

Outro (Bars 43–46)
The riff you played in the chorus is repeated here. This is the outro for this exam version, not the full track.

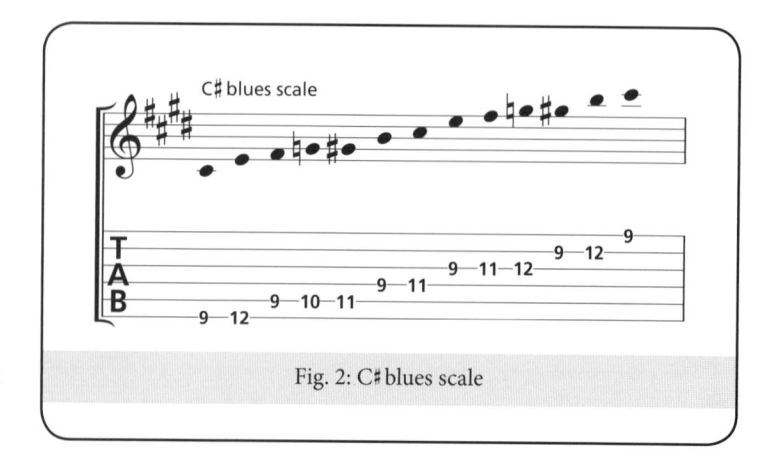

Fig. 1: Playing 16th-note pull-offs evenly

Fig. 2: C♯ blues scale

AC/DC

SONG TITLE: WHOLE LOTTA ROSIE
ALBUM: LET THERE BE ROCK
RELEASED: 1977
LABEL: ATCO
GENRE: HARD ROCK

PERSONNEL: BON SCOTT (VOX)
ANGUS YOUNG (GUITAR)
MALCOLM YOUNG (GUITAR)
CLIFF WILLIAMS (BASS)
PHIL RUDD (DRUMS)

UK CHART PEAK: 36
US CHART PEAK: N/A

© Simone Cecchetti/Corbis

BACKGROUND INFO

'Whole Lotta Rosie' is a great example of Bon Scott era AC/DC. We've TAB'ed the classic live version from the album *If You Want Blood, You've Got It* (1978).

THE BIGGER PICTURE

AC/DC was formed in Australia in 1973 by brothers Angus and Malcolm Young. Having achieved success in Australia, the group signed to Atlantic Records and moved to London in 1976 following the release of the album *High Voltage*. In Britain the band's formidable live show and brutal rock grooves were picked up on by members of the punk scene who mistook AC/DC for one of their own. The group was similarly confused with the New Wave Of British Heavy Metal but has always maintained that AC/DC is simply a good old-fashioned rock and roll band. *Let There Be Rock* was AC/DC's second album for Atlantic and gave the group its first chart success in Britain, reaching number 17. The success continued and for this incarnation of the band culminated in the brilliant *Highway To Hell* (1979), which cracked the top 20 in Britain and America. But tragedy struck when, on 20 February, 1980, singer Bon Scott was found dead in a friend's car after a night of heavy drinking. He was replaced by Brian Johnson.

NOTES

AC/DC's unmistakable sound is a combination of two things: Phil Rudd's basic but super tight drum groove and the Young brothers' raunchy guitar tone. Malcolm and Angus are instinctive guitarists who prefer to go with what feels good rather than plan out their parts based on any knowledge of music theory. This gives their playing an honesty and a spontaneity that appeals to fans all over the world. Theirs is the perfect hard rock tone, coaxed from a simple set-up of a Gretsch and a Gibson SG run straight into Marshall amps – no effects pedals – with the master volume turned up until the amps distort naturally, as opposed to using their amps' gain controls or overdrive pedals.

RECOMMENDED LISTENING

Bon Scott's last album, *Highway To Hell* (1979), was the moment when AC/DC reached its peak, creatively if not commercially. All the raunch that made the band such a hit with punks and fans of edgy rock and roll was there, and this time it was matched by a whole album's worth of classic tunes. *Back In Black* was just as good and helped launch the band onto greater commercial success. To hear AC/DC at its rawest, try the album *If You Want Blood, You've Got It*, recorded live in Glasgow in 1978.

Whole Lotta Rosie

CD 1 Tracks 15 & 16

AC/DC
Words & Music by Angus Young, Malcolm Young & Bon Scott

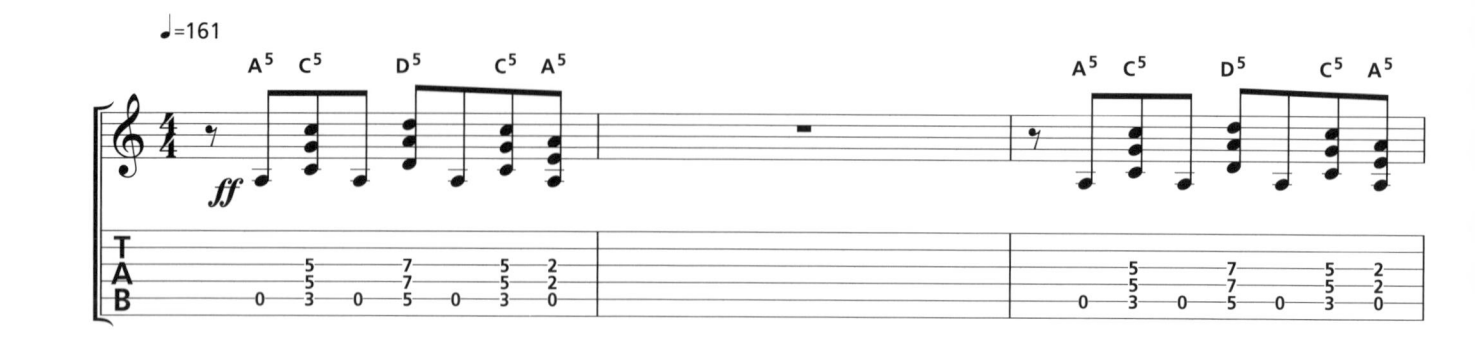

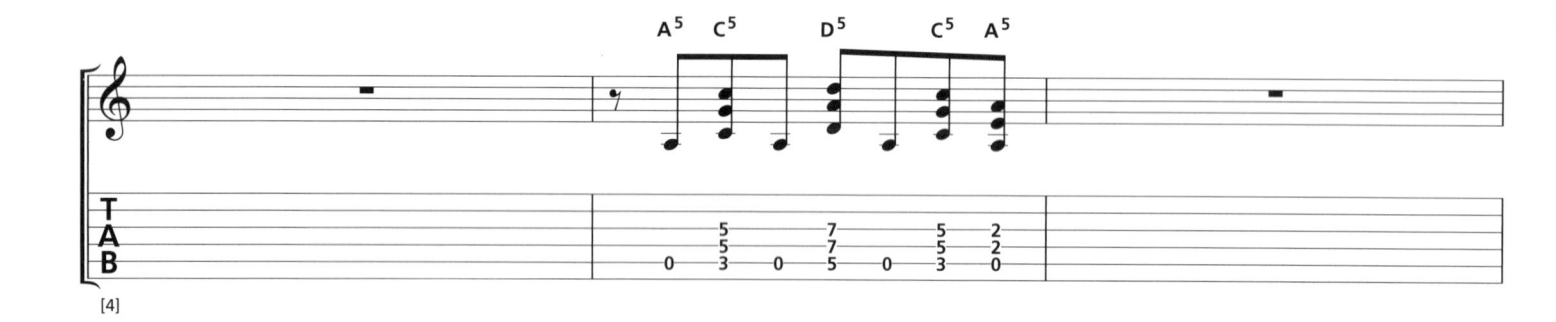

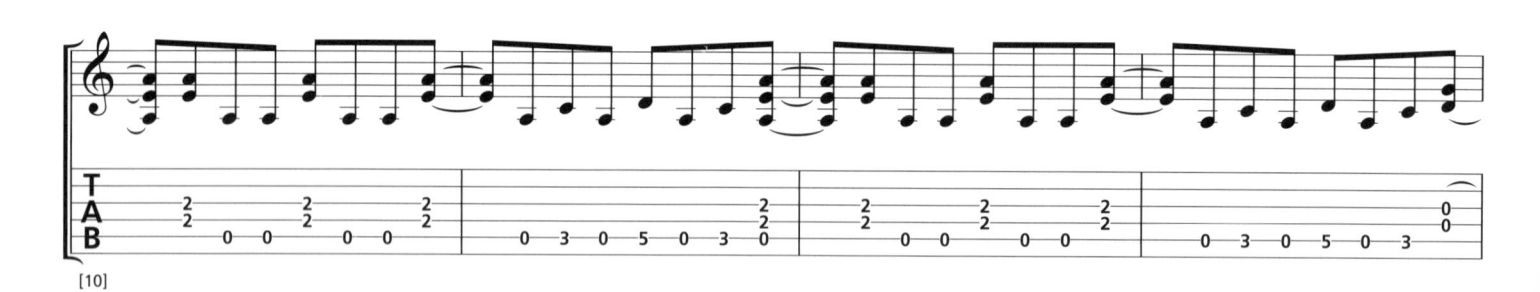

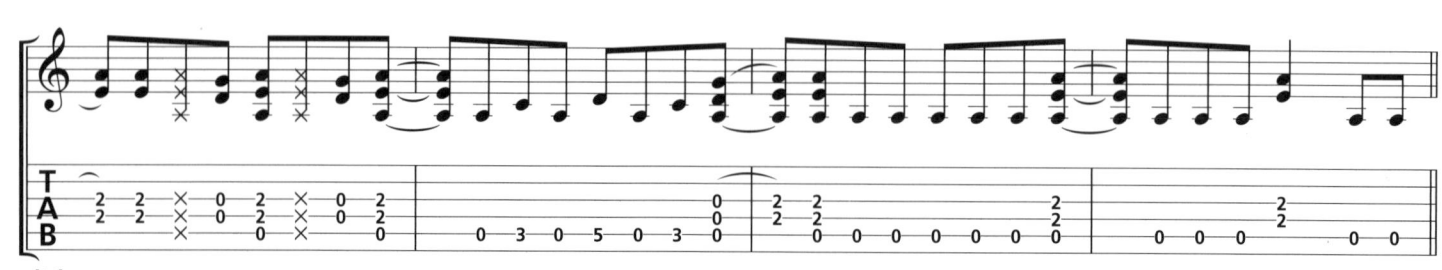

F
D5
[18]
A5
G5
A5
G5
[22]
A5
G5
G5
D/F♯
G5
D/F♯
G5
N.C.
[26]
Solo (16 bars)
A5
[30]
[34]
[38]

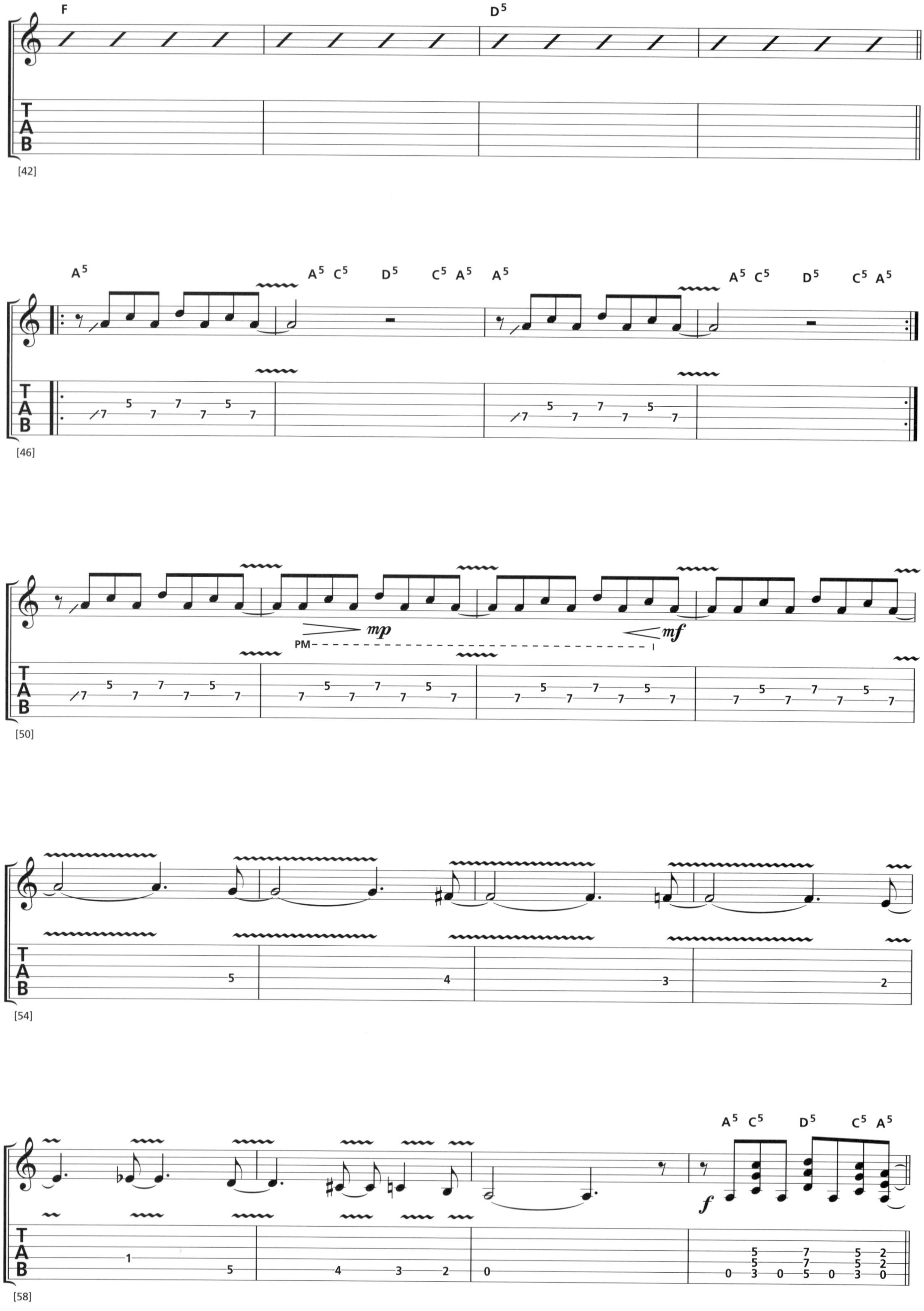

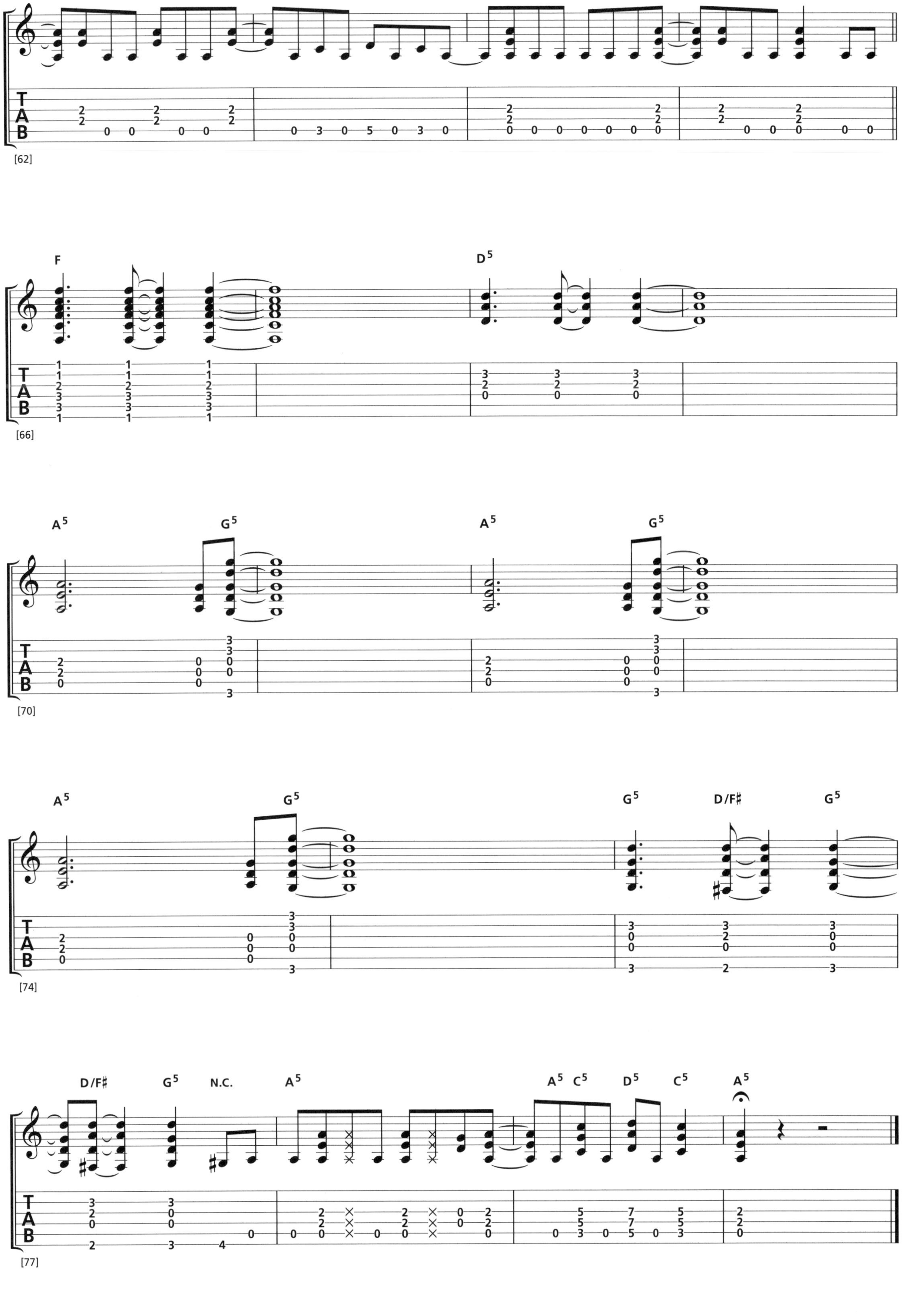
[62]
F
D5
[66]
A5
G5
A5
G5
[70]
A5
G5
G5
D/F♯
G5
[74]
D/F♯
G5
N.C.
A5
A5 C5
D5
C5
A5
[77]

Walkthrough

Tone

The guitar needs a 'crunch' tone – an overdriven sound that is not heavily distorted but not completely clean. Set your gain to around 6. This is just a guide. Your guitar's tone should be just breaking up, but not too distorted: you should still be able to hear every note of the chords in bars 5 and 6.

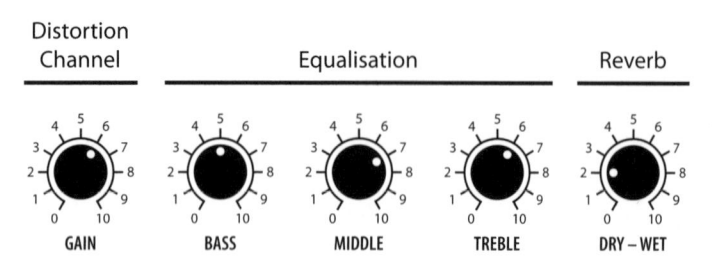

Bars 1–9 Intro/Main riff

The intro uses three-note powerchords and the open A string to create a fast, high-energy riff. This riff is the song's main musical idea and is varied in several sections.

Bars 1–2 | *Moving powerchords*
Think of the C^5 and D^5 powerchords in this riff as a single shape that is moved around the fretboard. Lock your hand into the powerchord shape when you play the C chord then think of moving your whole hand rather than individual fingers. Play the final A^5 chord with your first finger.

Bars 10–17 Verse

The verse is based on the open A5 powerchord and a variation of the main riff.

Bars 13–14 | *Double-stop hammer-on*
Hammer on with your first finger barred across the D and G strings. Make sure the pad of your finger is flat as it hits the fretboard so both strings are played. This can be practised in isolation until both notes ring out clearly (Fig. 1).

Bars 18–29 Chorus

The chorus is based on open chords and features some fast changes in the last two bars.

Bars 28–29 | *D/F♯ chord*
The D/F♯ is played by fretting a conventional chord then hooking your thumb over the top of the fretboard to play the F♯ on the sixth string. It is possible to fret this chord using conventional fingering, but the song's tempo and the speed of the chord changes would make this difficult (Fig. 2).

Bars 30–45 Solo

This is an opportunity for you to create your own solo over the verse section of the song.

Bars 30–45 | *Building solos*
The improvised section is 16 bars in length. This is quite a long time to be improvising for, so you will need to have a basic idea of the direction of your solo. Starting with slower, low register phrases before moving to busier licks in a higher register is one way in which you could give your solo shape.

Bars 46–61 Interlude

The interlude is a question and answer between the lead guitar and the band. It is based on variations of the main riff.

Bars 46–53 | *Finger rolls*
When two or more notes follow each other on the same fret but different strings you must roll your finger to prevent the notes bleeding into each other. Play the first note with the tip of your finger and play the second note with the pad of your finger by pushing down with your first knuckle. Play the third note by rolling onto the tip of your finger by bending the finger at the first knuckle.

Bars 62–80 Verse 2, Chorus 2 & Outro

Theses three sections are reprises of sections found earlier in the song and bring the piece to a close.

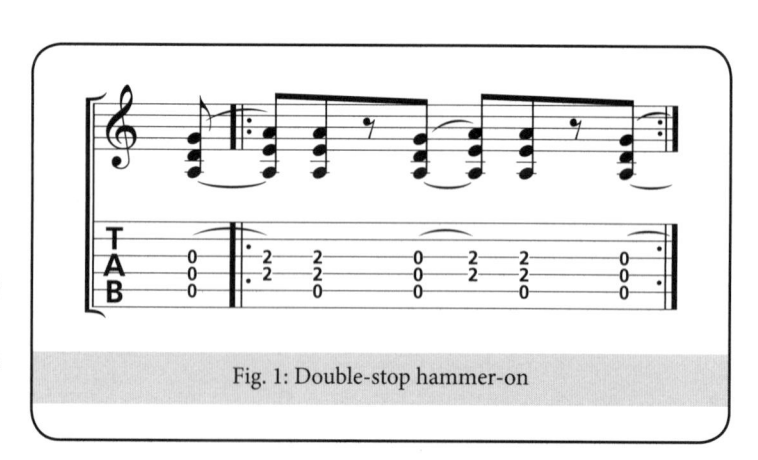

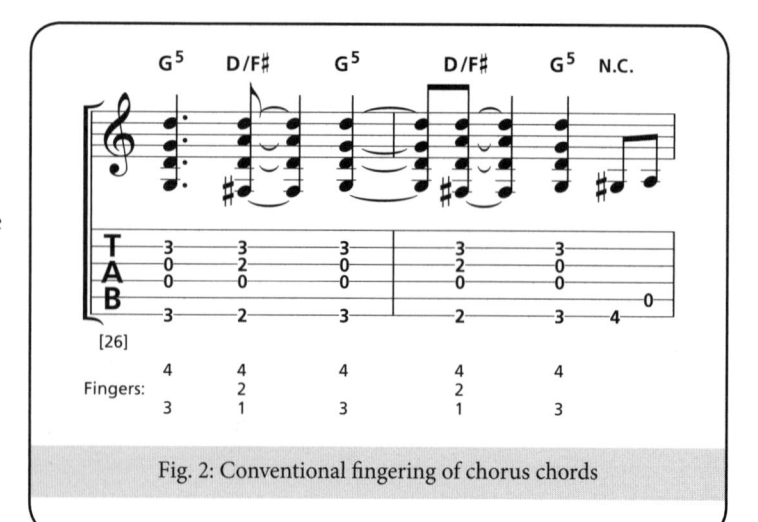

Fig. 1: Double-stop hammer-on

Fig. 2: Conventional fingering of chorus chords

Full Transcriptions

This section contains the full transcriptions of the pieces. These have been prepared for players who would like to perform them in public examinations or for their own sake.

These transcriptions are each accompanied by a Walkthrough. Many of the sections of these songs are similar to the exam versions found in the first half of the book; therefore, the Walkthroughs focus on the parts of the tracks and techniques which are different to the exam versions. In most cases this involves an in-depth analysis of the technique required to play the solo sections.

The accompanying audio for these arrangements can be found on CD 2. There are two tracks for each song: the first is the full performance including the guitar part, while the second is the backing track without the main guitar part. Where parts are doubled-tracked on the original recording (different guitars playing identical parts) both parts have been removed to avoid confusion and make room for the part being performed by the candidate.

© Henry Ruggeri/Corbis

Before I Fall To Pieces

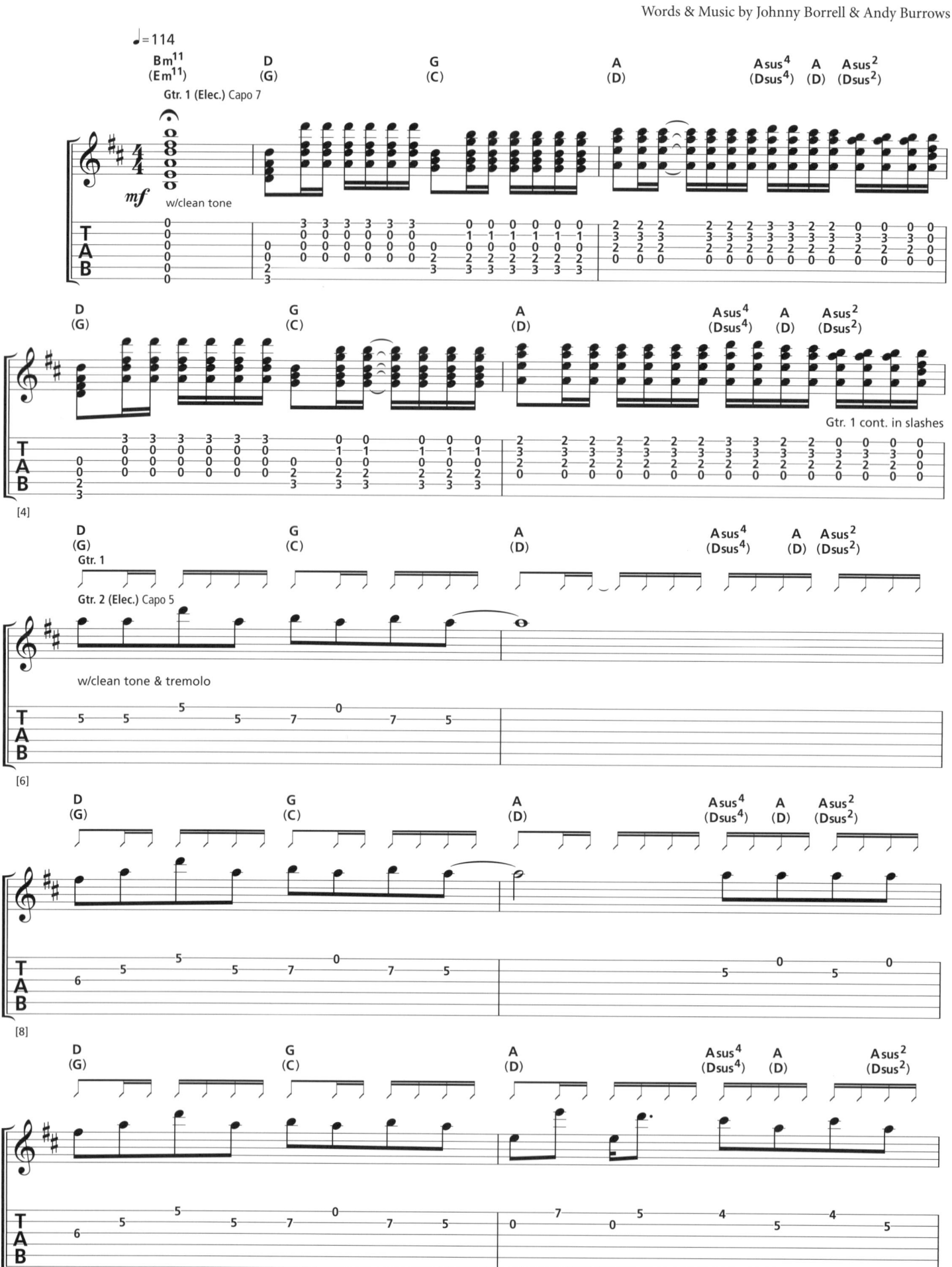

CD 2 Tracks 1 & 2

Razorlight
Words & Music by Johnny Borrell & Andy Burrows

© Copyright 2006 Sony/ATV Music Publishing.
All Rights Reserved. International Copyright Secured.

D (G) G (C) A (D) Asus4 (Dsus4) A (D) Asus2 (Dsus2)
Oh,
TAB
[12]
Verse
D (G) G (C) A (D) D (G) G (C)
one more drink and then I'll go, (se - ri - ous - ly). But there's one more thing I've got to know.
let's just get this whole thing straight, I don't wan - na kid - nap the truth then ne - go - ti - ate.
8va
TAB
[14]
A (D) D (G) G (C) A (D)
Does he take you pla - ces that I don't? And what
Or miss the point and aim at you, just wan - na
2° Gtr. 2
8va
NH
TAB
[17]

D (G) G (C) A (D) D (G) G (C)
hap-pened to the sto-ry that we wrote? You just say you don't know, you don't know.
hear you say some-thing that you be - lieve to be true. But you say you don't know, you don't know.
8va
NH
[20]
A (D) Asus4 (Dsus4) A (D) D (G) G (C) A (D)
1.
Oh, no you don't know, you don't know. Whoo!
You just say you don't know, you don't know.
[23]
D (G) G (C) A (D) Asus4 (Dsus4) A (D) Asus2 (Dsus2) D (G) G (C)
[26]

2.
A (D)
Asus4 (Dsus4)
Asus2 (Dsus2)
D (G)
G (C)
Oh, What it feels like.
[29]
What it feels like. And so I'll go,
[32]
be - fore I fall to pie - ces. Yes I'll go,
f
[35]
be - fore I fall to pie - ces. Now I'm just
[37]

Em (Am) A (D) D (G) G (C) Em (Am) A (D)
wait - ing for some - thing that might nev - er come. If it's a mil - lion to one shot, I'll make
[39]
D (G) G (C) Bm (Em) A (D) D (G) G (C)
sure I'm one. Seems that no - thing is cer - tain, 'cept that truth turns to lies. Nev-er
[42]
D (G) G (C) D (G) A (D)
fig-ured it out or found out why. So I'll go,
[45]
Interlude
D (G) G (C) A (D) D (G) G (C)
mp
yes I'll go. Yes I'll go, yes I'll go.
[48]

A (D)
D (G)
G (C)
A (D)
Oh ba-by I'll go, oh, yes I'll go. Yes I'll go,
mf
[51]
D (G)
G (C)
A (D)
ah yes I'll go.
Chorus
D (G)
G (C)
Be-fore I fall to pie-
f
[54]
A (D)
Asus4 (Dsus4)
A (D)
Asus2 (Dsus2)
D (G)
G (C)
A (D)
Asus4 (Dsus4)
A (D)
Asus2 (Dsus2)
-ces. Be-fore I fall to pie-ces. Yes I'll go,
[57]
D (G)
G (C)
A (D)
Asus4 (Dsus4)
A (D)
Asus2 (Dsus2)
D (G)
G (C)
be-fore I fall to pie-ces. Yes I'll go, be-fore I fall to pie-
[60]

A (D) Asus4 (Dsus4) A (D) Asus2 (Dsus2) D (G) G (C) A (D) Asus4 (Dsus4) A (D) Asus2 (Dsus2)
- ces.
Oh,
[63]
D (G) G (C) A (D) Asus4 (Dsus4) A (D) Asus2 (Dsus2) D (G) G (C)
oh,
oh.
Oh,
oh,
oh.
[66]
A (D) Asus4 (Dsus4) A (D) Asus2 (Dsus2) D (G) G (C) A (D) Asus4 (Dsus4) A (D) Asus2 (Dsus2)
Oh,
oh,
oh.
[69]
D (G) G (C) A (D) D (G) G (C) A (D)
[72]
D (G) G (C) D (G) A (D) D (G) G (C) Bm (Em) A (D)
[76]

Notes On The Full Transcription

Using A Capo
The capo should be placed close to but not on top of the fret in a position parallel to the fret. Set it up so that there is just enough (i.e. not too much) pressure on the strings as this could put them out of tune. Make sure that you place the capo directly on top of the strings as you clamp it down (in the position you intend it to be in once it's clamped) so that the strings aren't bent out of tune.

Bars 1–79 | *Capo notation*
The numbers in the TAB notation are relative to the position of the capo. This means a note marked as '6' indicates that you should play six frets higher than the capo. Capo notation can seem confusing at first, so work slowly through the first few sections of the piece and bear in mind that there are two different guitars with capos at different frets.

Bars 1–79 | *Capo chord notation*
The chords above the notation show the actual pitches of the chords. However, because of the capo, playing the regular open chord shapes that match these symbols will produce the wrong chord. The chords in brackets show the open chord shapes that will produce the correct sound.

Bar 1 | *Opening chord*
The opening 'chord' is simply the open strings strummed once. This produces an unresolved sound that creates a feeling of anticipation before the song's first proper chords.

Bar 1 | *Fermata*
At first glance it looks as if the note in bar 1 should last only four beats. However, it is marked with a *fermata* which means you should hold the note for longer than the specified notation. In the original version of the song the first chord rings for a period of time that doesn't fit a specific number of beats or bars. In this recording the chord lasts for two bars and a count is included to help you start the strumming at the correct time.

Bars 2–5 | *16th-note strumming*
It can be difficult to play these bars fluently because your hand has to move four times per beat at a high tempo. Aim to reduce the distance your hand has to travel back and forth, and therefore reduce the amount of effort you have to make to strum the part. This will help you with your stamina, particularly in the latter part of the song.

Bars 2–5 | *Fretting accuracy*
The capo's location for this part means there is much less room for your fingers to fret the chords than in open position. This can make accuracy a problem, especially on the suspended chords at the end of bars 3 and 5 when you will have to move your fingers quickly and precisely. Make sure you fret the chords with the tips of your fingers to avoid accidentally muting the strings with the underside of your fingers. Adjusting the position of your thumb may help.

Rhythm Notation
If you have worked your way through the main guitar parts, you might like to play the rhythm notation above the stave. This is the part played by the guitar that opens the song and then complements the main part. Start by strumming the chords without following the rhythm notation, then add the rhythms when you are more comfortable with the changes. Some are quite complex, especially taking into account the high tempo, so count slowly through the bar to work out exactly where each note falls (Fig. 1).

Bars 10-13 | *Playing smoothly*
Play this melodic guitar part as smoothly as possible by holding down each note for its full duration so that the notes bleed into each other and there is no discernible gap between each note.

Bars 18-21 | *Natural harmonics*
Natural harmonics are sounded by lightly placing your finger *directly over* the frets. Don't make contact with any part of the fretboard. Your finger placement for the 7th-fret harmonic must be fairly precise, so don't be discouraged if it takes a while to sound it correctly. If you are new to natural harmonics spend some time playing them at the 12th fret as these are the easiest to sound (Fig. 2).

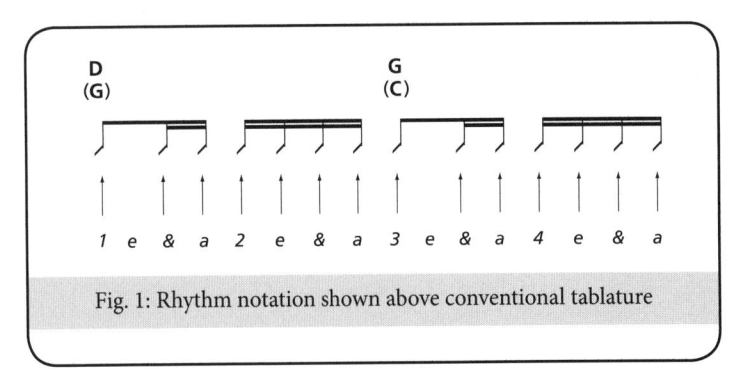

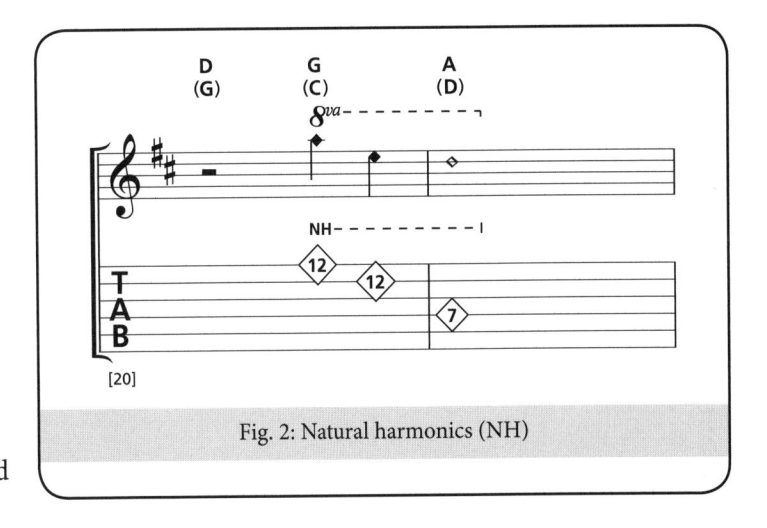

Fig. 1: Rhythm notation shown above conventional tablature

Fig. 2: Natural harmonics (NH)

The Boys Are Back In Town

Thin Lizzy
Words & Music by Phil Lynott

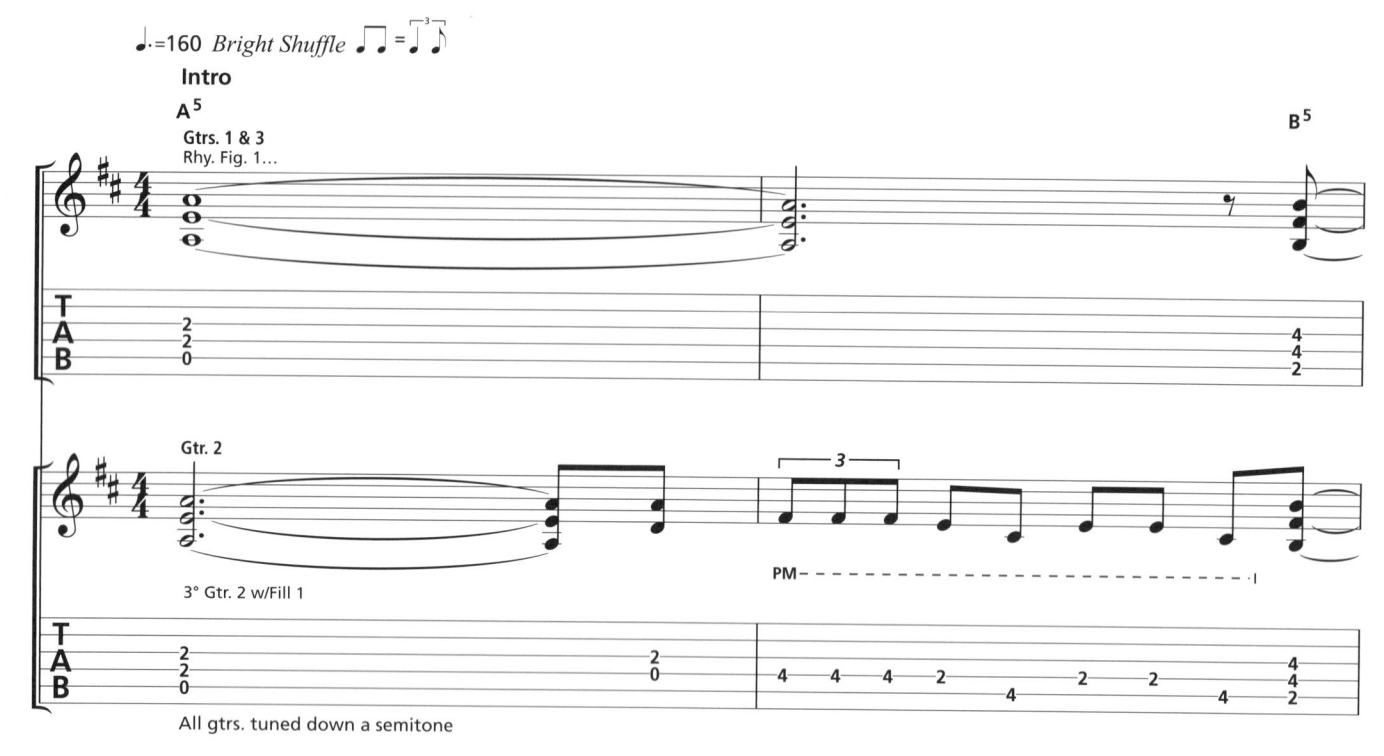

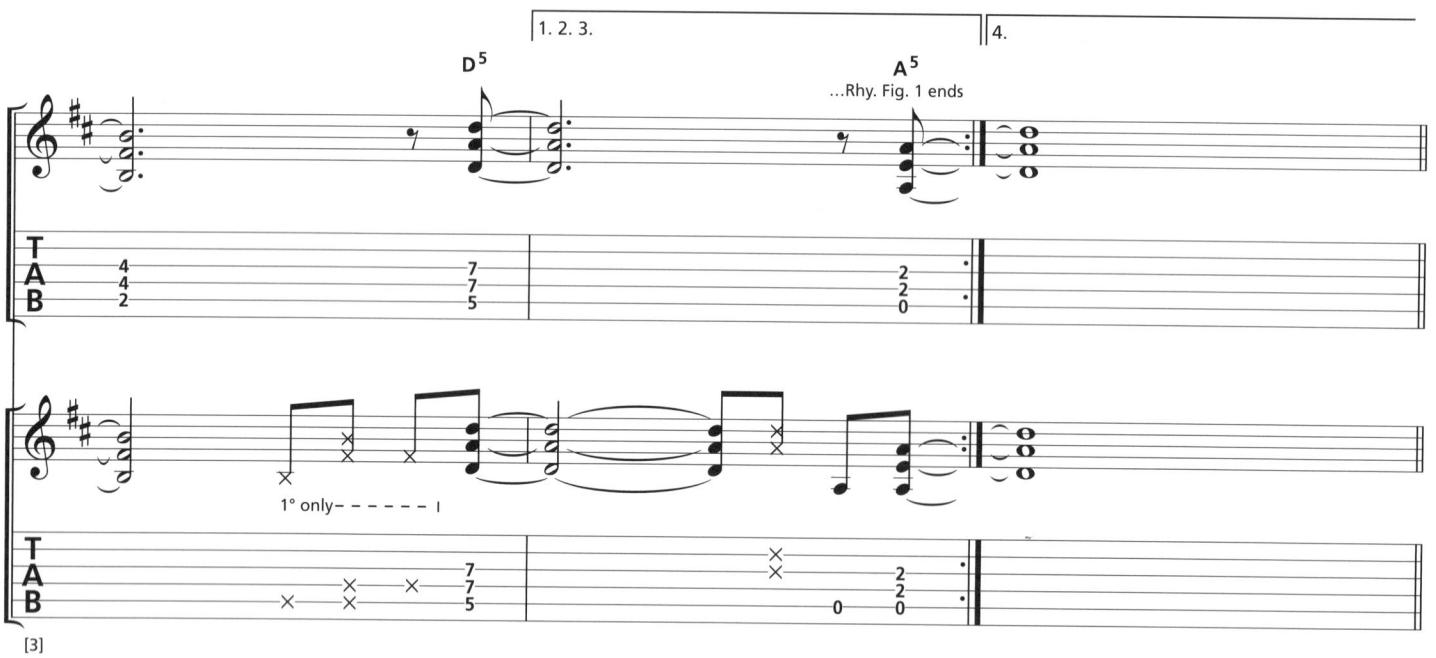

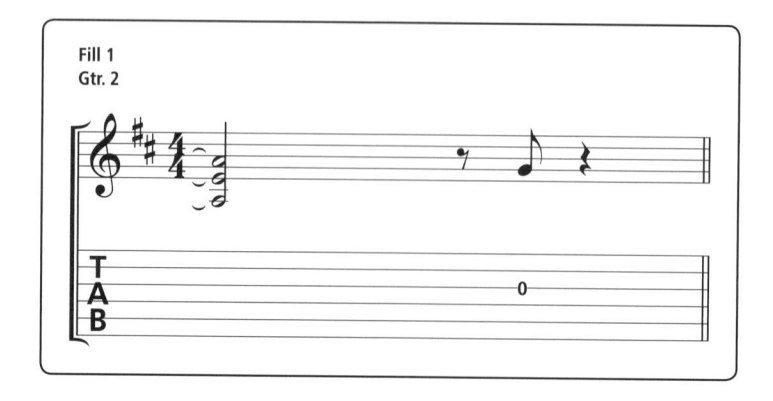

CD 2 Tracks 3 & 4

© Copyright 1976 Pippin The Friendly Ranger Music Company Limited.
Universal Music Publishing Limited.
All Rights Reserved. International Copyright Secured.

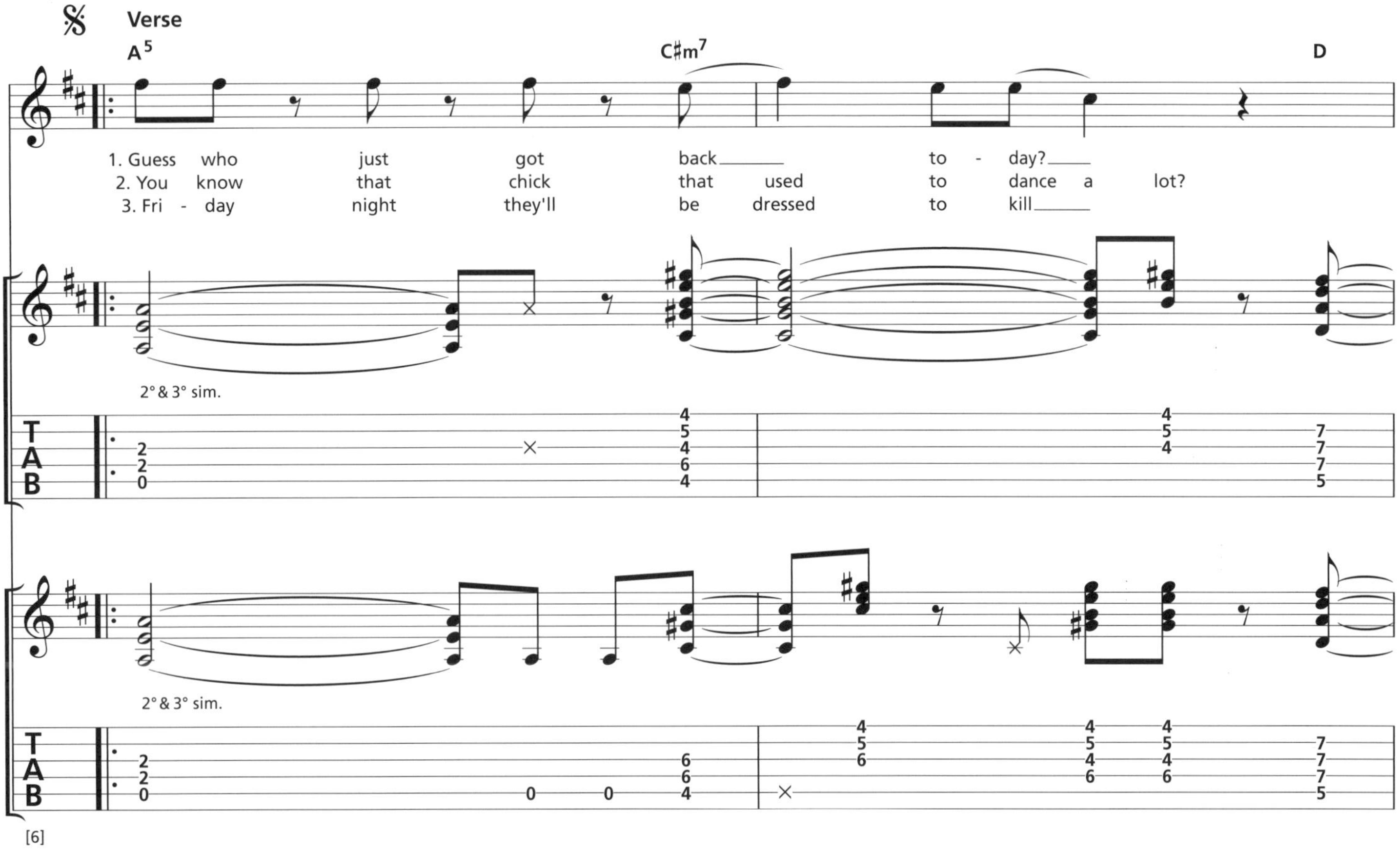
Verse
A5
C♯m7
D
1. Guess who just got back to - day?
2. You know that chick that used to dance a lot?
3. Fri - day night they'll be dressed to kill
2° & 3° sim.
2° & 3° sim.
[6]

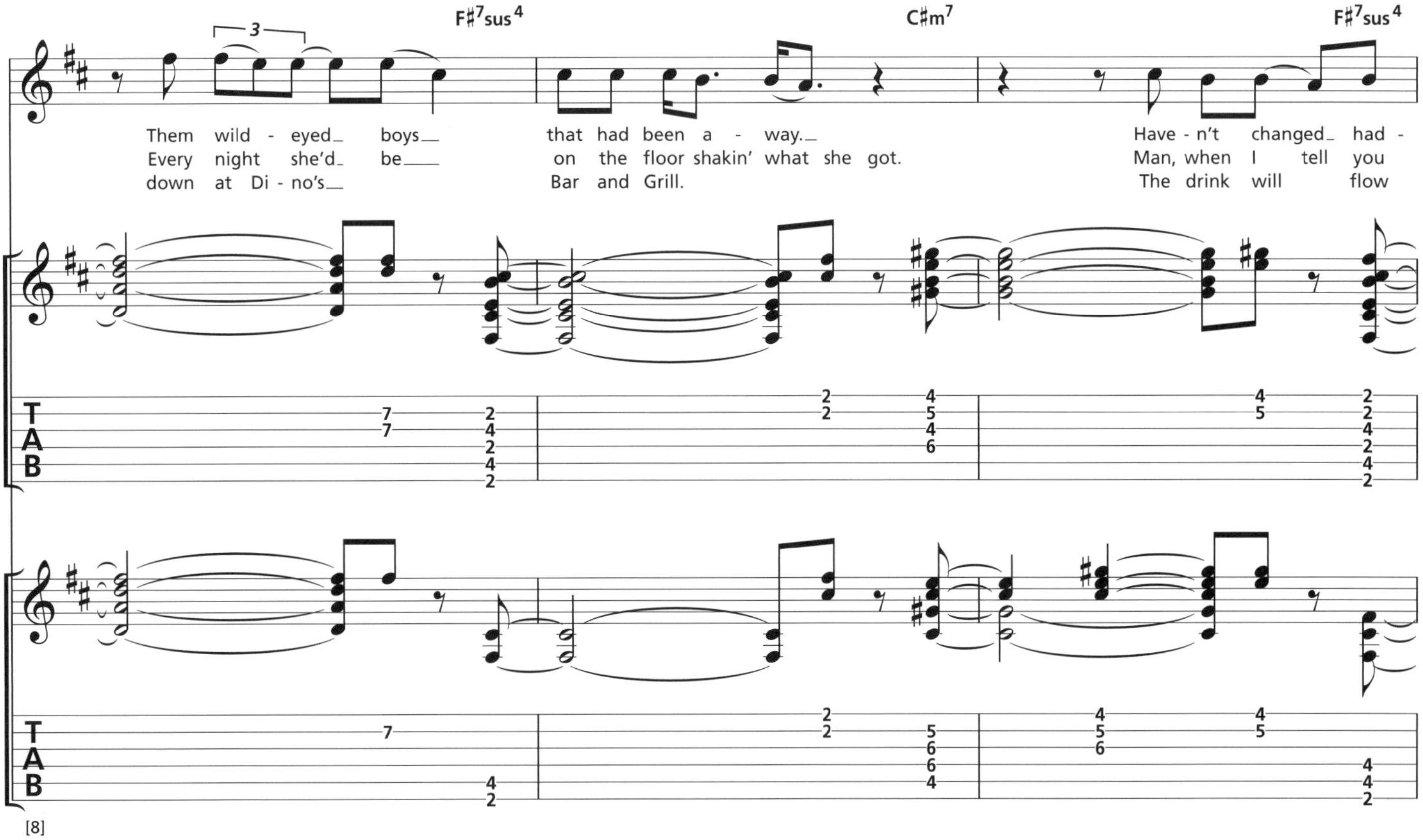
F♯7sus4
C♯m7
F♯7sus4
Them wild - eyed boys that had been a - way. Have - n't changed had -
Every night she'd be on the floor shakin' what she got. Man, when I tell you
down at Di - no's Bar and Grill. The drink will flow
[8]

Bm7
Bm7/E*
A5
– n't much to say, but man, I still think them cats are cra - zy.
she was cool, she was red hot! I mean she was steam-in'!
and blood will spill, and if the boys wan - na fight you better let 'em.
2° Gtr. 3 w/Fill 2
* mute A string w/1st finger of left hand
3° Gtr. 2 w/Fill 4
[11]
C♯m7
D
F
They were ask - in' if you were a - round, how you was, where you could
And that time over at John - ny's place, well this chick got up and
That juke box in the corn - er blast - in' out my favourite song. The nights are get - ting warm and it
[14]
Fill 2
Gtr. 3
BUBD
Fill 4
Gtr. 2
let ring

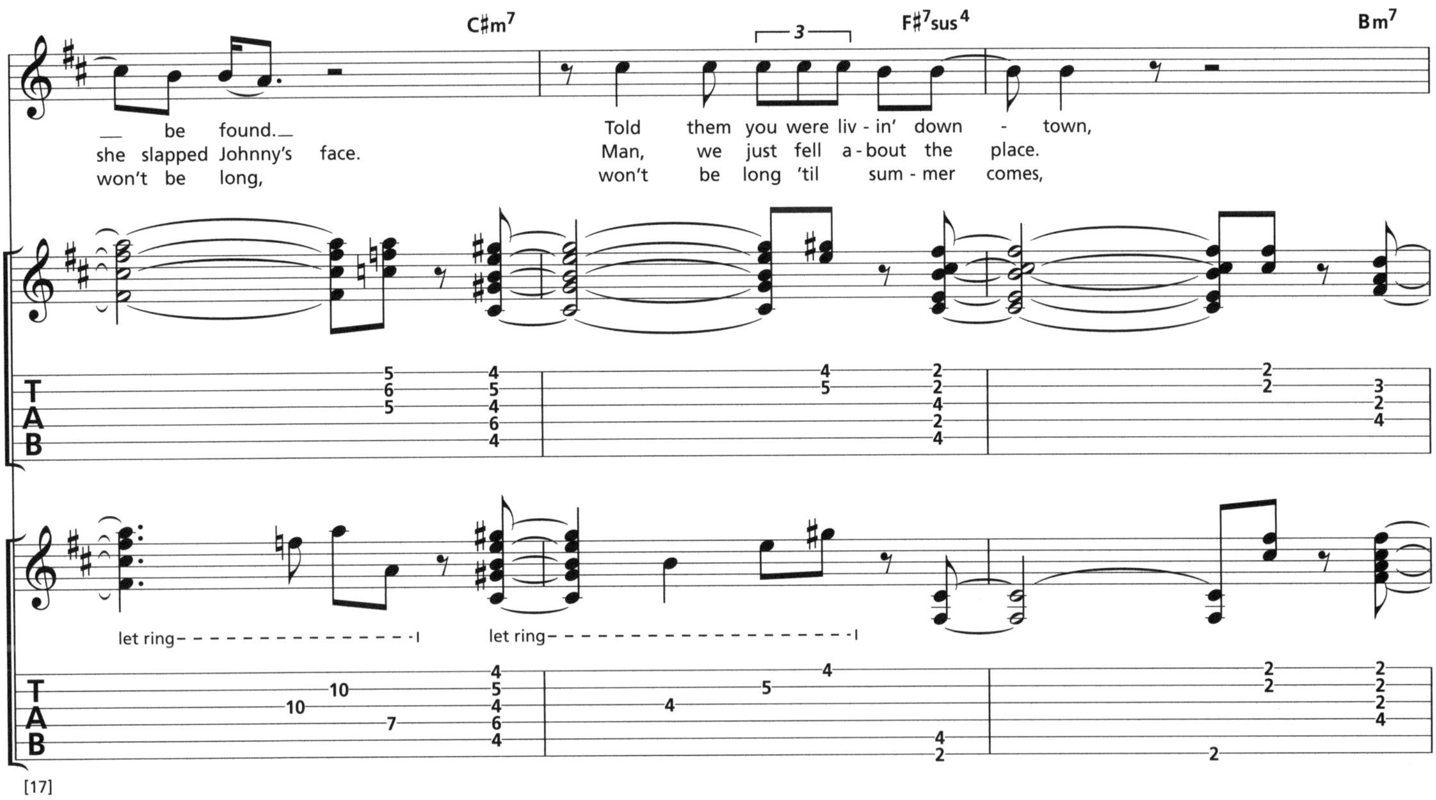
C♯m7
F♯7sus4
Bm7
— be found. —
she slapped Johnny's face.
won't be long,
Told them you were liv - in' down - town,
Man, we just fell a - bout the place.
won't be long 'til sum - mer comes,
let ring
let ring
[17]

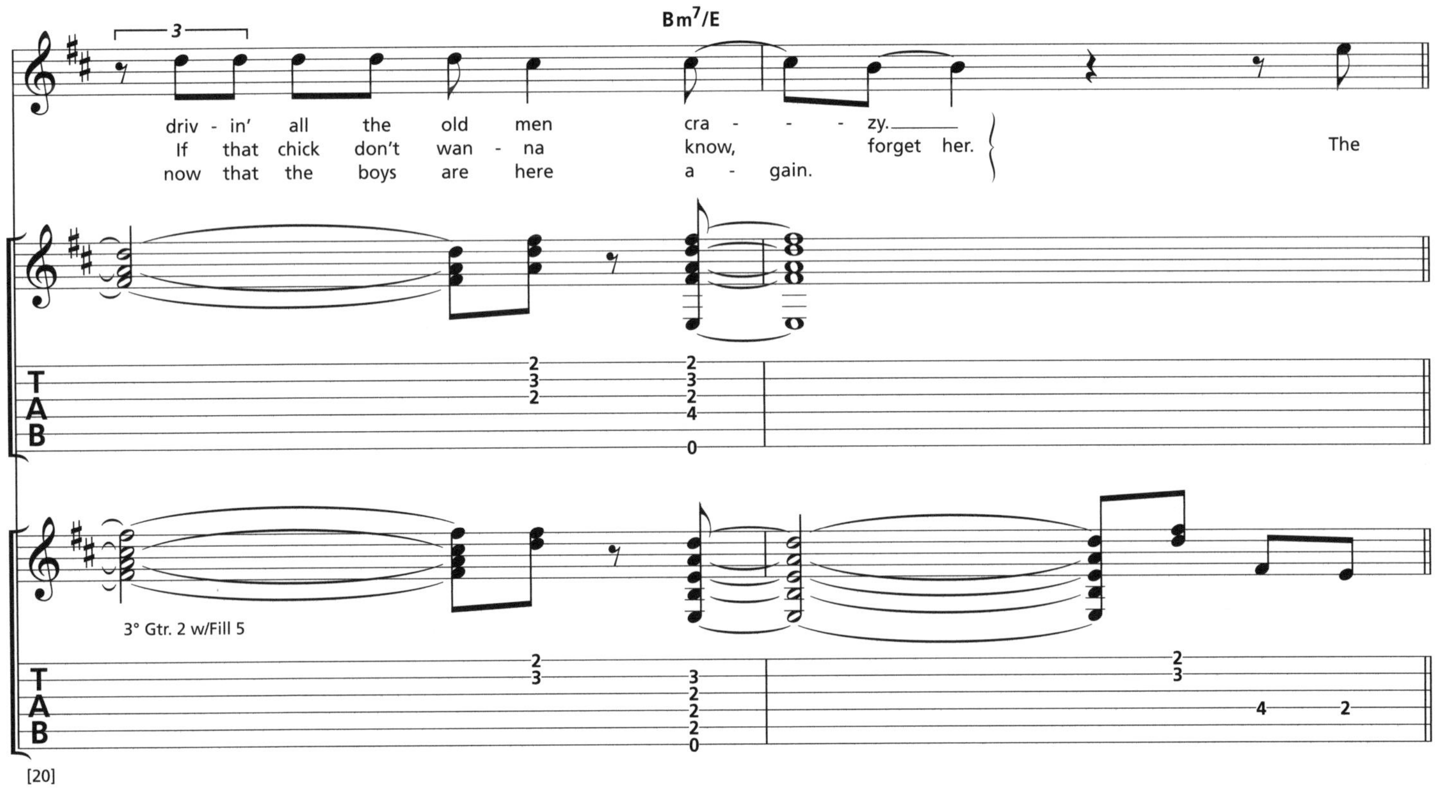
Bm7/E
driv - in' all the old men cra - - zy. —
If that chick don't wan - na know, forget her.
now that the boys are here a - gain.
The
3° Gtr. 2 w/Fill 5
[20]

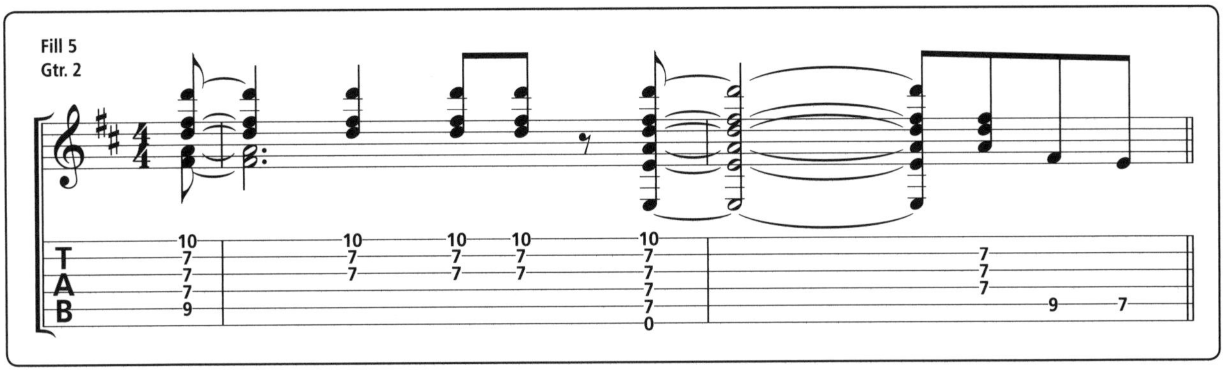
Fill 5
Gtr. 2

Chorus
A5
B5
boys are back in town. The boys are back in town.
Gtr. 2
Gtrs. 1 & 3 w/Rhy. Fig. 1 (3 times)
[22]
D5
A5
I said the boys are back in town.
[24]
To Coda
B5
D5
A5
The boys are back in town. The
[27]

B5
D5
boys are back in town. The boys are back in town. The boys are back in town.
(Backing vocals:) The boys
TAB
[30]
are back in town.
N.C.
Gtr. 1
Rhy. Fig. 3…
Gtr. 3 tacet
Gtr. 2
Rhy. Fig. 4…
[33]
…Rhy. Fig. 3 ends
A5
…Rhy. Fig. 4 ends
[36]

Bridge

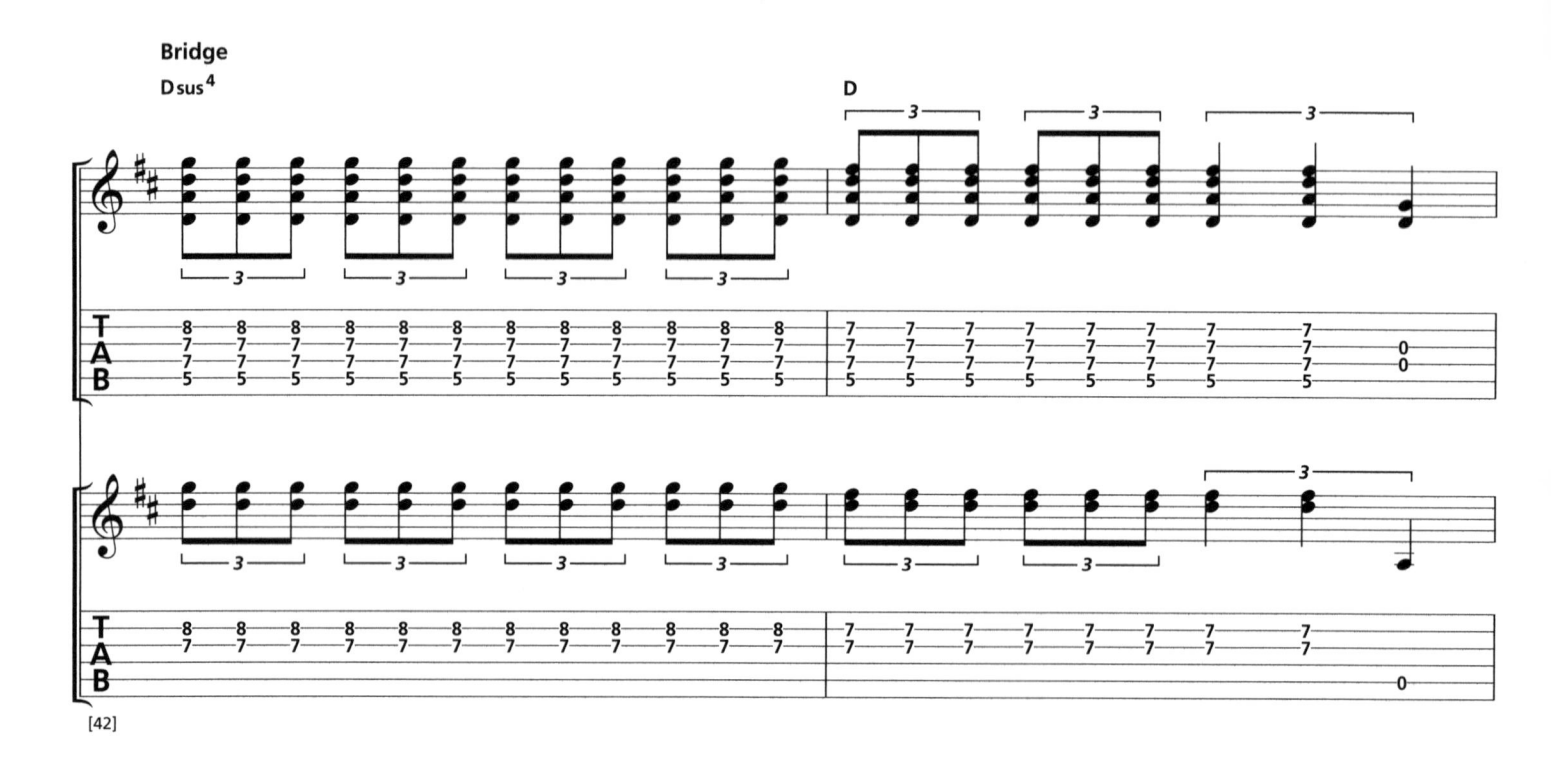

Dsus4 ... D

Fill 3
Gtr. 2

Spread the word a-round. Guess who's back in town.

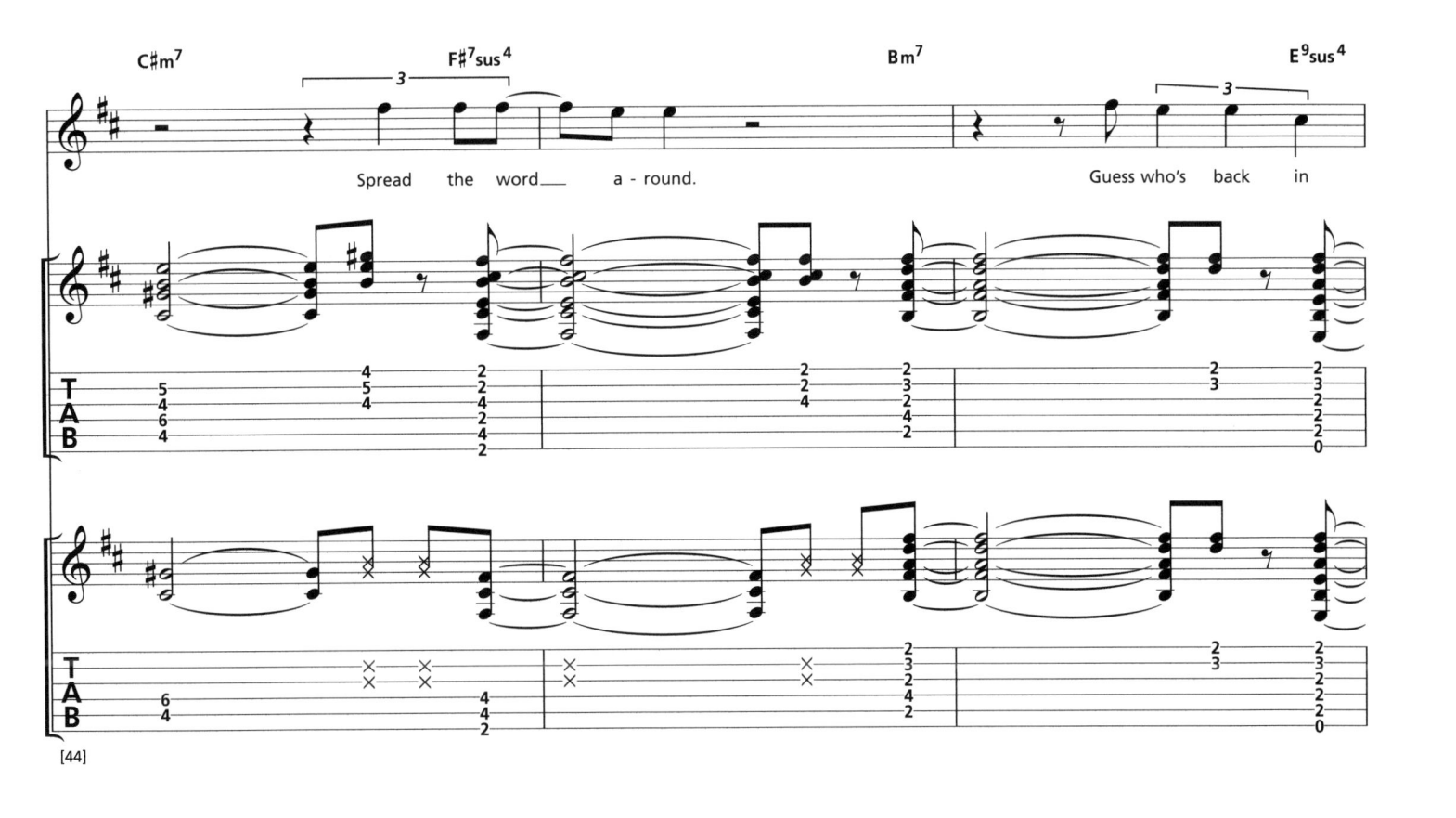

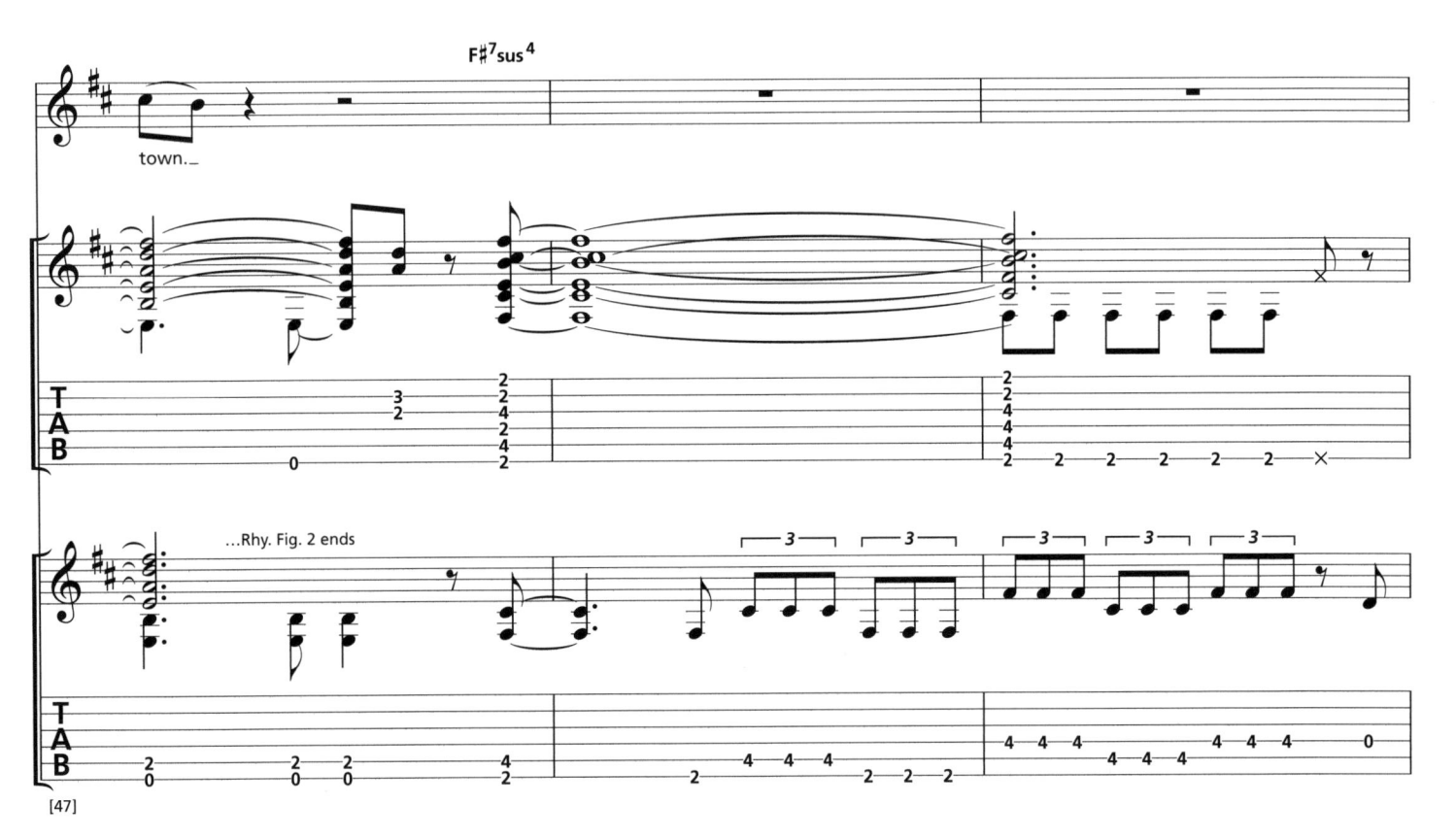

...Rhy. Fig. 2 ends

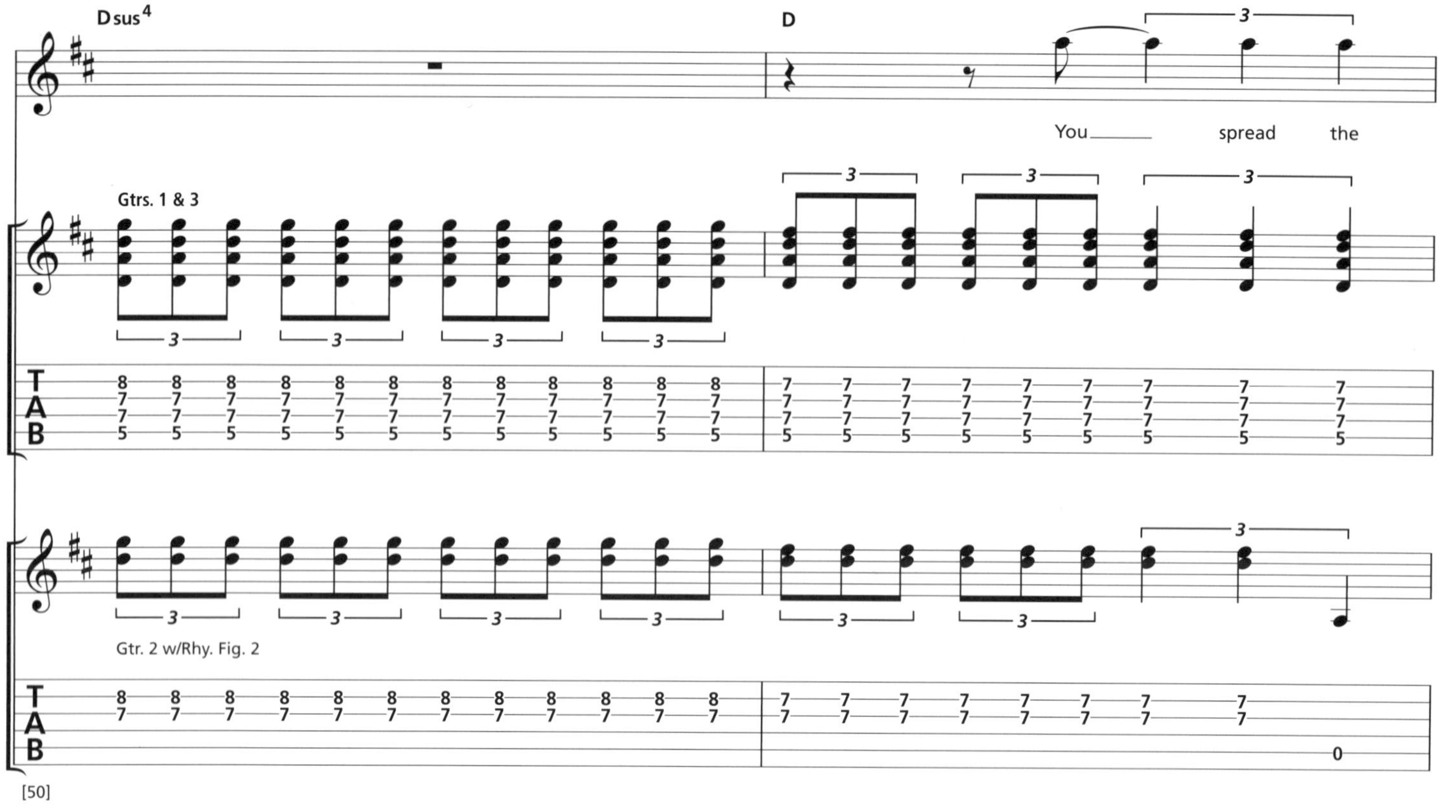
Dsus4
D
You spread the
Gtrs. 1 & 3
Gtr. 2 w/Rhy. Fig. 2
[50]

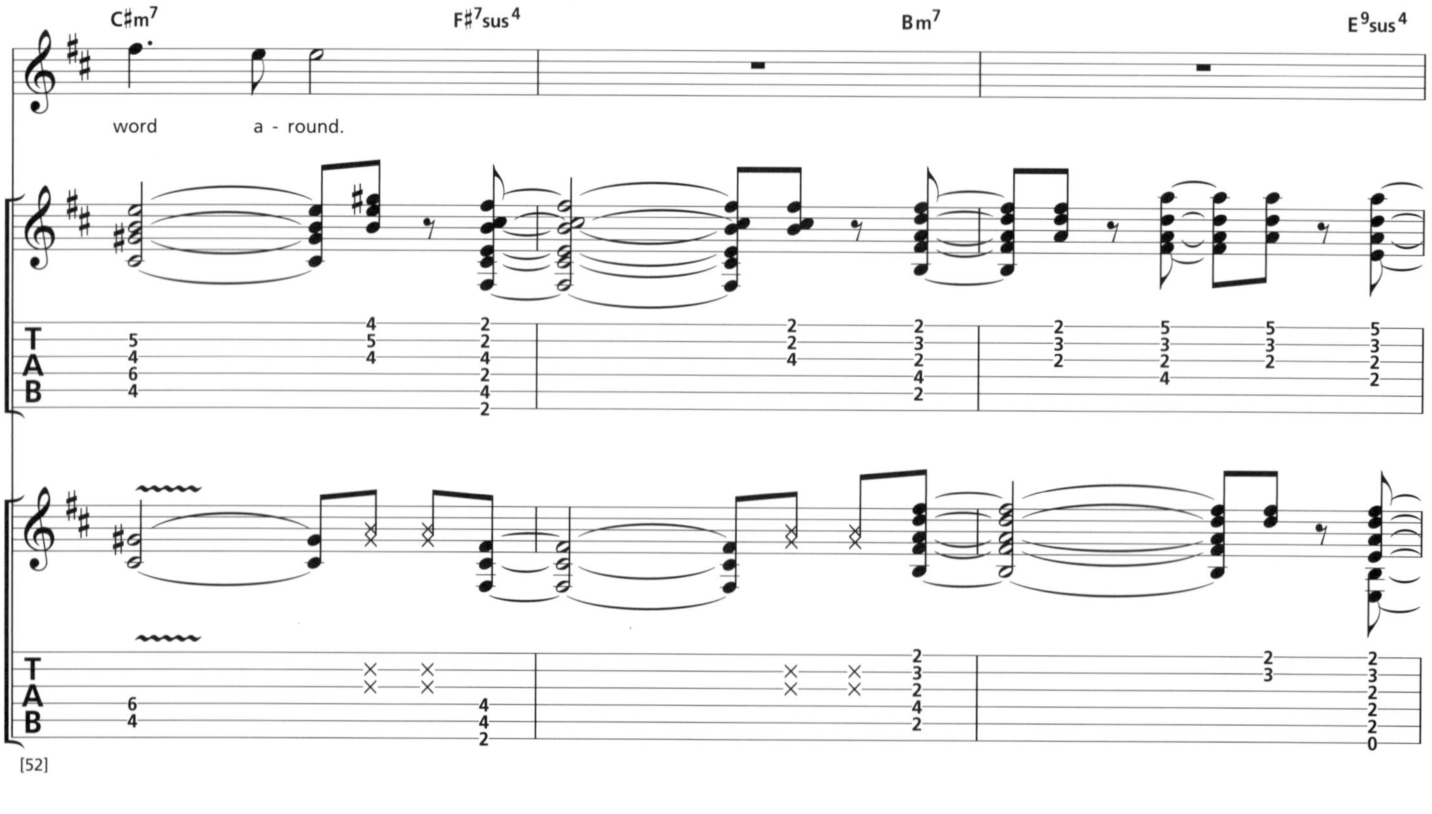
C♯m7
F♯7sus4
Bm7
E9sus4
word a - round.
[52]

F♯7sus4
D.%. al Coda
[55]
Coda
A5
Gtr. 2
B5
boys are back in town. the boys are back in town.
Gtr. 1
Gtr. 1 cont. in slashes
Gtr. 3
PM
[58]
D5
A5
(Spread the word a - round.) The boys are back in town. The
PM
[60]

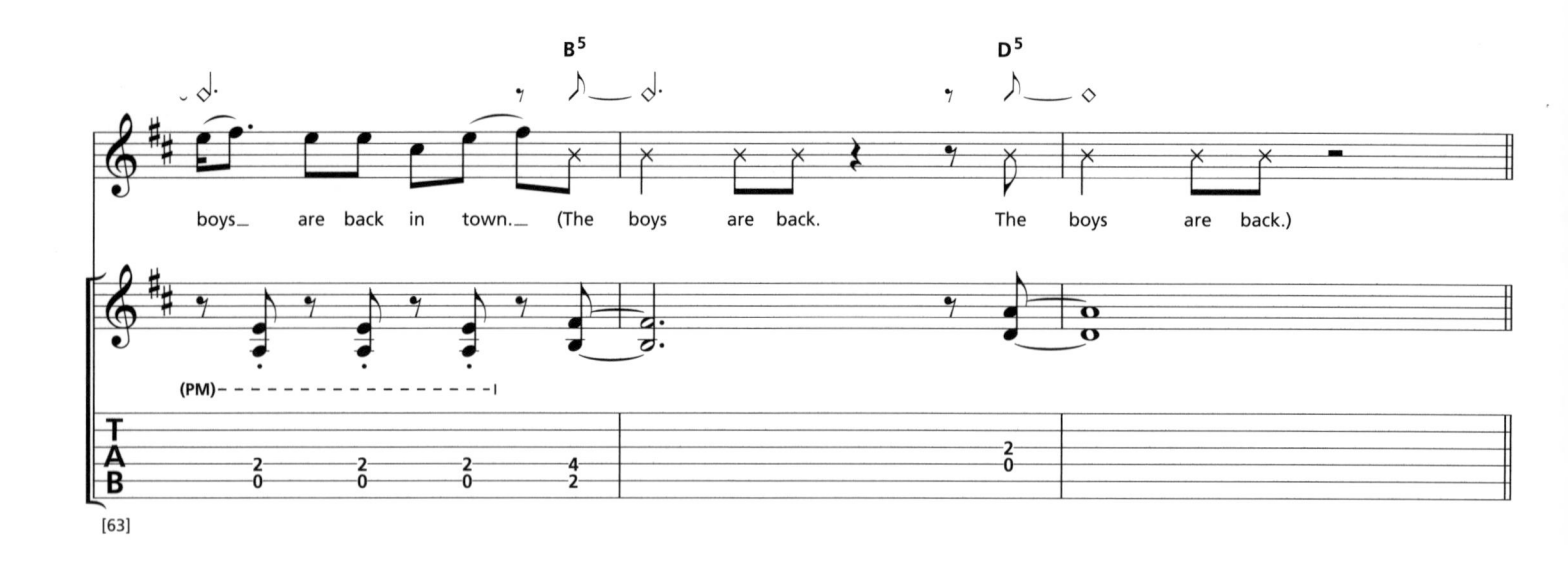

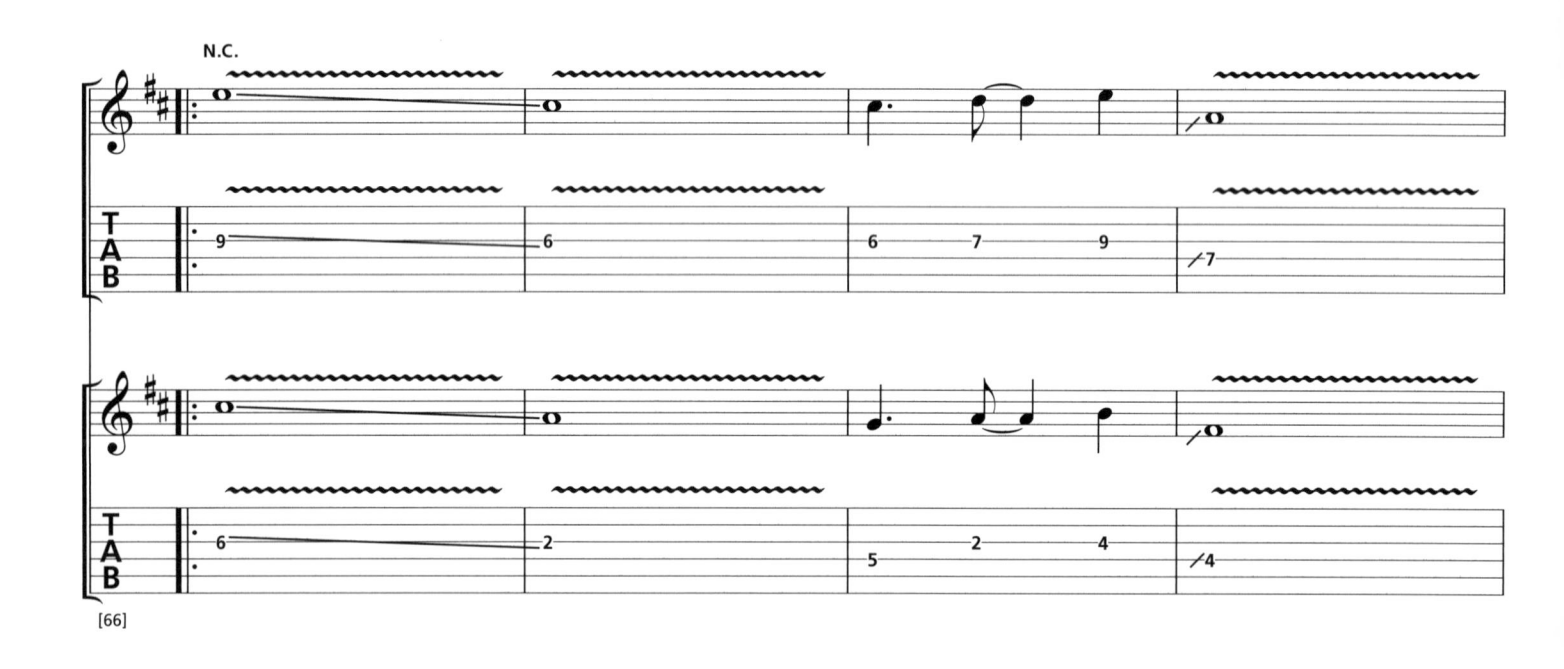

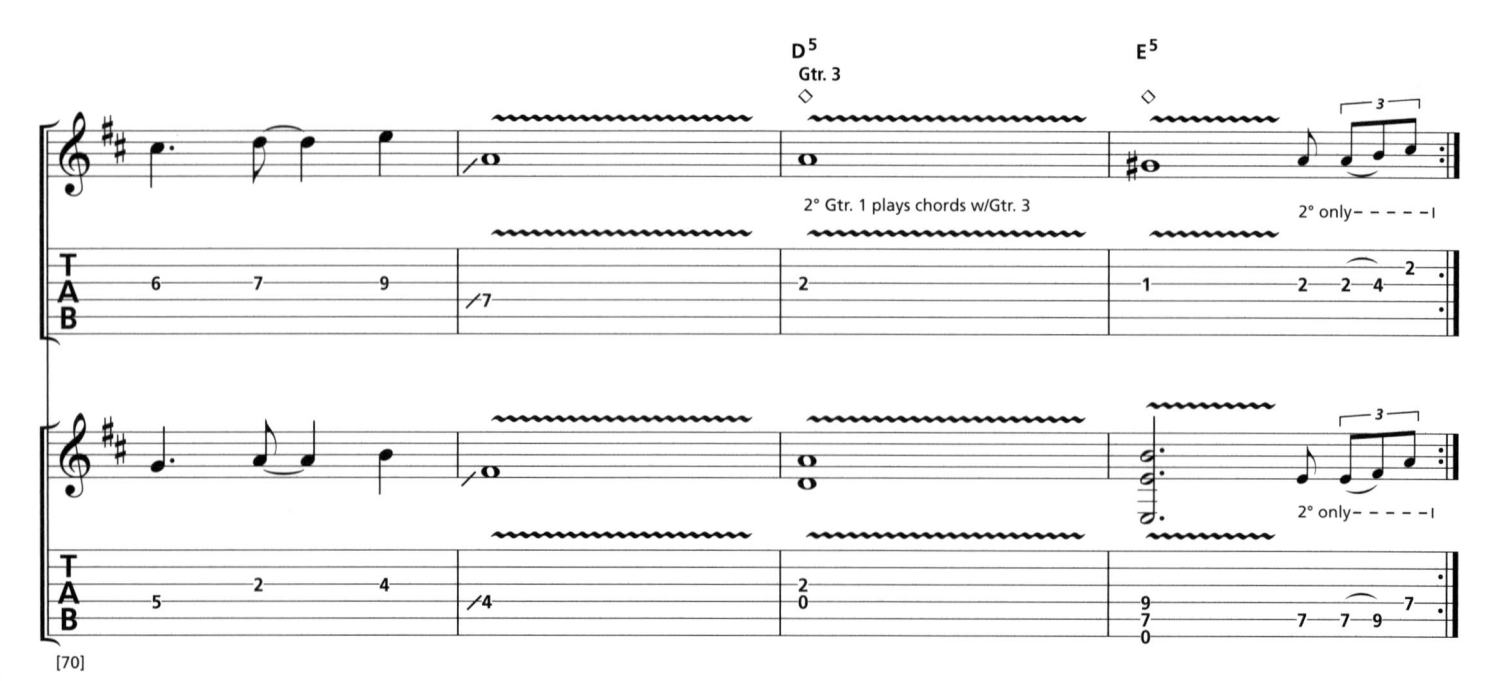

boys are back in town. (The boys are back. The boys are back.)

N.C.
Gtr. 2 w/Rhy. Fig. 4 (7 times)
[74]
The boys_ are back_ in town
[78]
Gtr. 3 w/Fill 6 (2 times)
_ a - gain._
'Been hang - in' down_ at
[82]
Gtr. 4 w/Fill 7
Di - no's._
[86]
Fill 6
Gtr. 3
Fill 7
Gtr. 4

Gtr. 3
The boys are back_ in town
Gtr. 4
[90]
— a - gain._
RP
BU
BD
[94]
RP
BU
BD
[98]

Notes On The Full Transcription

Bars 1–101 | *E♭ tuning*
In the original version of this song all the guitars are tuned one semi-tone lower than standard pitch. This can also be referred to as 'E♭ tuning' or 'tuning down a half-step'. To play along to the recordings on the CD you will need to re-tune your guitar, low to high, to E♭ A♭ D♭ G♭ B♭ E♭. The notation is written as if the guitar were in standard tuning. If you don't want to play to the backing track (you may wish to play the song in a group where the other members of the band don't play in E♭ tuning) you don't have to re-tune the guitar.

Bars 1–4 | *Performance figures*
There are several performance figure directions throughout this transcription. The first occurs in bar 1 where you will see the direction 'Rhy. Fig. 1…' and the next is in bar 4 where you will see '…Rhy. Fig. 1 ends'. This means these two bars make up Fig. 1, so in bar 22 where you see the direction 'Gtrs. 1 & 3 w/Rhy. Fig. 1' you would play bars 1–4. Follow this procedure for all the other performance figures.

Bars 6–21 | *Ghost strumming*
Keeping your hand in a constant strumming motion between chord hits will make the rhythm parts more fluent. When you don't want to strike the strings move your pick a small amount away from them. These are 'ghost strums'.

Bars 6–21 | *Swing rhythm strumming*
Your eighth-note strumming pattern should be uneven to reflect the swing feel. The downstrokes should last slightly longer than the upstrokes to produce this lopsided feel.

Bar 8 | *F♯^{7}sus^4*
An F♯m^7 chord consists of the root (F♯), the ♭3rd (A), the 5th (C♯) and the ♭7th (E). A suspended 4th chord is created by replacing the 3rd with the 4th (in this case, F♯, B, C♯, E). A chord is major or minor based on whether the chord has a major or minor third. Because the 4th in a suspended chord replaces the 3rd a suspended chord is neither major or minor so the chord is written as the root note followed by sus^4 (e.g. Dsus^4). This chord also contains the 7th and so is written as F♯^{7}sus^4 (Fig. 1).

Bar 20 | *Slash chords*
A 'slash chord' indicates when a chord uses a bass note that is not the root note of the chord. The information to the left of the slash is the name of the chord, while the information to the right is the bass note. The Bm^7/E chord in bar 20 indicates the chord is a Bminor^7 with an E bass note (Fig. 2).

Bars 33–41 | *Vibrato*
Vibrato varies tremendously from one player to another; it is one of the most distinctive aspects of a guitarist's style. Whether your vibrato is fast and wide or slow and shallow, make sure that the movement is even and consistent or else you'll sound out of tune. One way to practise vibrato is to do 'push-ups' with a metronome. Watch and listen to how far you move the string in your normal vibrato action. Aim to move the string *exactly* this amount *every* time and in time. Set your metronome to around 65–100 BPM and perform your normal vibrato action slowly in time with the metronome. Be sure not to exaggerate your normal action; you're aiming to build a consistent vibrato, not change your style. This will help your vibrato sing sweetly and, most importantly, sound in tune.

Bars 42–43 | *Triplet strumming*
The fast pattern should be played with alternate strumming. Because the notes are grouped in threes rather than the more common groupings of two or four, the second and fourth beats of the bar will start with upstrokes not downstrokes. This may feel unusual at first.

Bars 94–101 | *Harmony bends*
Pay close attention to the timing and pitch of the bends. Normally a player would have some room for interpretation, but the fact that this is a harmony part means the bends must synchronise *exactly* with the other guitar. As well as solo practice, ensure you devote time to playing with the backing track to lock in with the harmony guitar part.

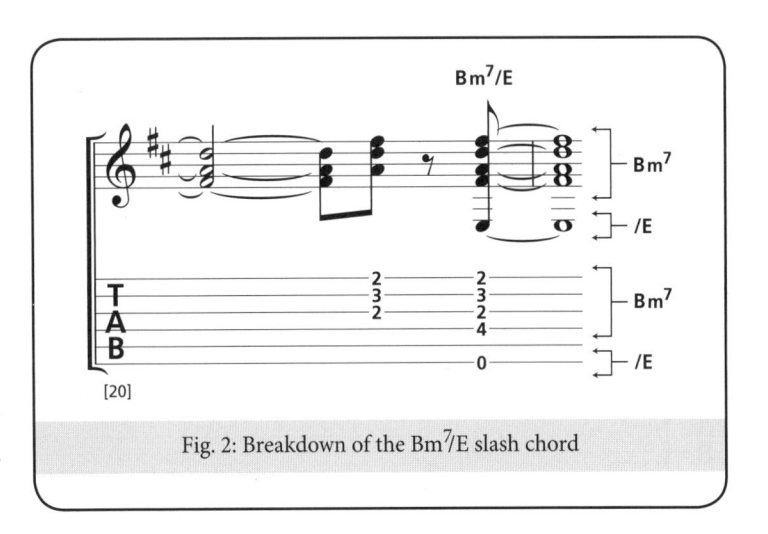

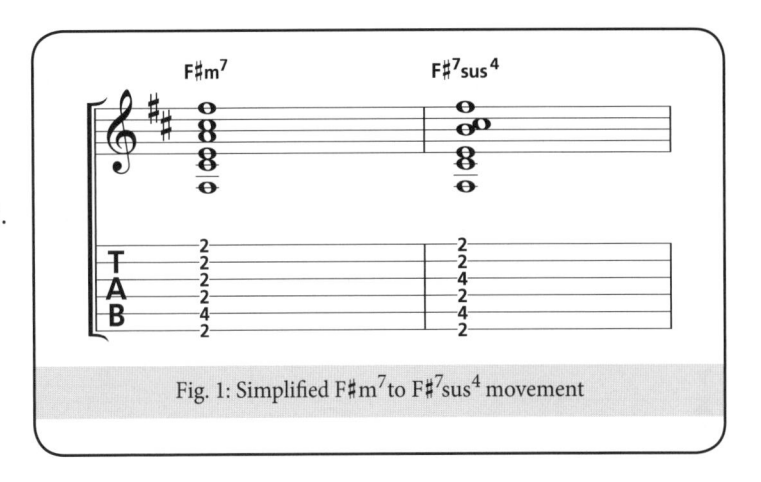

Fig. 2: Breakdown of the Bm^7/E slash chord

Fig. 1: Simplified F♯m^7 to F♯^{7}sus^4 movement

Don't Look Back In Anger

Oasis

Words & Music by Noel Gallagher

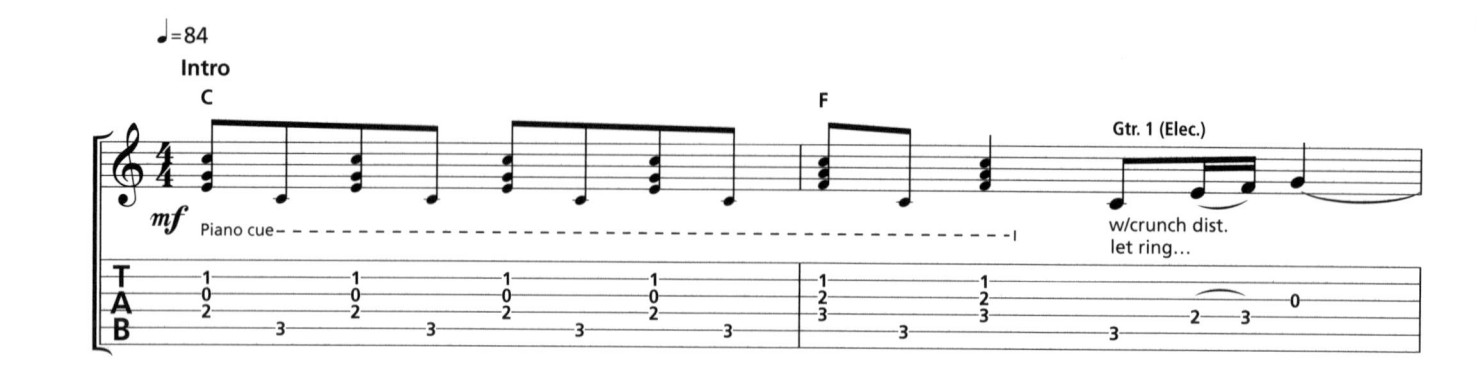

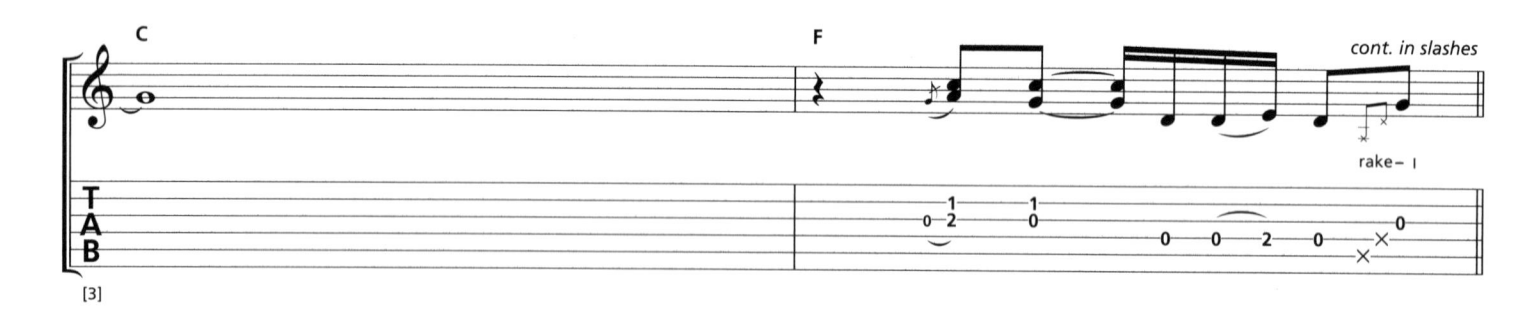

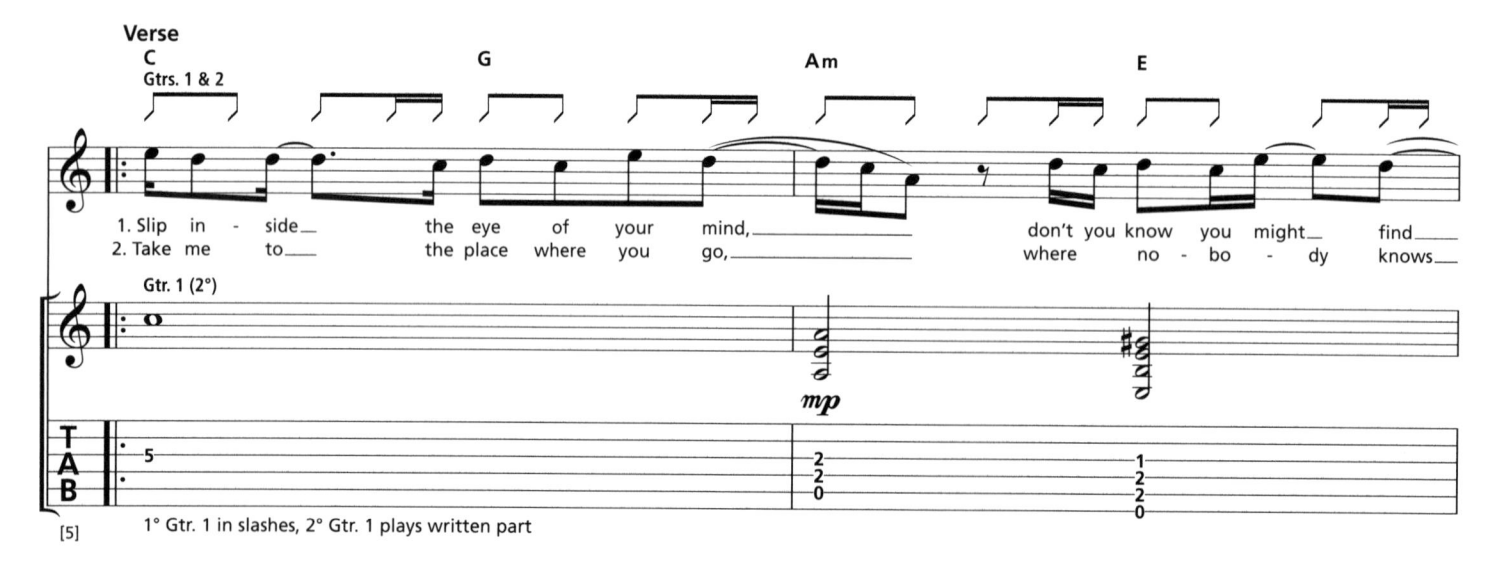

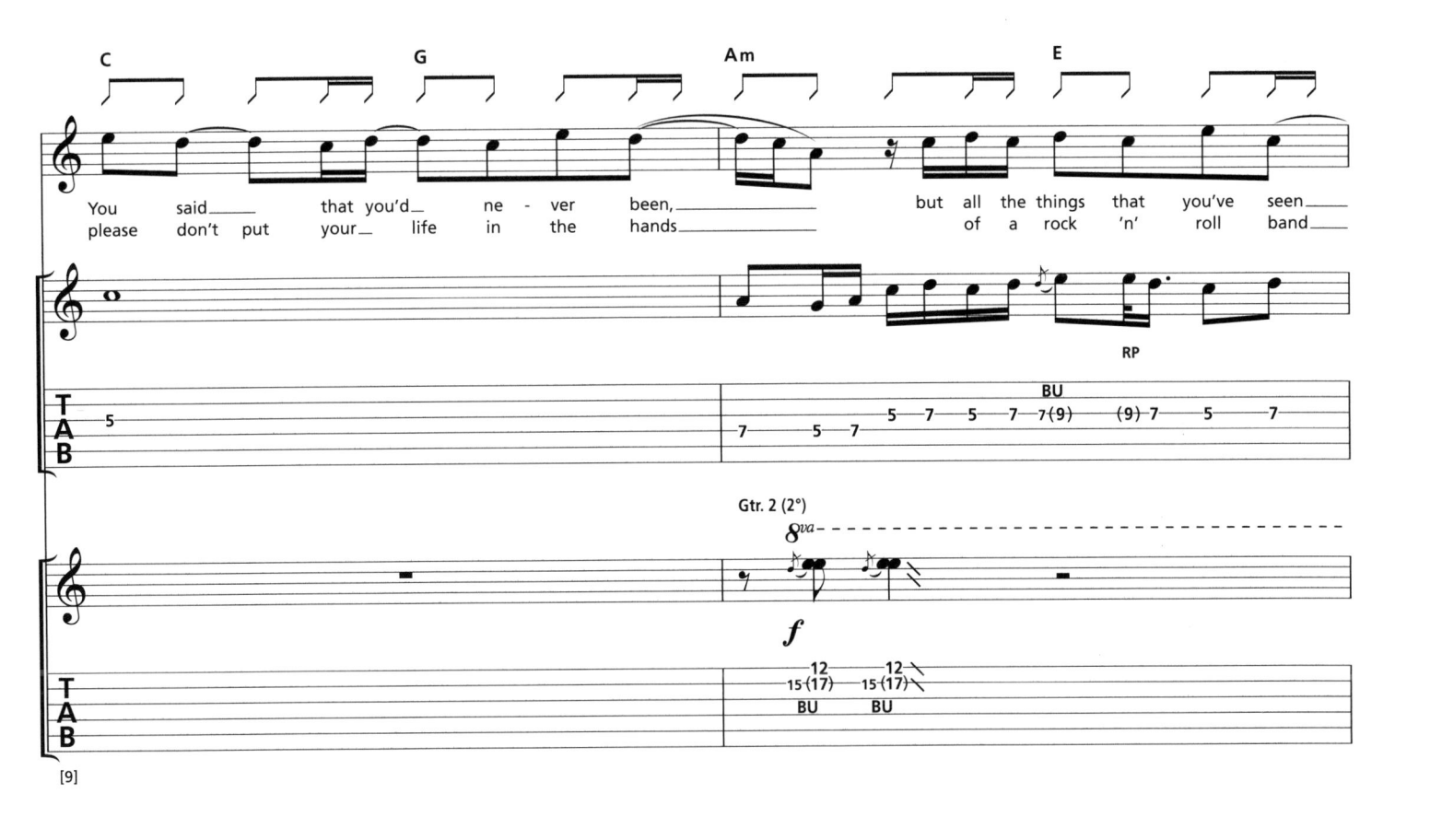

Lyrics:
You said that you'd never been, but all the things that you've seen are gonna fade away.
Please don't put your life in the hands of a rock 'n' roll band who'll throw it all away.

Bridge
F
Fm
C
So I start a re - vo - lu - tion from_ my bed, 'cause you
I'm gon - na start a re - vo - lu - tion from_ my bed, 'cause you
Gtr. 3 (Elec.)
1° cont. rhythm
2°
Gtr. 4 (Elec.)
[13]

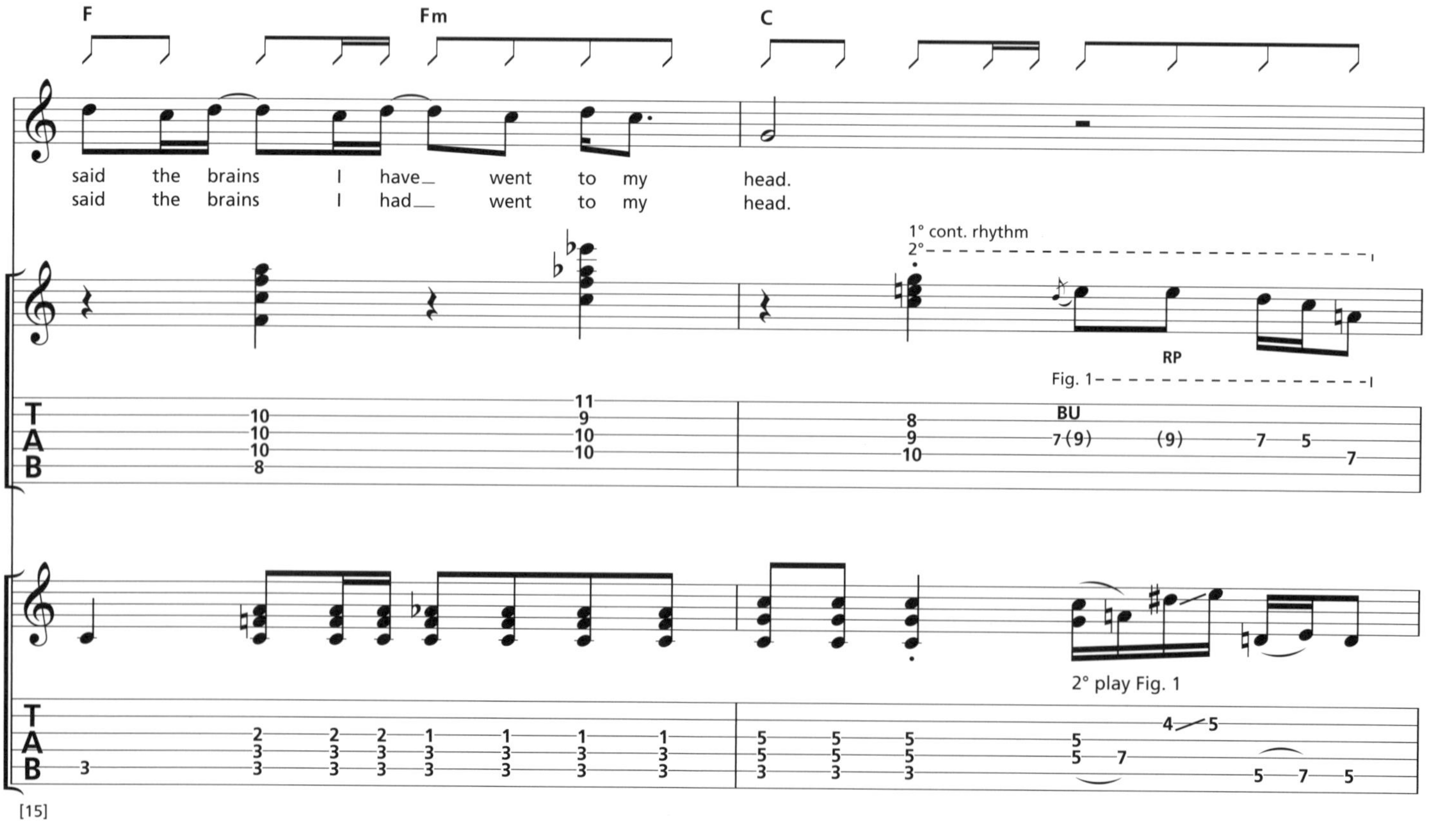
F
Fm
C
said the brains I have_ went to my head.
said the brains I had_ went to my head.
1° cont. rhythm
2°
RP
Fig. 1
BU
2° play Fig. 1
[15]

[Sheet music page — Hot Rock Guitar Grade 4, p. 77]

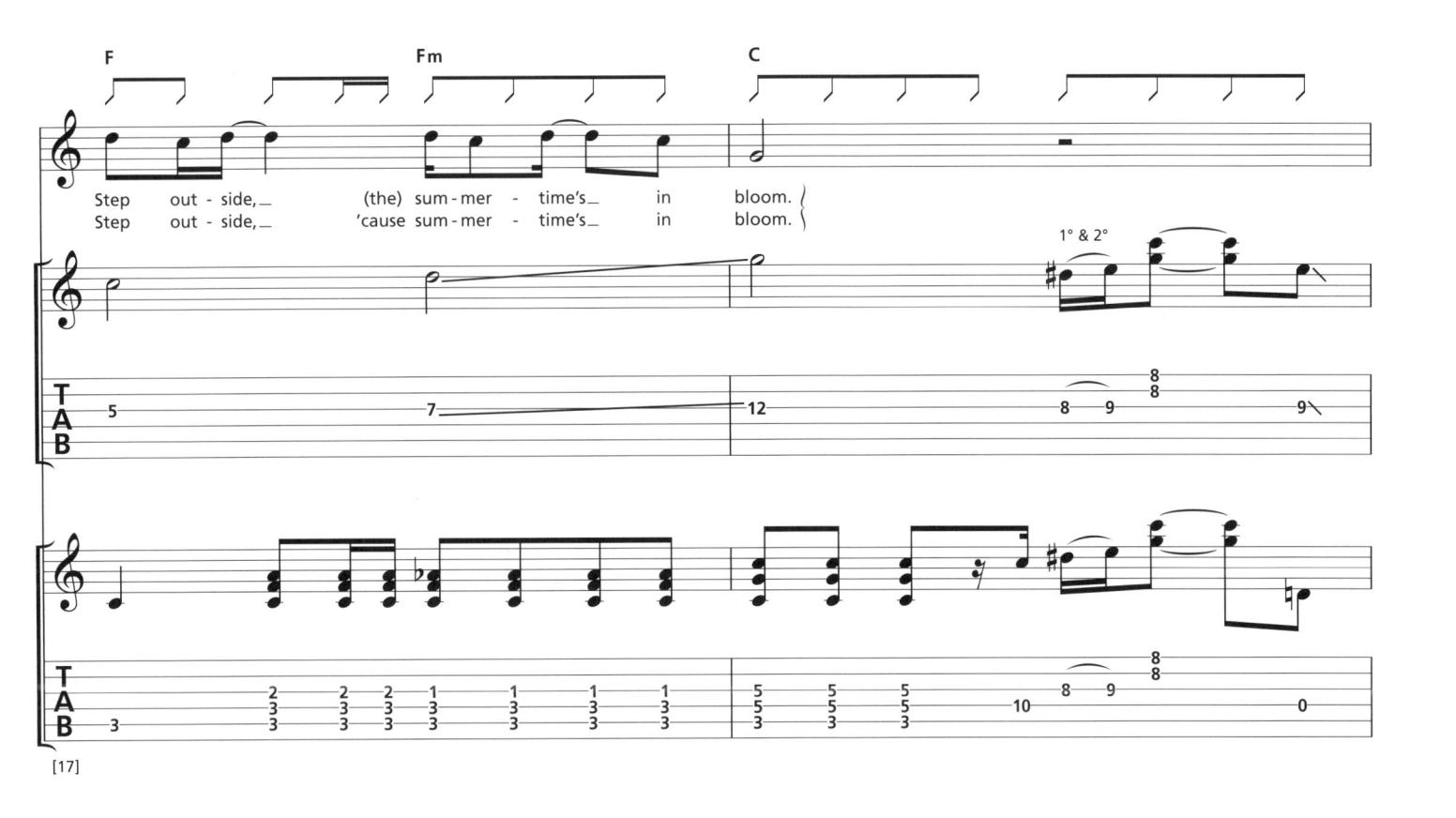

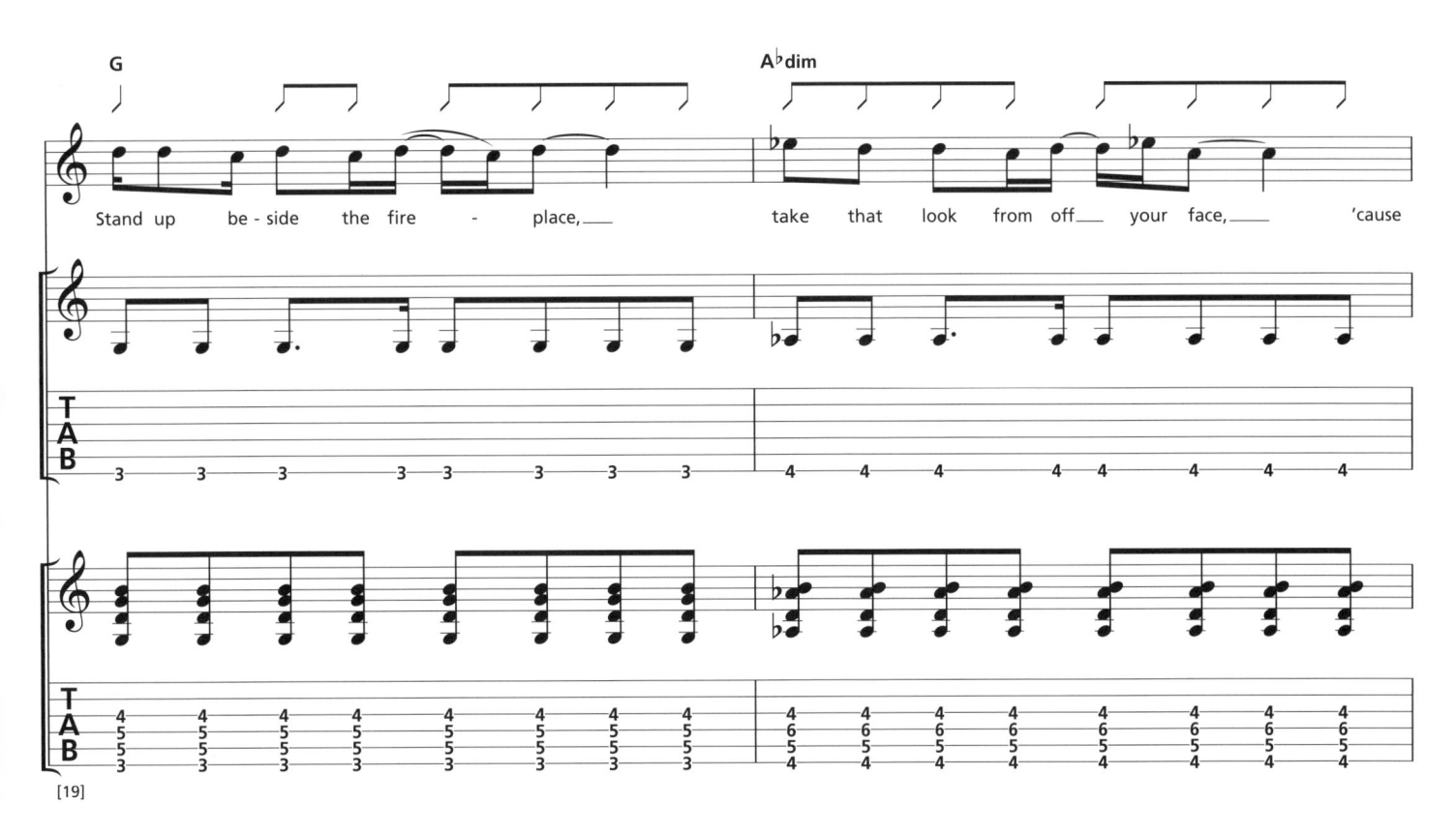

Lyrics:
Step outside, (the) summertime's in bloom.
Step outside, 'cause summertime's in bloom.
Stand up beside the fireplace, take that look from off your face, 'cause

you ain't ev - er gon - na burn my heart out.

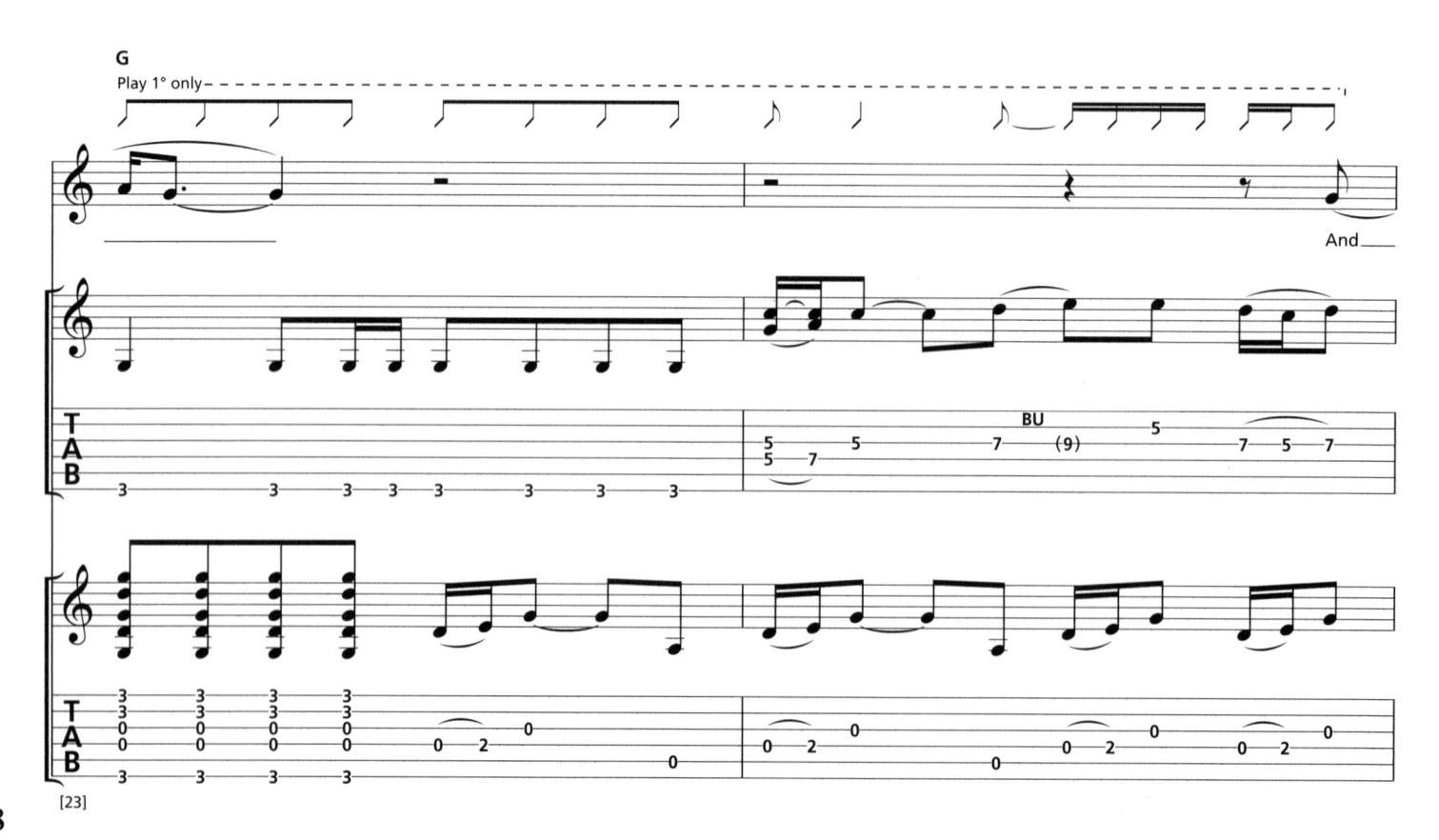

[21]

Play 1° only

And

[23]

G
Play 2° only
And
BU BD
BU
[25]
Chorus
C G Am E F G
(1. 3.) so (2.) Sal - ly can wait, she knows it's too late as we're / she's walk - ing on by.
Gtr. 3. tacet
cont. in slashes
[27]
To Coda
C Am G C G Am E
Her / My soul slides a - way, but don't look back
[30]

in an-ger, I heard you say.

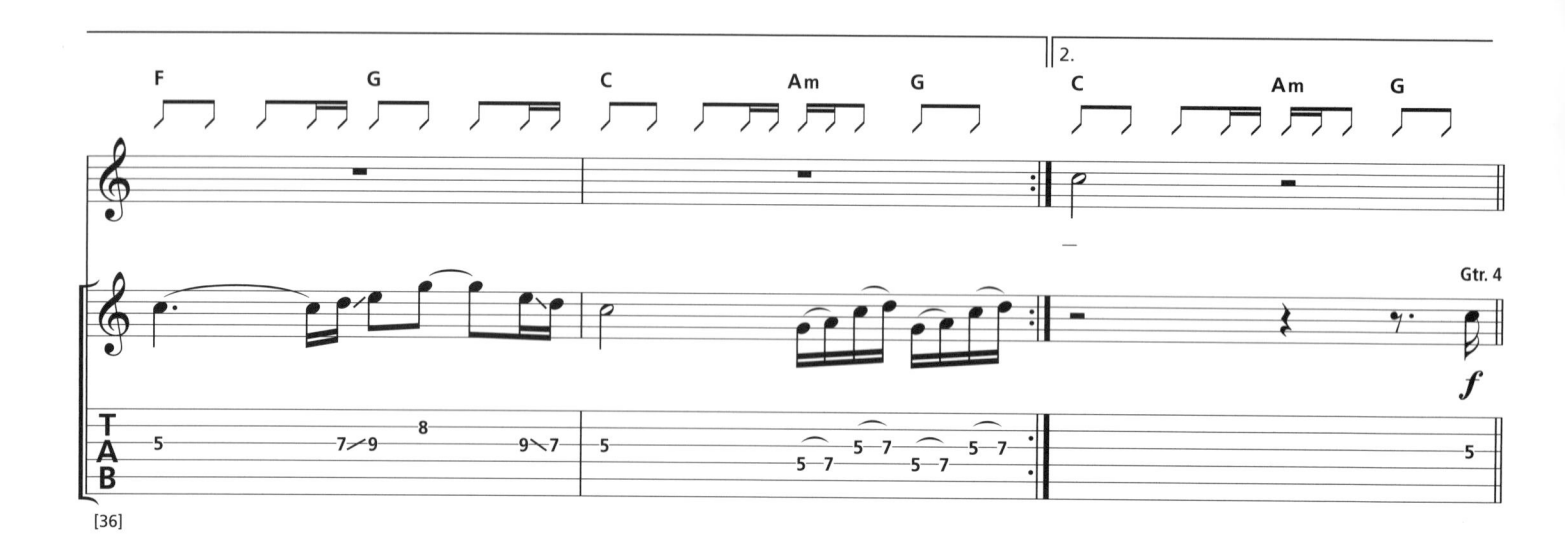

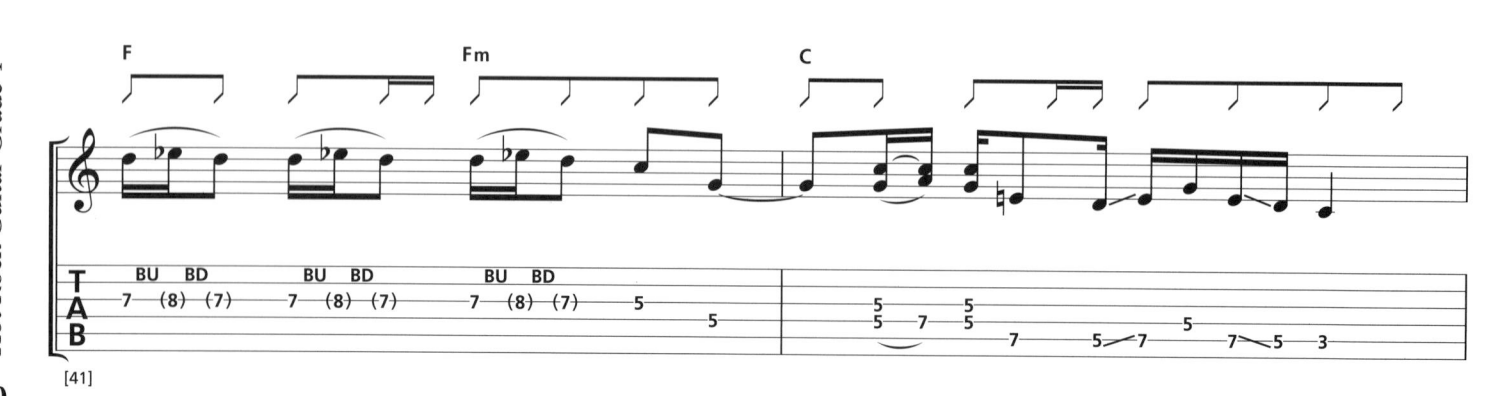

F
Fm
C
G
A♭dim
Am
G
F
G
D.%. al Coda
Coda
F
G
C
Am
G
C
G
cont. sim.
in an - ger, heard you say.
So Sal - ly can wait,
Gtr. 4
mf
BU
BD
[43]
[45]
[47]
[49]
[51]

Am Em F G C Am G
— she knows it's too late as she's walk - ing on by. My
[54]
C G Am Fsus2
soul slides a - way, but don't look back in an - ger, don't look
mp
[57]
Fm C G
Freely
Gtrs. 1 & 2
back in an - ger, I heard you say.
Gtr. 4
w/mellow tone
BU BD
[60]
Am E F Fm C
(At least not to - day.)
BU
[63]

Notes On The Full Transcription

Bars 1–2 | *Piano cue*
The opening bars of this piece are played by the piano. This part has been arranged for guitar so you can play along.

Bars 1–65 | *Layered parts*
'Don't Look Back In Anger' contains many different guitar parts. There are electric and acoustic rhythm guitars and several lead guitar parts. The best way to approach this dense track is to build your own arrangement from the different part. Throughout the notation there are notes advising you on the most appropriate part to play.

Bars 1–65 | *Rhythm notation*
If you have worked your way through the main guitar parts, you might like to play the acoustic guitar which is written as rhythm notation above the stave. Start by strumming the chords without following the rhythm notation, then add the rhythms in when you are comfortable with the changes.

Bar 11 | *Unison bends*
A unison bend is where one note is fretted normally and a note on the next lowest string is simultaneously bent until it reaches the pitch of the un-bent note. Practise the bend slowly and you will be able to hear the change in pitch of the bent note. If you have a floating bridge (where the bridge of your guitar 'floats' above the body of the guitar, e.g. a Floyd Rose style unit), the two notes will never sound exactly in tune as bending the note up will raise the floating bridge slightly, which will cause the un-bent note's pitch to drop. The more you bend, the more the other note's pitch will drop, so the two pitches will never meet.

Bar 16 | *Performance directions*
The performance direction in bar 16 indicates that the first time through you should ignore the notation in the last half of this bar and instead repeat beats 1 and 2 on beats 3 and 4 as shown in Fig. 1. The second time through you should play the part as written.

Bar 24 | *Complex rhythm*
This complex, syncopated (offbeat) rhythm may take some time to play smoothly and accurately. If you have trouble reproducing the rhythm, count through the bar in 16th notes ("1 e & a, 2 e & a") to help you place the notes correctly. Fig. 2 shows where the notes in bar 7 fall against the count.

Bars 39–50 | *Solo*
This solo features lots of melodic hooks, so it was probably composed rather than improvised. On the surface it looks fairly easy, but you must pay close attention to the timing of the hammer-ons and bends to play the phrases accurately.

Bars 39–41 | *Rhythmic bends*
The bends in this bar must be played accurately or the intended feel will be lost. Make sure that the original note as well as the bend up, bend down and pull-off all last for the correct duration.

Bars 45–46 | *Playing evenly*
The first three beats of these two bars are a steady stream of 16th notes. Count through the bar in 16th notes ("1 e & a, 2 e & a…") and make sure that all the notes are the same length. Pay particular attention to the hammer-ons because it's common to rush these, which makes the first note shorter than the second when they should be identical.

Bar 49 | *Unison bend lick*
Play the unison bend as described in the earlier step. As you complete the bend, release pressure on the bent note but continue to fret the E note on the B string. This is quite an awkward movement and may take some time to master.

Bar 60 | *Rall.*
Rall. is short for 'rallentando', an Italian musical term that means 'gradually getting slower'. It is quite common for a song to gradually slow down as it comes to the end. 'Don't Look Back In Anger' slows down in bar 60.

Bar 65 | *Fermata*
At first glance it looks as if the note in bar 65 should last four beats. However, it is marked with a *fermata* which means you should hold the note for longer than the specified duration. The *fermata* is notated above the final chord of the song, which means you can silence the note when you feel the time is right.

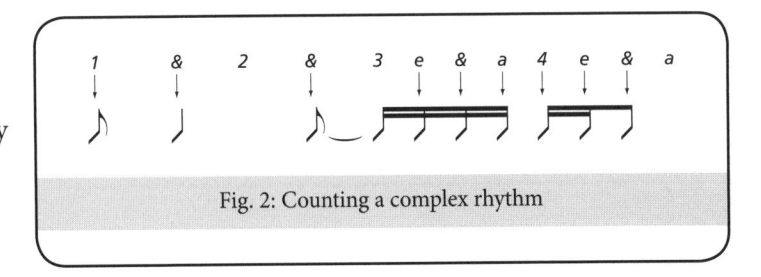

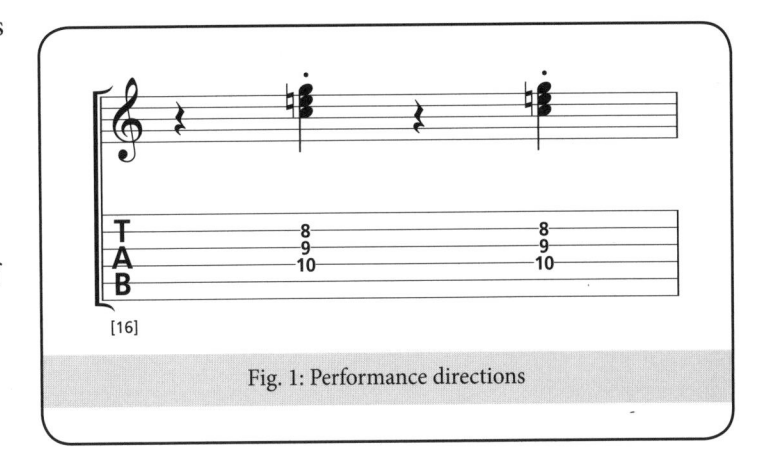

Fig. 2: Counting a complex rhythm

Fig. 1: Performance directions

Edge Of Darkness

CD 2 Tracks 7 & 8

Eric Clapton
Music by Eric Clapton & Michael Kamen

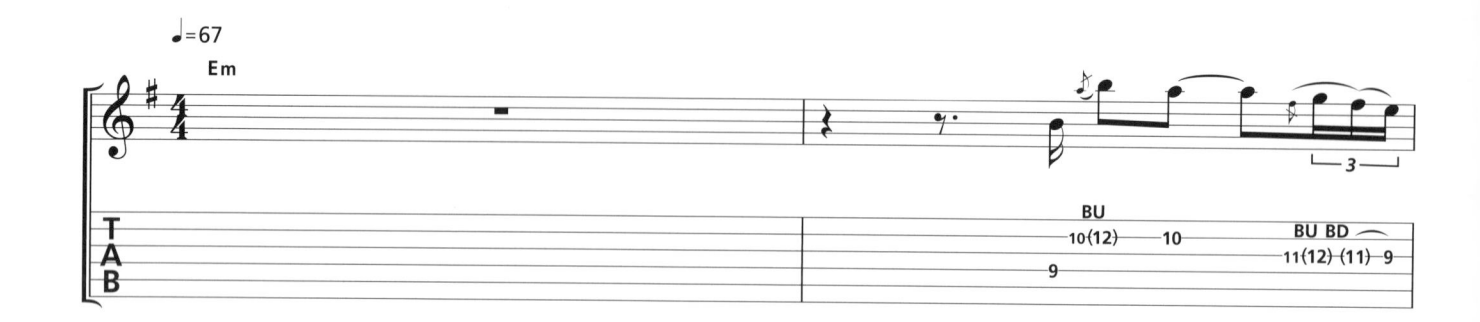

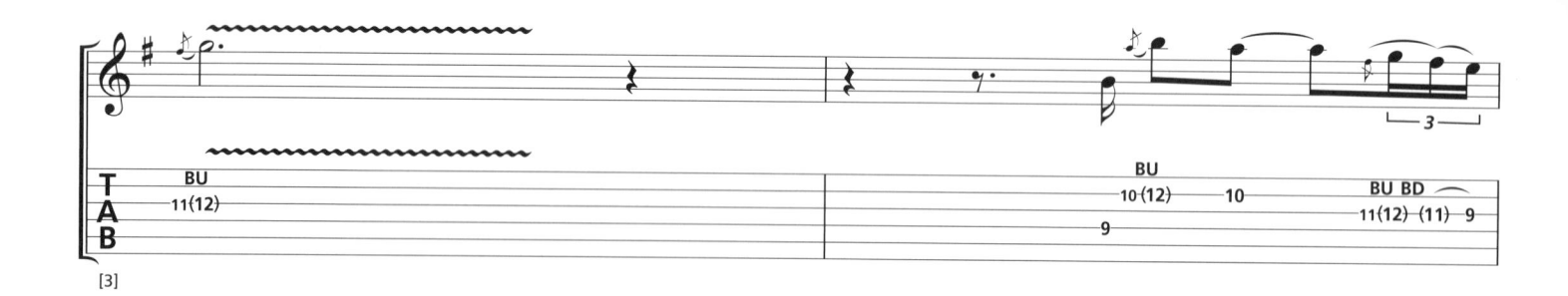

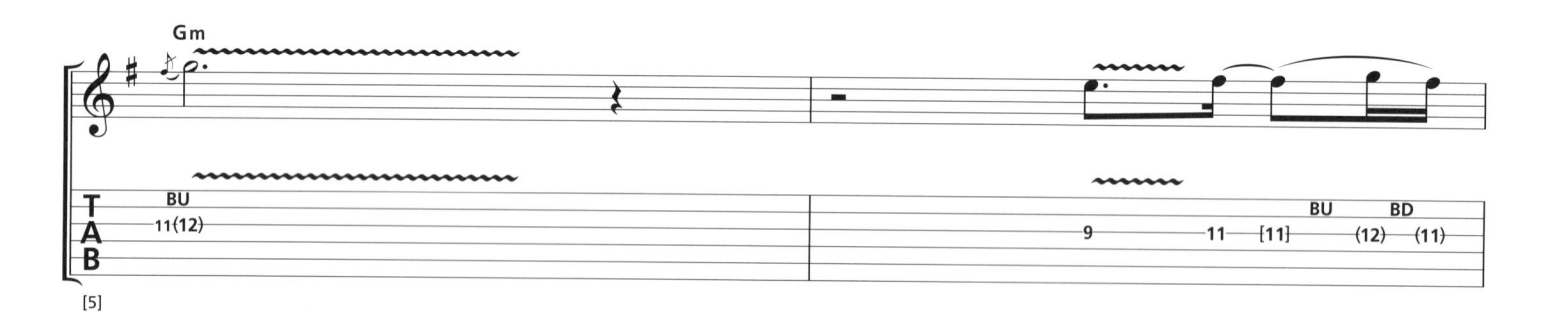

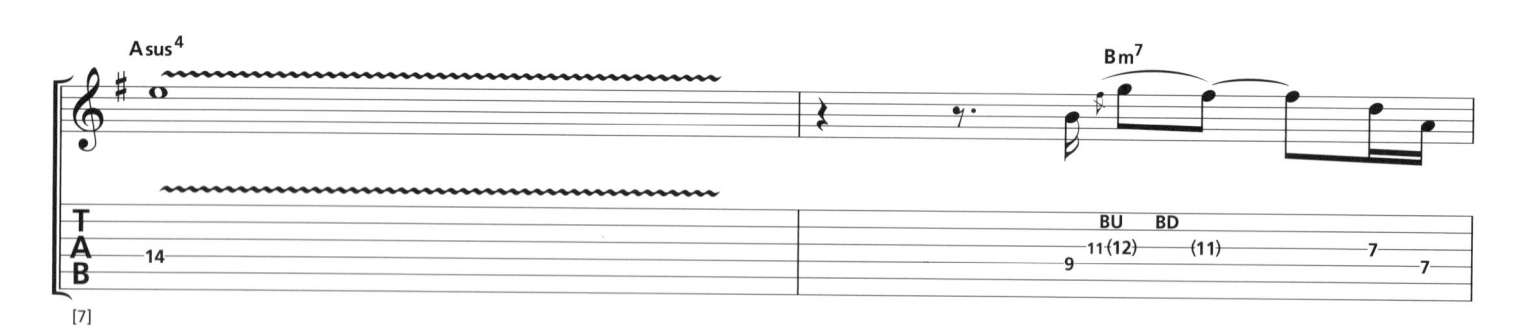

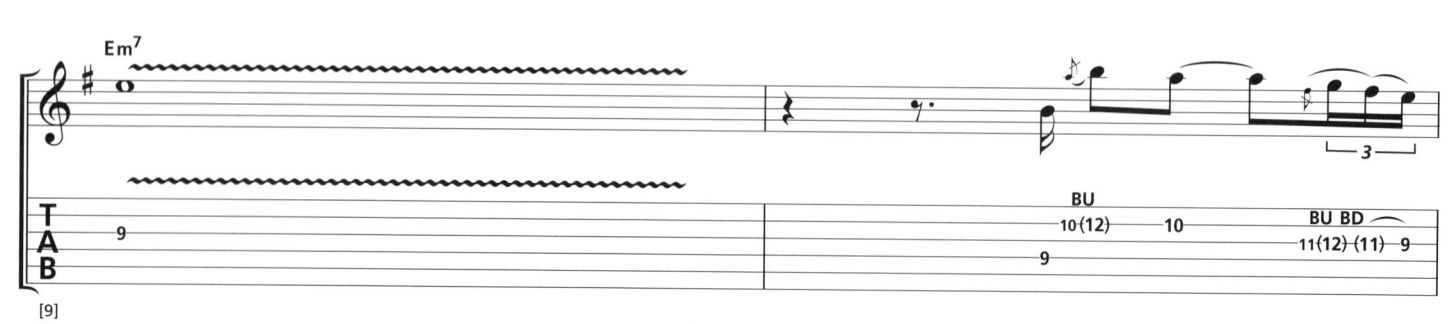

© Copyright 1985 & 1991 E.C. Music Limited/Mother Fortune Inc.
E.C. Music Limited/Intersong Music Ltd.
All Rights Reserved. International Copyright Secured.

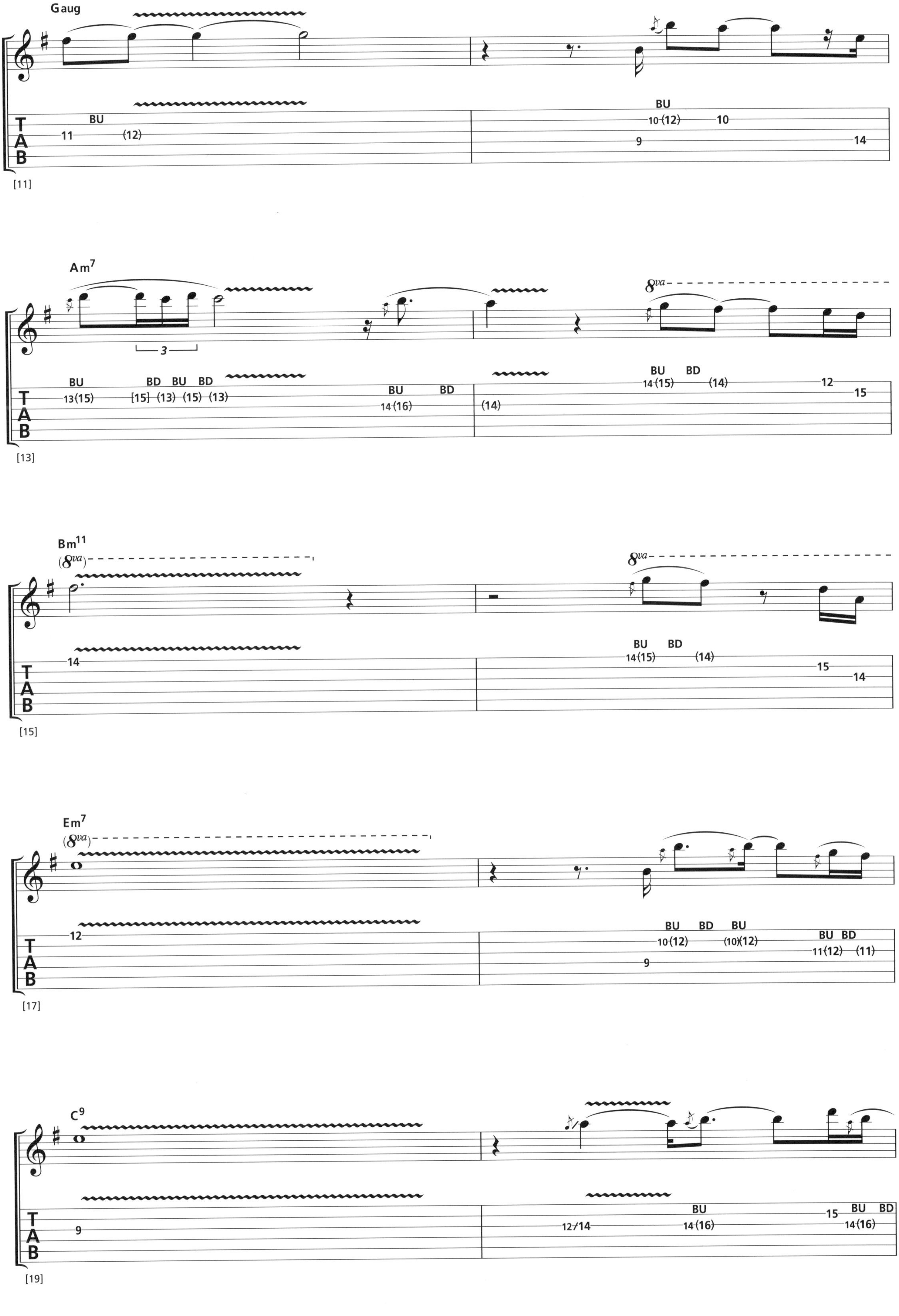
Gaug
[11]
Am7
[13]
Bm11
[15]
Em7
[17]
C9
[19]

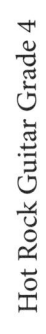

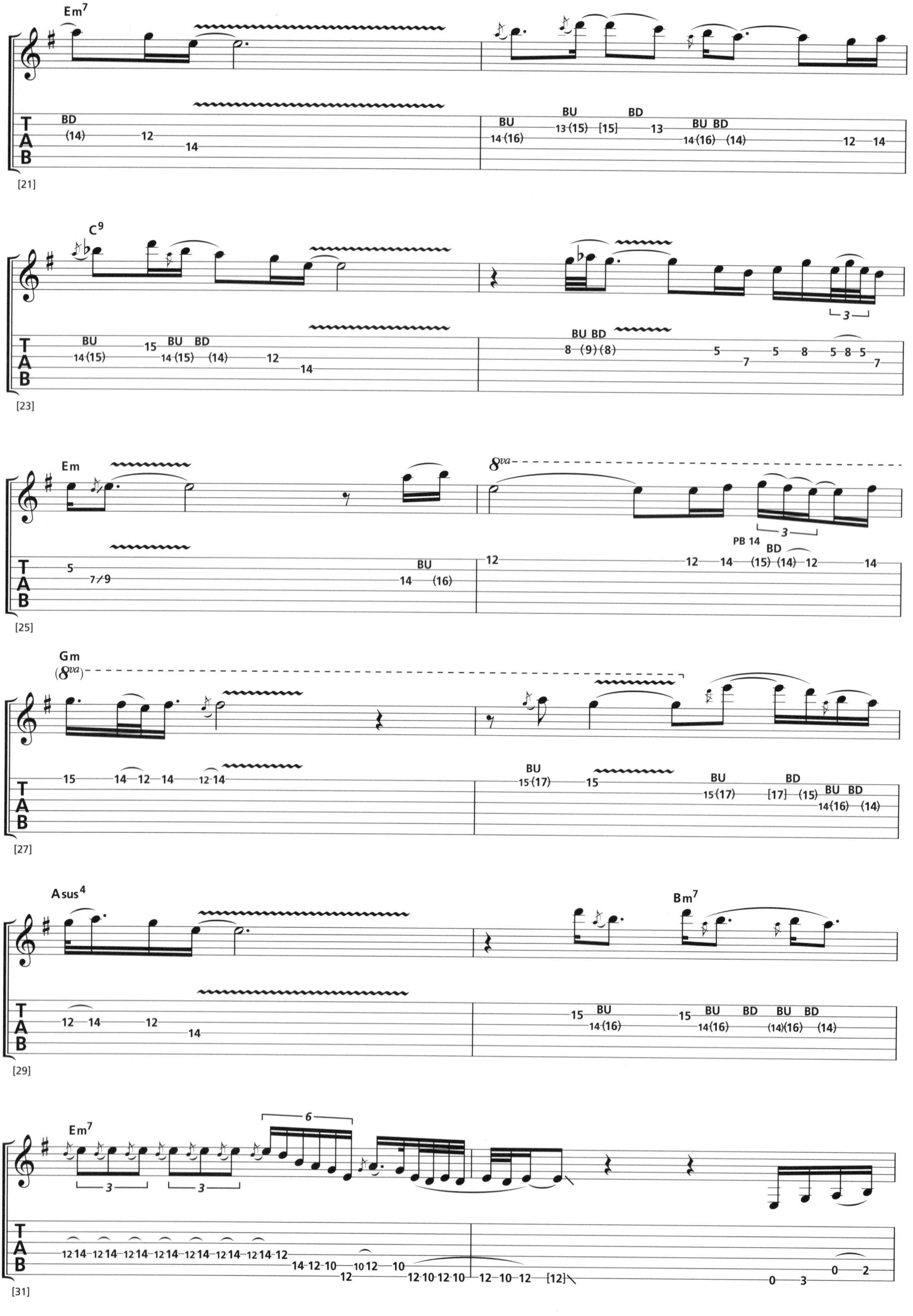
Em7
[21]
C9
[23]
Em
8va
[25]
Gm
(8va)
[27]
Asus4
Bm7
[29]
Em7
[31]

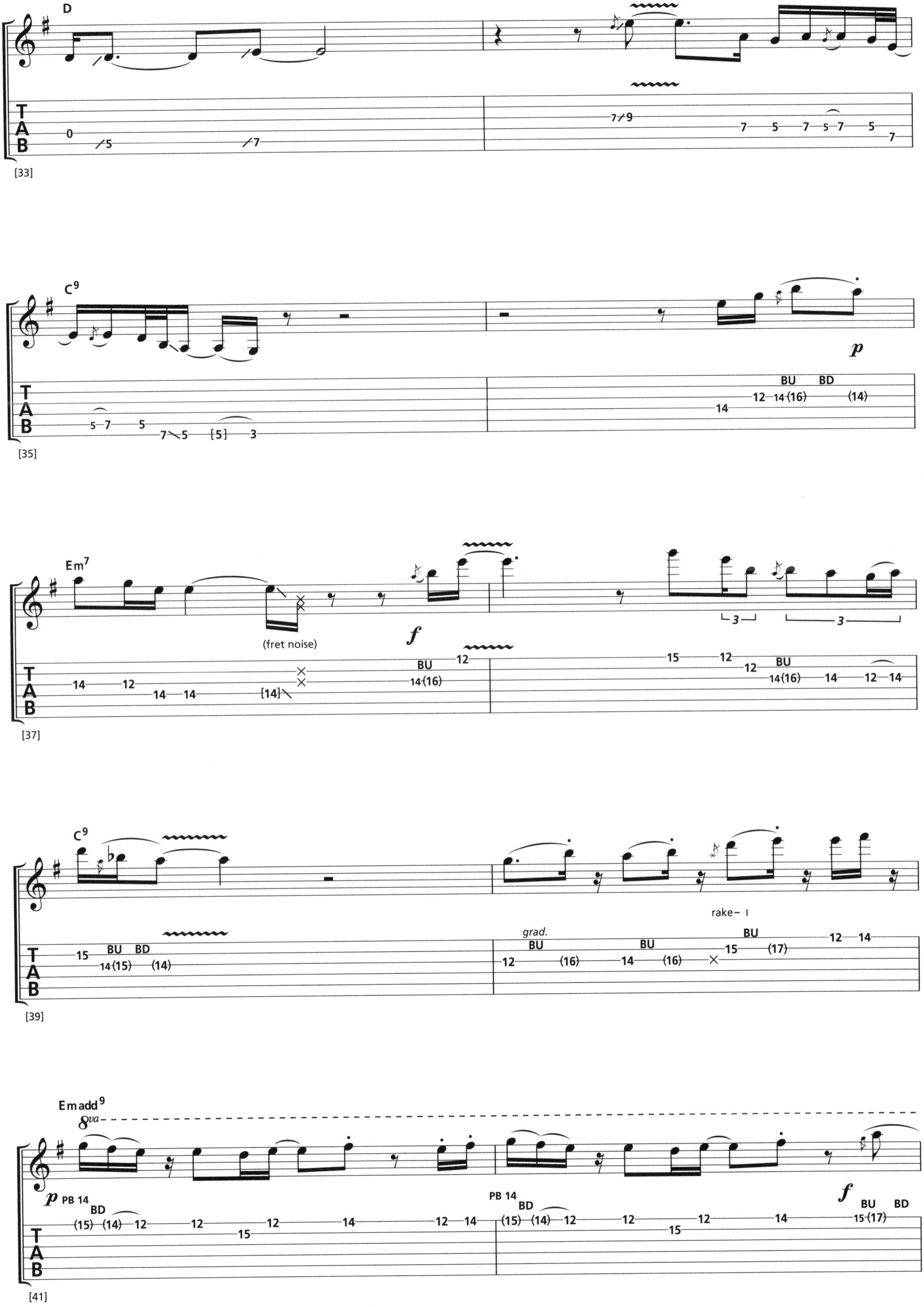
D
[33]
C9
[35]
Em7
(fret noise)
[37]
C9
rake-
grad.
[39]
Emadd9
8va
[41]

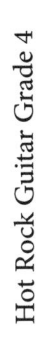

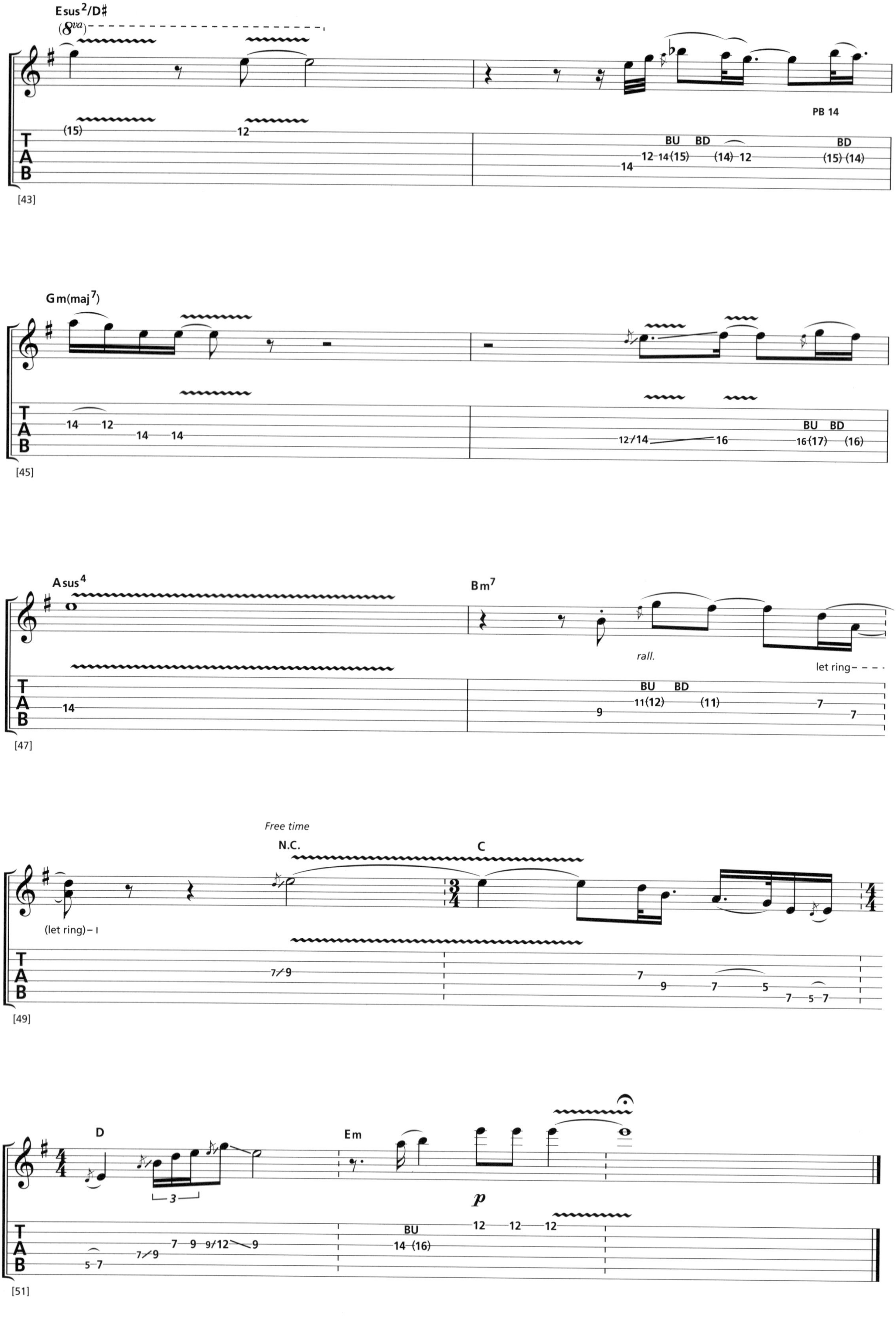
Esus²/D♯
(8va)
PB 14
BU
BD
[43]
Gm(maj⁷)
[45]
Asus⁴
Bm⁷
rall.
let ring
[47]
Free time
N.C.
C
(let ring)
[49]
D
Em
p
[51]

Notes On The Full Transcription

Bars 1–53 | *Complex notation*
The slow tempo of this piece means that phrases that are simple to recreate by ear can look intimidating when written down. Listen to the track several times before attempting to play it so you are familiar with the melody. It may also help to play along with the audio track with the guitar melody.

Bars 1–53 | *Beyond notation*
An excellent performance of this piece will involve the performer going beyond the printed notation. There are many subtleties involving things like the volume and attack of individual notes and phrases that are impossible to capture in notation. Once you have prepared at least four bars of music try playing them in different ways, making some phrases louder or softer than others until you have a set of phrases you are happy with. The way you interpret each phrase is what will make your performance unique.

Bars 1–53 | *Bending accuracy*
'Edge Of Darkness' features many string bends of both tones and semi-tones. These bends use lots of different articulations. Whatever the interval or technique, your primary concern should always be to ensure your bends are in tune. Practise each phrase slowly, making sure that the bend reaches the target note (the note in brackets).

Bars 1–14 | *Applying vibrato to bends*
This advanced technique requires a lot of control to articulate. Focus first on getting the initial bend to sound in tune then add vibrato. Some players apply vibrato by releasing the bend a *tiny* amount and returning it to its 'in-tune' position. Others prefer to apply vibrato from the in-tune position in the same way you do to an unbent string. Experiment with both approaches and see which you prefer.

Bars 31–32 | *Fast lick*
Work through this challenging lick a beat at time (the following step will get you started). Gradually piece together each beat while ensuring the original rhythm is preserved.

Bar 31 | *Grace note hammer-ons*
The first two beats of bar 31 consist of two triplets, each note of which is preceded by a fast grace note hammer-on. While the grace notes are an important part of the phrase's sound, they shouldn't interfere with the triplet rhythm. Start by playing the triplets without the hammer-ons so you are sure of the rhythms, then alternate between triplets with hammer-ons and the triplets without. This will help keep the triplet rhythm fresh in your mind (Fig. 1).

Bars 40–41 | *Dynamic contrast*
These two bars feature a wide dynamic contrast. Bar 40 is a series of aggressive ascending bends immediately followed by the next bar's delicate phrases. Practise these two bars in isolation for the sole purpose of creating the biggest possible contrast between the dynamics of each phrase.

Bar 40 | *Rake*
The raking technique in bar 40 creates an aggressive attack. Place the heel of your picking hand on the strings below the one you intend to play and drive your pick aggressively through the strings to produce a percussive sound. The aggressive attack will mean that more of your pick will strike the destination note, resulting in a stronger sound than a normal picking technique would produce (Fig. 2).

Bar 48 | *Rall.*
Rall. is short for 'rallentando', an Italian musical term that means 'gradually getting slower'. It is common for a song to slow gradually as it comes to its end. In 'Edge Of Darkness' the song slows down in bars 48 and 49 as it enters free time, which lasts for the remainder of the track.

Bars 49–53 | *Free time*
Music in free time has no regular pulse and the notes are played when the performer feels it is right to do so. A *freely* performance direction indicates that although the music is written in bars and given note values this should be treated only as a guide by the performer.

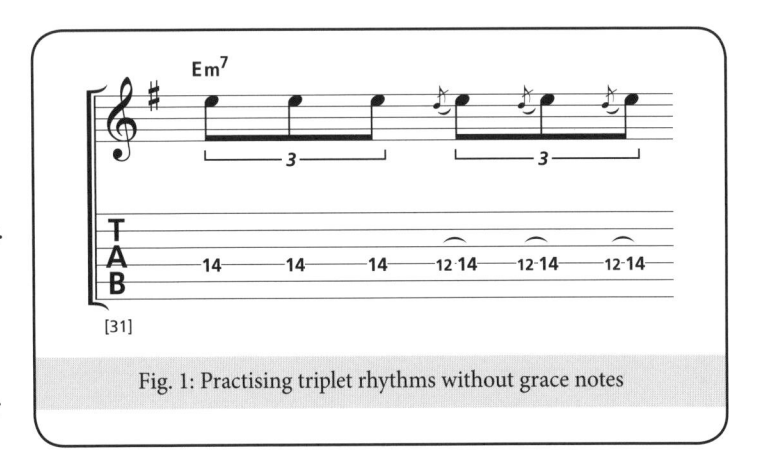

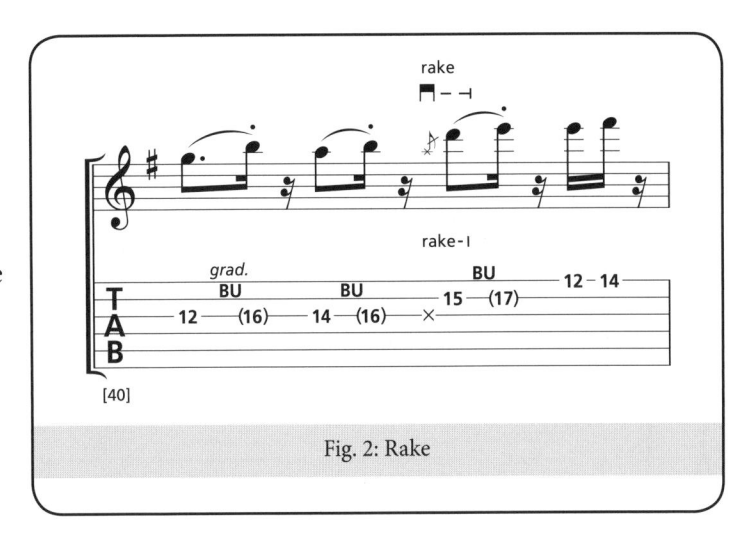

Fig. 1: Practising triplet rhythms without grace notes

Fig. 2: Rake

For Whom The Bell Tolls

Metallica

Words & Music by James Hetfield, Lars Ulrich & Cliff Burton

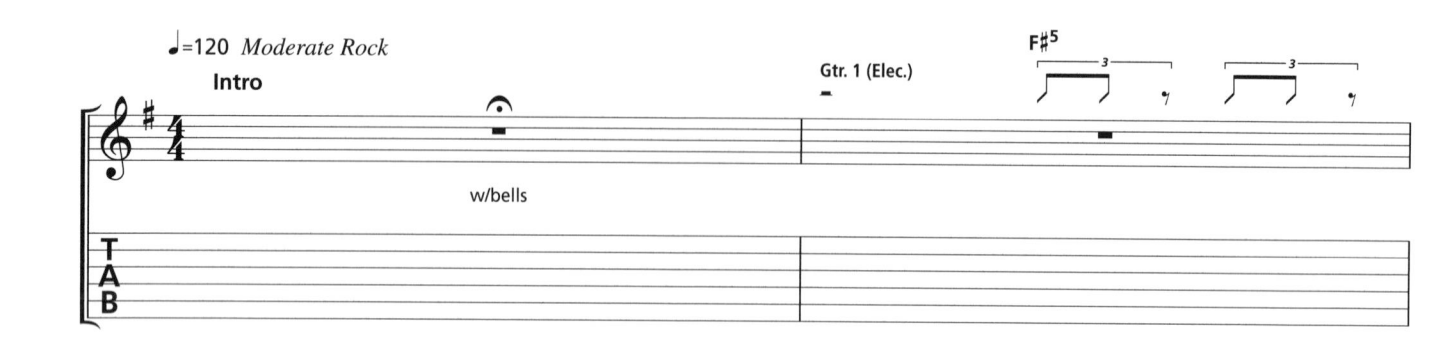

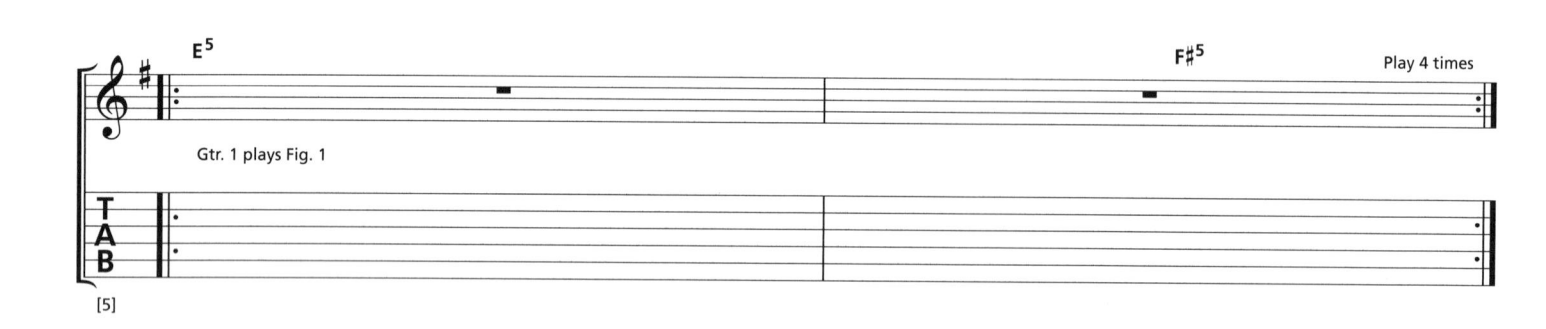

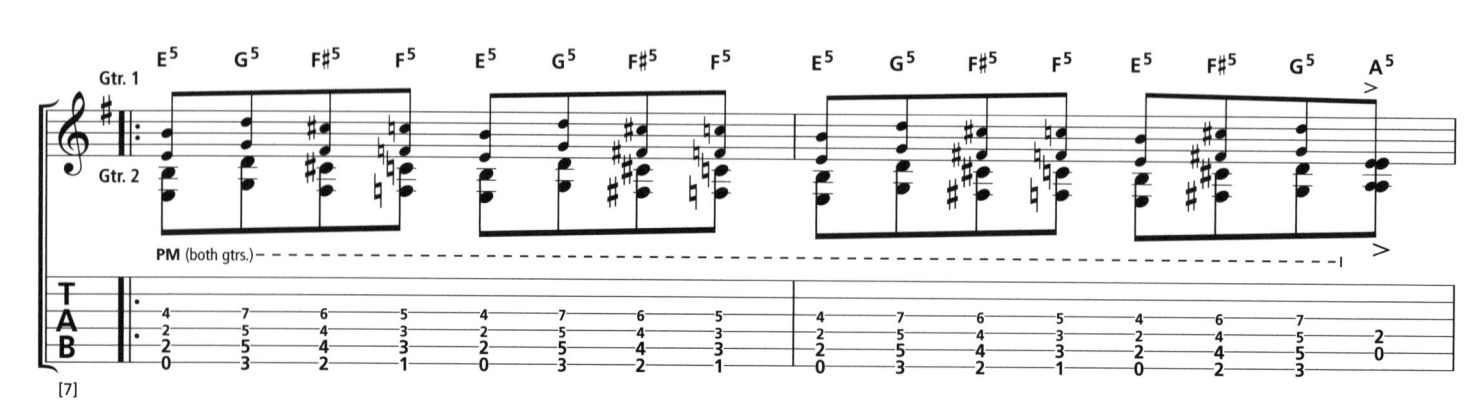

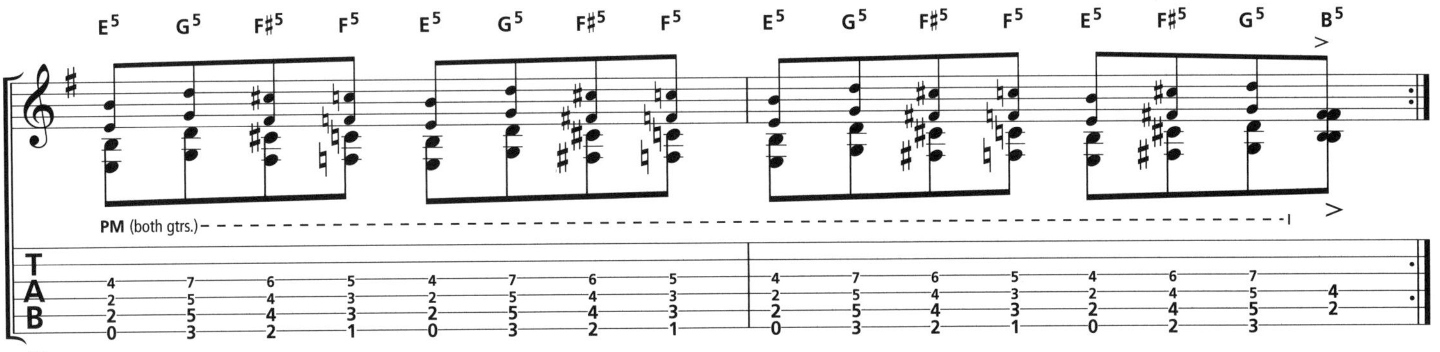
E5 G5 F♯5 F5 E5 G5 F♯5 F5 E5 G5 F♯5 F5 E5 F♯5 G5 B5
PM (both gtrs.)
T
A
B
[9]

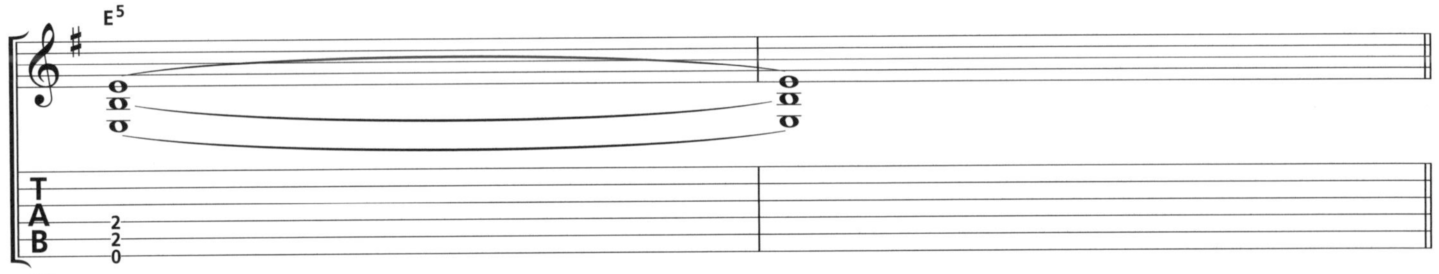
E5
T
A
B
[11]

E5
Gtr. 1
Fig. 2…
Gtr. 2
PM
T
A
B
[13]

G5
(PM)
T
A
B
[15]

E5
(PM)
[17]
G5
C5
A5
...Fig. 2 ends
(PM)
[19]
N.C.
Gtrs. 1 & 2
G5
A5
B♭5
F♯5
PM
Fig. 3...
[21]
F5
...Fig. 3 ends
[23]
T
A
B

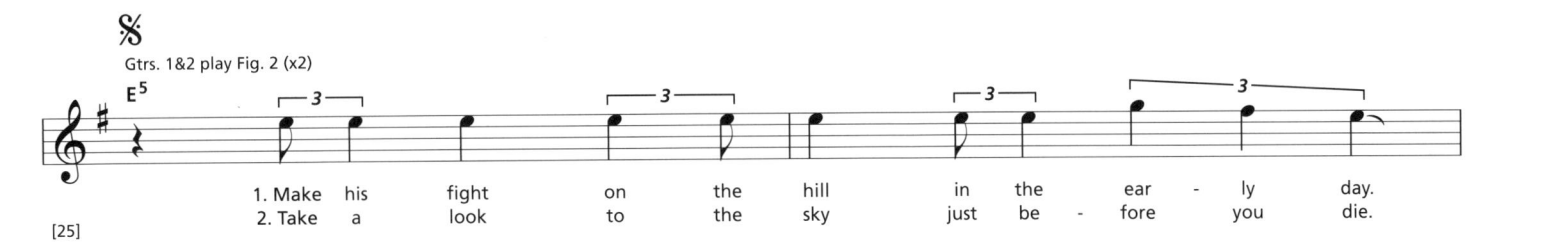

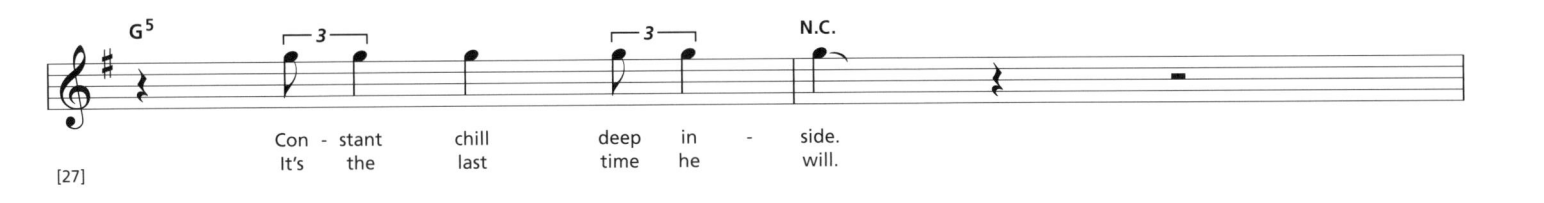

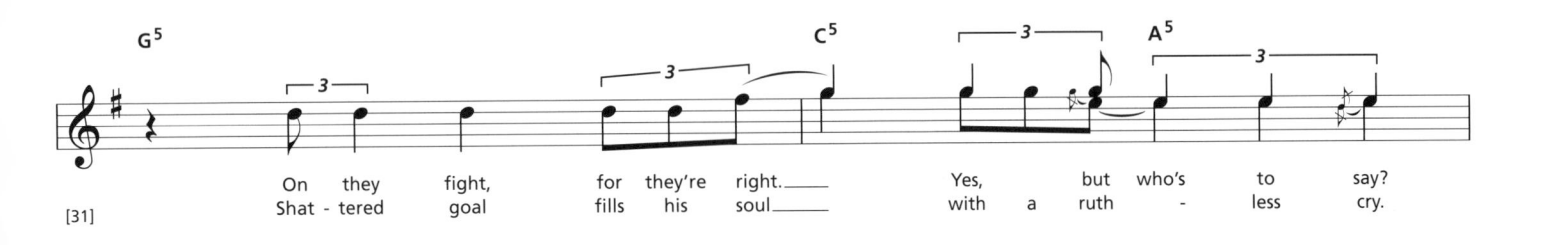

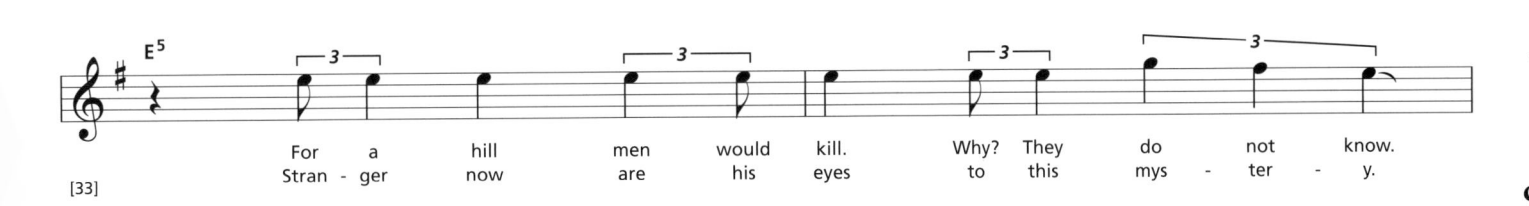

[25] E5 — Gtrs. 1&2 play Fig. 2 (x2)
1. Make his fight on the hill in the ear-ly day.
2. Take a look to the sky just be-fore you die.

[27] G5 / N.C.
Con-stant chill deep in-side.
It's the last time he will.

[29] E5
Shout-ing gun, on the run through the end-less grey.
Black-ened roar, mas-sive roar fills the crum-bling sky.

[31] G5 / C5 / A5
On they fight, for they're right. Yes, but who's to say?
Shat-tered goal fills his soul with a ruth-less cry.

[33] E5
For a hill men would kill. Why? They do not know.
Stran-ger now are his eyes to this mys-ter-y.

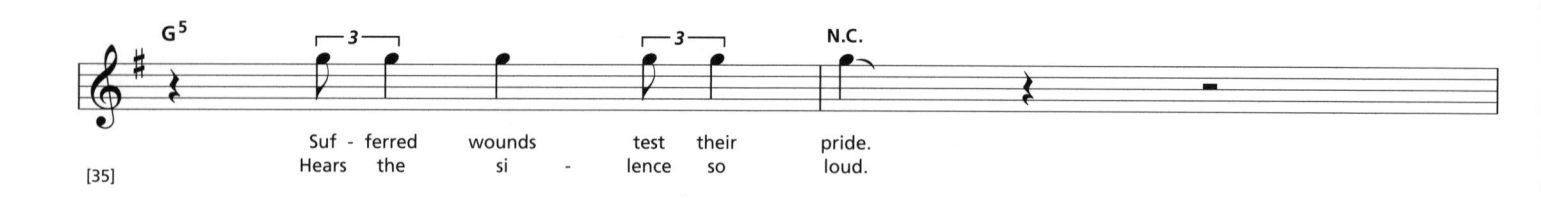

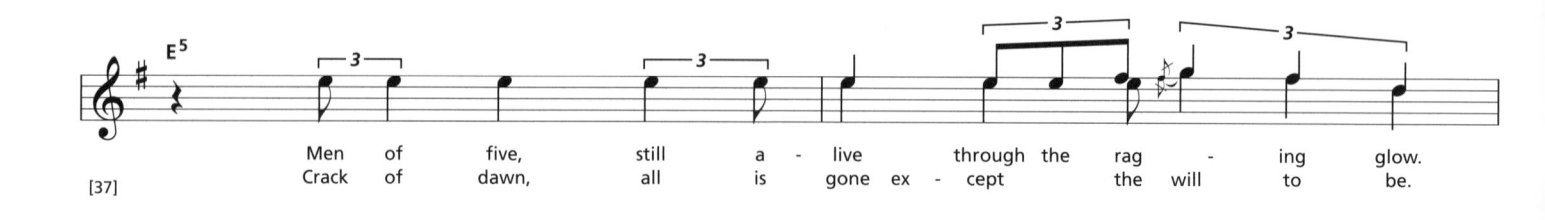

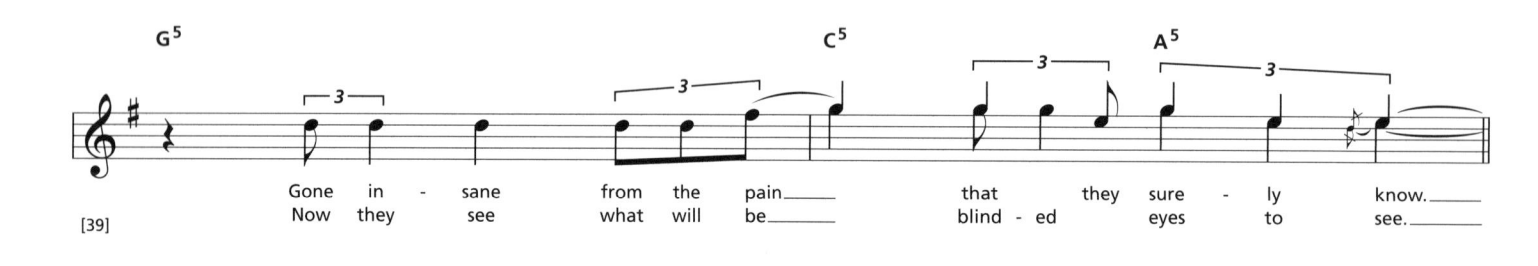

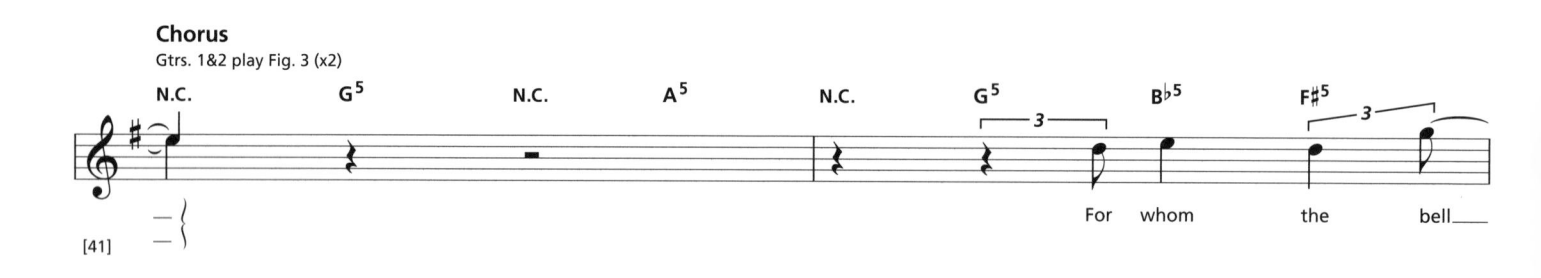

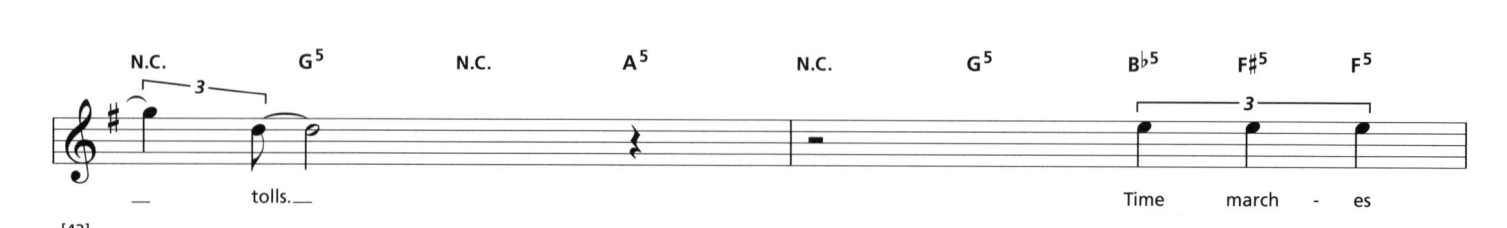

Suf - ferred wounds test their pride.
Hears the si - lence so loud.

Men of five, still a - live through the rag - ing glow.
Crack of dawn, all is gone ex - cept the will to be.

Gone in - sane from the pain that they sure - ly know.
Now they see what will be blind - ed eyes to see.

Chorus
Gtrs. 1&2 play Fig. 3 (x2)

For whom the bell

tolls. Time march - es

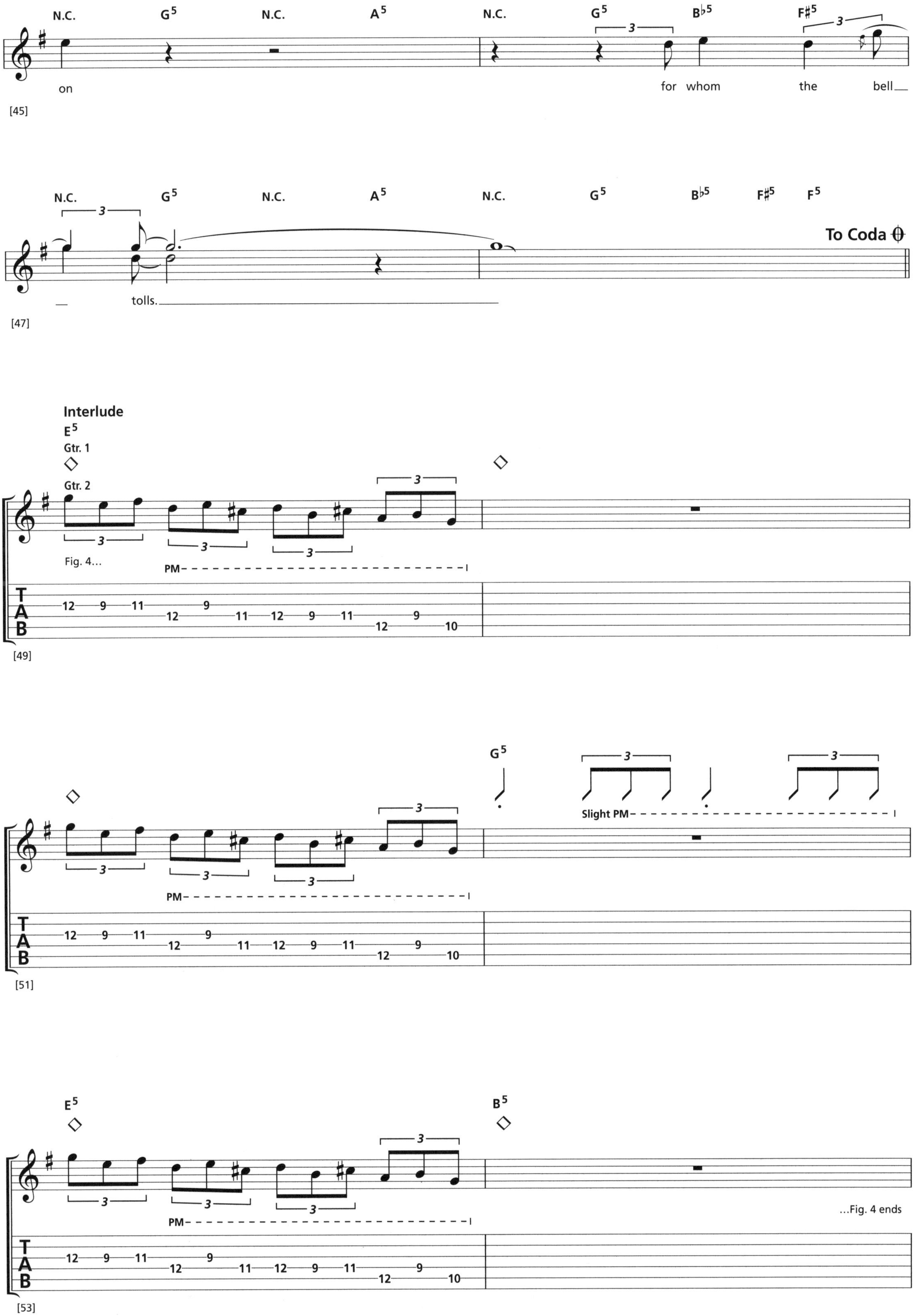
N.C. G5 N.C. A5 N.C. G5 B♭5 F♯5
on for whom the bell
[45]
N.C. G5 N.C. A5 N.C. G5 B♭5 F♯5 F5
To Coda
tolls.
[47]
Interlude
E5
Gtr. 1
Gtr. 2
Fig. 4…
PM
[49]
G5
Slight PM
PM
[51]
E5
B5
PM
…Fig. 4 ends
[53]

E5
Gtr. 3
Gtr. 4
PM (Gtr. 4)
Gtr. 2 plays Fig. 4
[55]
PM (Gtr. 4)
G5
Slight PM
[57]
E5
B5
D.𝄋. al Coda 𝄌
PM (Gtr. 4)
[59]
𝄌 Coda
E5
F♯5
E5
F♯5
G5
2° w/tremolo bar fx (till fade)
w/bells
[61]

Notes On The Full Transcription

Bars 1–63 | *Different types of palm muting*
There are many sections in 'For Whom The Bell Tolls' that feature palm muting; however, they are not all played in the same way. The sound of a palm-muted part can change depending on how much pressure is applied. For example, the riff in bars 7–10 must be played with a heavy palm mute so the strings produce an almost choked sound, whereas the picking riff in bars 13–20 should be played with a much lighter mute to stop the notes bleeding into each other while still maintaining fluency. Experiment with different degrees of palm muting to see what works best for each section.

Bars 2–63 | *Rhythm notation*
Several of the sections in this transcription include rhythm notation above the stave. All of the chords in the piece are two- or three-note powerchords which will allow you to focus on the rhythms.

Bars 3–5 | *Wah as a filter*
To achieve an authentic sound for this part of the song you need to use a wah pedal in a slightly unusual way. Rather than moving up and down in a rhythm or accenting certain notes, the pedal is left partially open to create a thin, nasal tone. This technique has been used by guitarists such as Slash, Joe Satriani and Michael Schenker.

Bars 3–7 | *Performance figures*
There are several performance figure directions throughout this transcription. The first occurs in bar 3 where you will see the direction 'Fig. 1…' and the next is in bar 4 where you will see 'Fig. 1 ends'. This means these two bars make up Fig. 1, so in bar 5 where you see the direction 'Gtr. 1 plays Fig. 1' you would play bars 3 and 4. Follow this procedure for all the other performance figures.

Bars 7–10 | *Twin rhythm guitar parts*
This section features two guitars playing the same rhythm part an octave apart. This creates a very dense sound. Unless you are playing with another guitarist the lowest sounding part is the best to play (Fig. 1).

Bars 13–20 | *Picking stamina*
This deceptively difficult picked riff will require considerable stamina to play accurately and in time for the whole 16 bars. Use a relaxed picking motion and aim to move the pick the smallest possible amount past the string after you strike it to minimise excess motion. Reducing motion like this will preserve your energy and stop your hand from tiring. You should also look to remove any tension in your body, as this will also cause you to tire prematurely. Raised shoulders are an obvious sign of tension.

Bars 49–58 | *Harmony guitar parts*
This section consists of a variation of the picking riff in bars 13–20. The section starts with a single guitar playing a descending line which is then joined by two more guitars playing harmony parts. These additional parts are unusual in that they don't follow the shape of the original. This means that instead of a harmonised descending line the end result is a dense bar of music that sounds more like block chords than a melodic part.

Bars 61–63 | *Quarter-note triplets*
The $F\#^5$ and G^5 chords in this section are grouped in quarter-note triplets, which means each triplet is spread across two beats (rather than the usual one). However, you play only the first two notes of each triplet here. Try counting out loud "ev-en-ly" (where each syllable relates to a different note of each triplet) as you play through this section. On the quarter-note triplets you should play only on the "ev-en" part of "ev-en-ly" (Fig. 2).

Bars 61–63 | *Tremolo bar effects*
The sound effects at the end of the song are played by multiple guitars using the tremolo arm to create wide vibrato and divebomb effects. These parts were undoubtedly improvised and would be virtually impossible to write in any meaningful way using traditional notation, so they are not transcribed here.

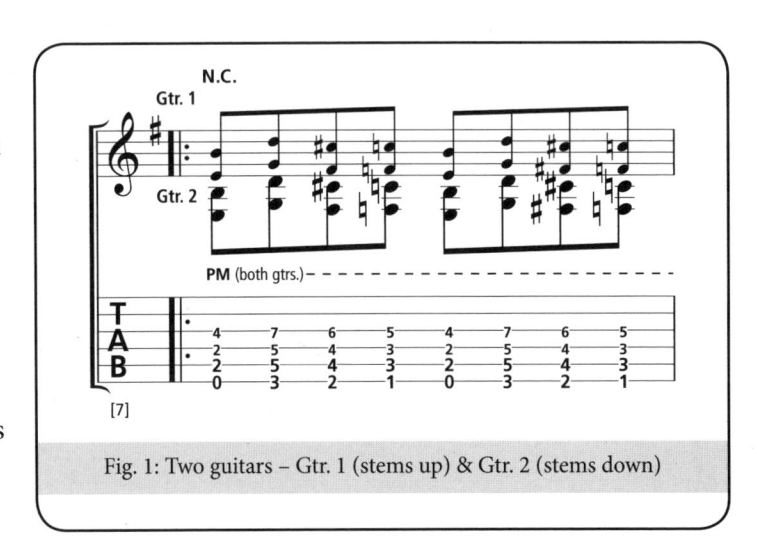

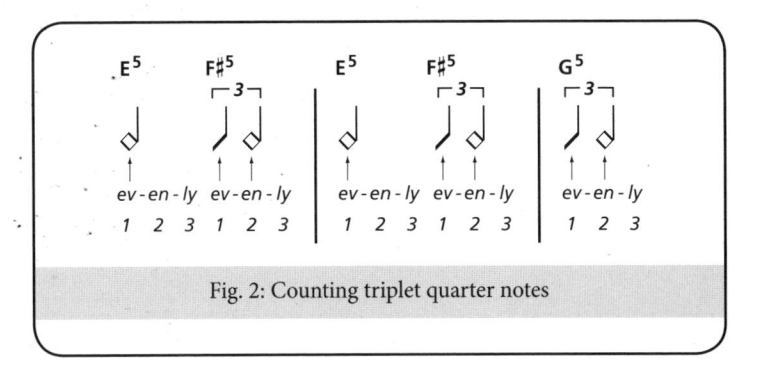

Fig. 1: Two guitars – Gtr. 1 (stems up) & Gtr. 2 (stems down)

Fig. 2: Counting triplet quarter notes

Ice 9

CD 2 Tracks 11 & 12

Joe Satriani
Music by Joe Satriani

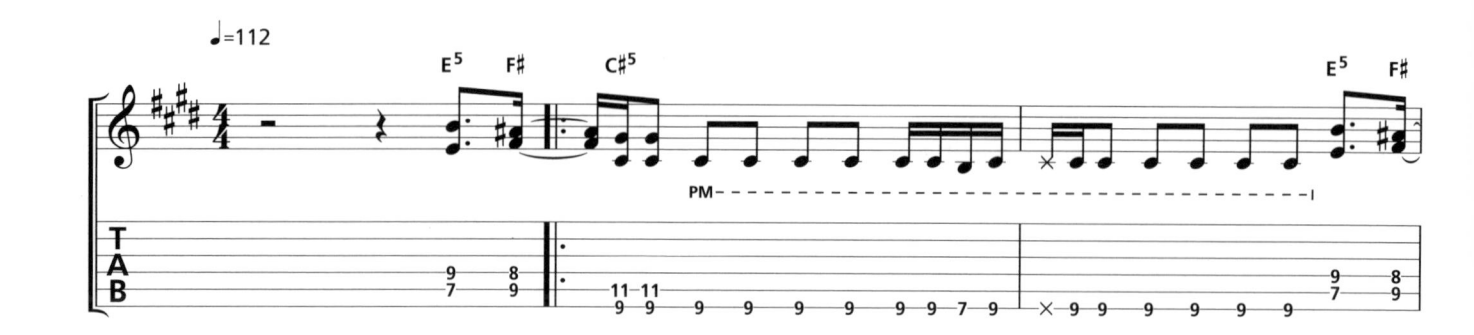

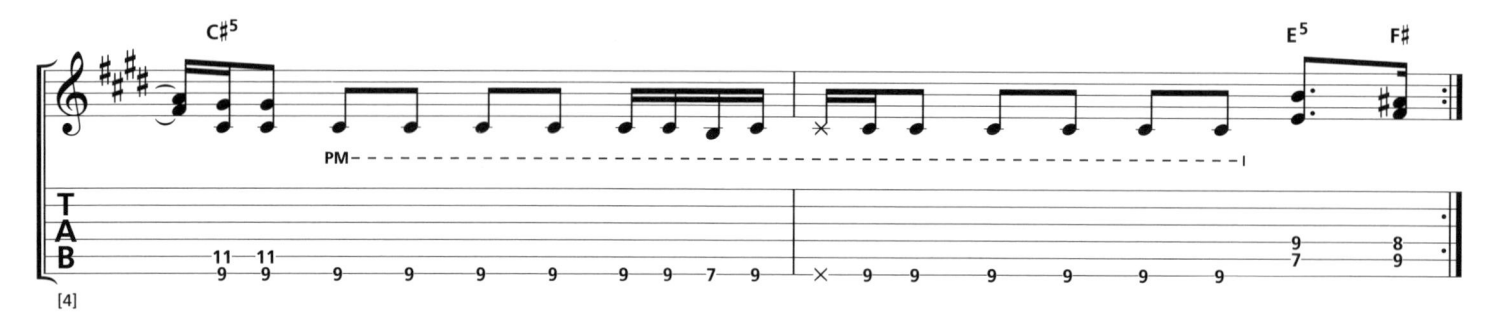

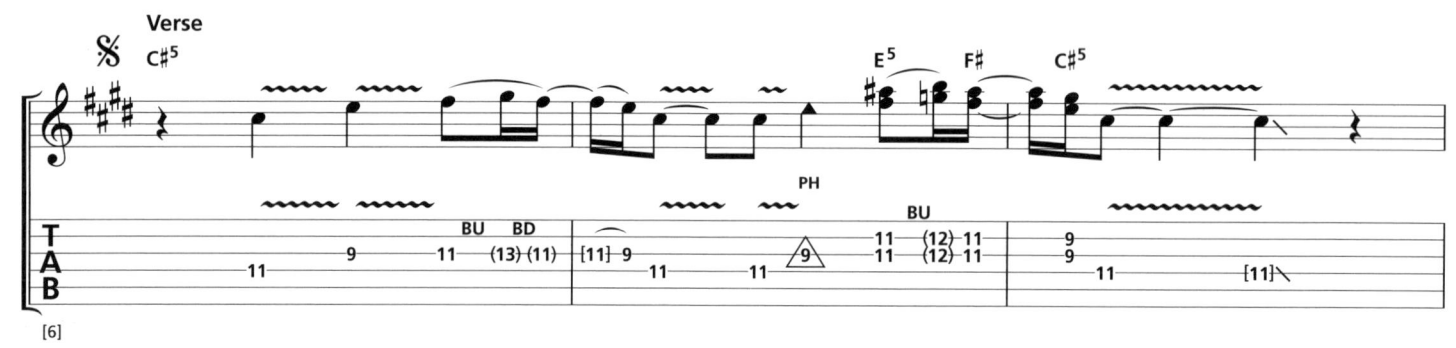

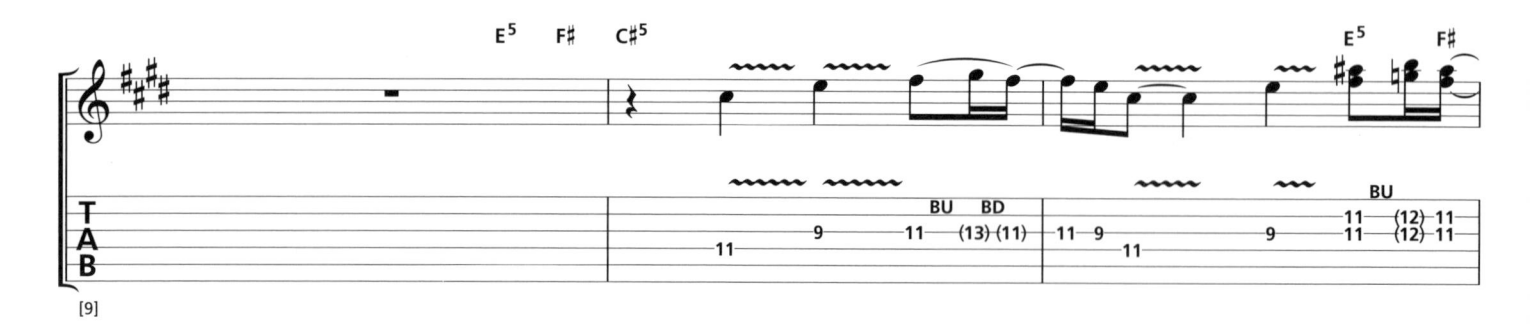

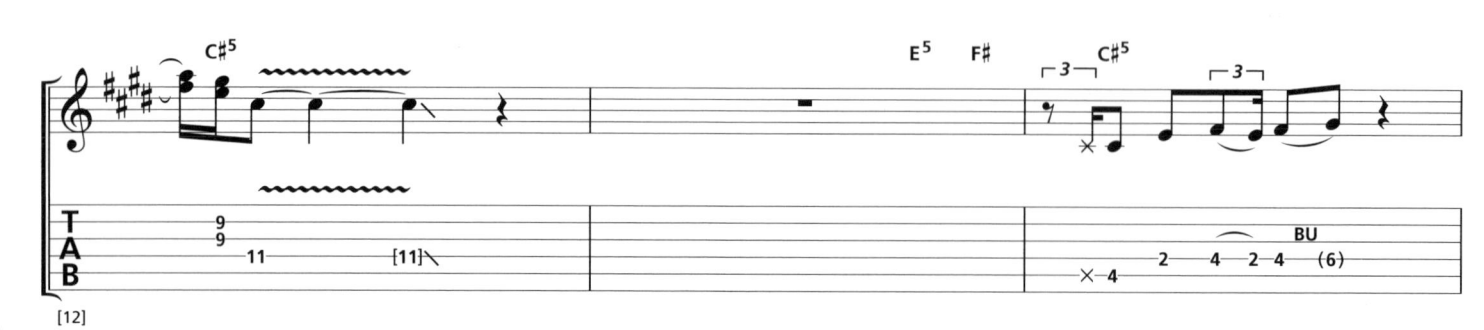

E5 F♯ C♯5 E5 F♯
PH
[15]
C♯5 E5 F♯ C♯5
PH
BU
[18]
Chorus
N.C. G♯5 F♯5 C♯5 A5
1/4
BU
[21]
8va
D♯5 G♯5
w/bar
BU
[24]
F♯5 (8va) C♯5 E5 G♯5 E5 F♯
1/4
BU
To Coda
[27]

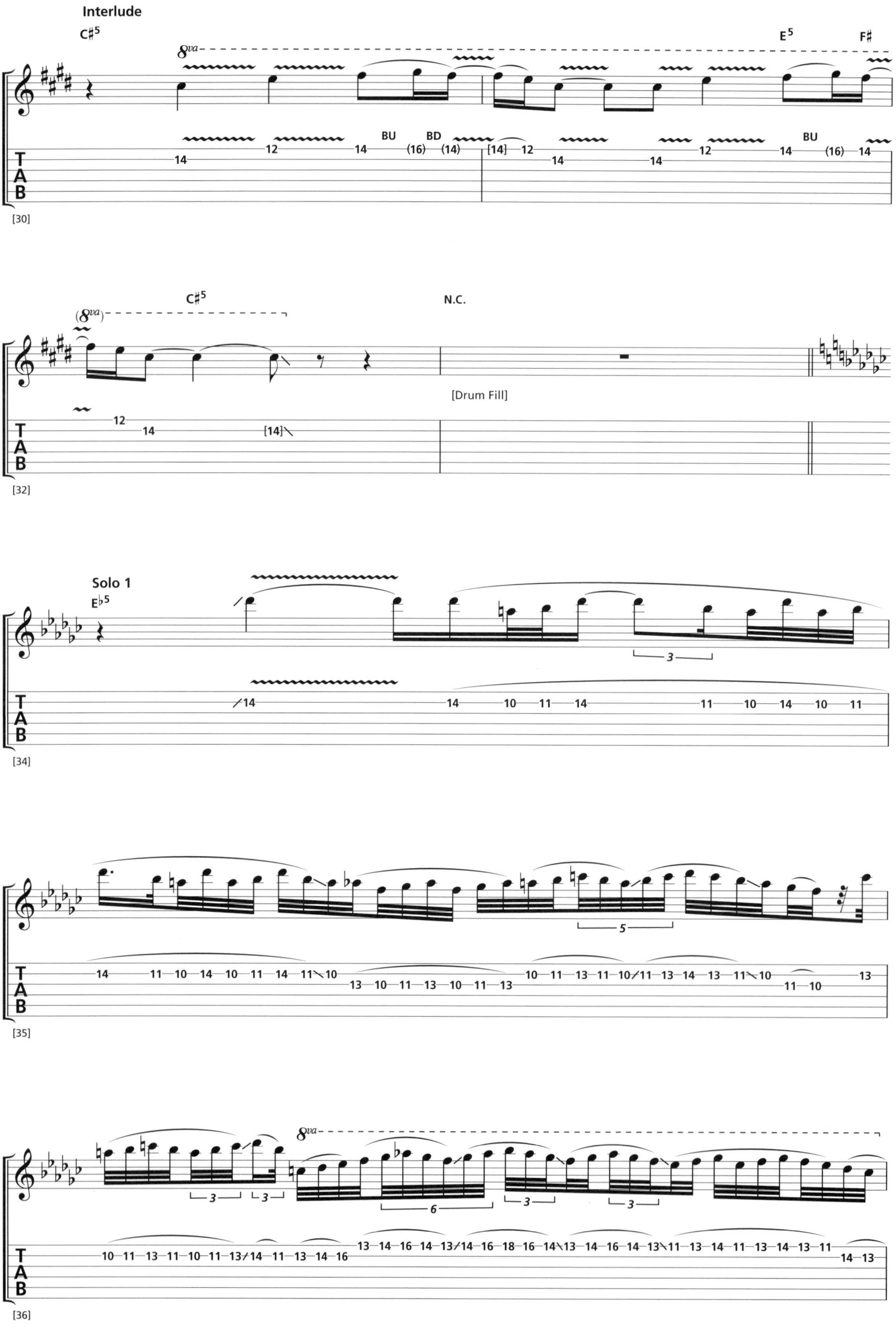
Interlude
C♯5
8va
E5
F♯
BU
BD
[30]
(8va)
C♯5
N.C.
[Drum Fill]
[32]
Solo 1
E♭5
[34]
[35]
8va
[36]

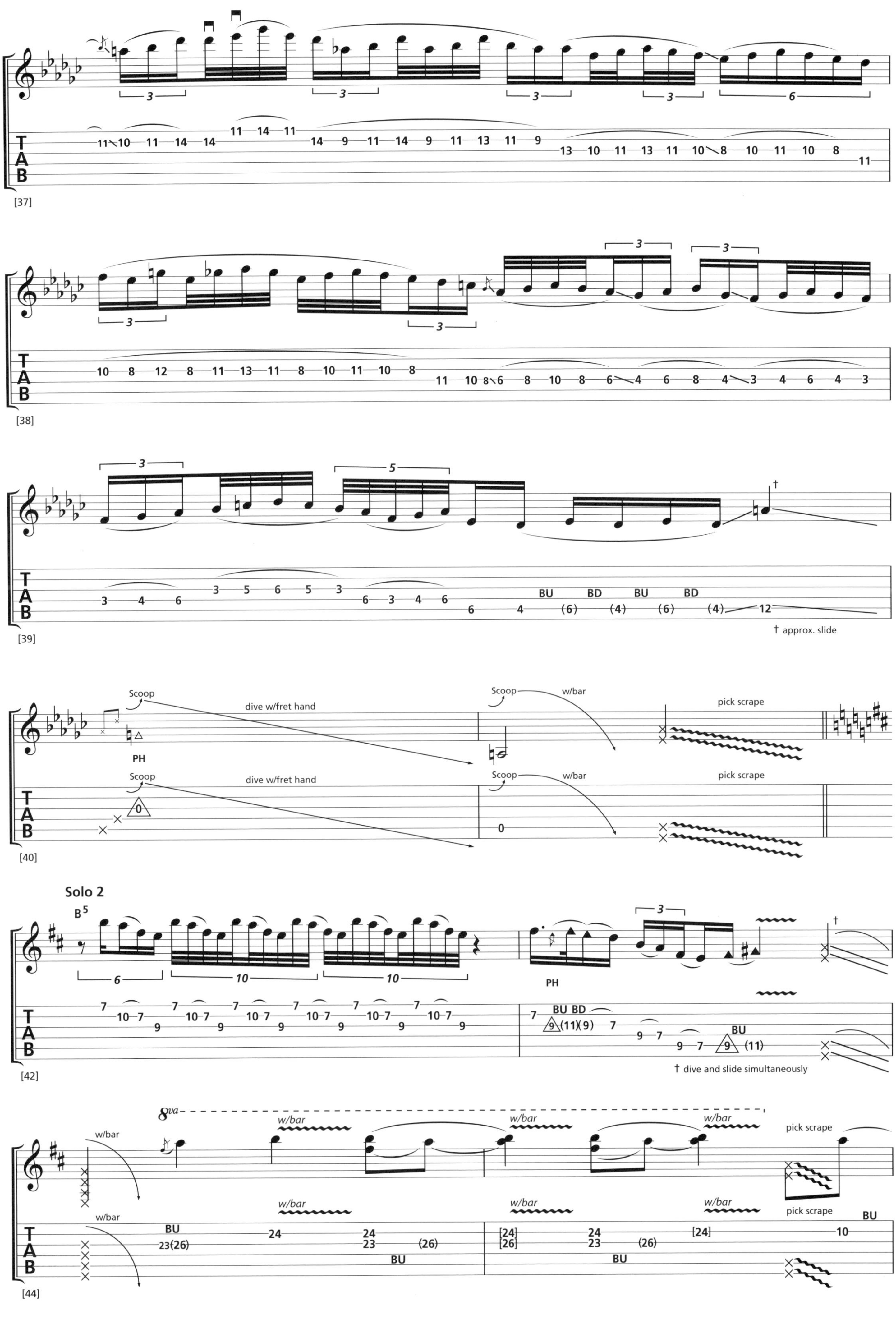
[37]
[38]
[39]
† approx. slide
Scoop
dive w/fret hand
w/bar
pick scrape
PH
[40]
Solo 2
B5
BU
BD
† dive and slide simultaneously
[42]
8va
[44]

† pre-depress bar then release from slack

† 'lizard down the throat' – as hand slides up and down fretboard the whammy bar is raised or lowered to compensate, keeping pitch at approx. fret 2

D.%. al Coda ⊕

Coda
Outro Solo
G♯5
F♯5
C♯5
A5
D♯5
[58]
G♯5
F♯5
C♯5
E5
BU
BD
[61]
† Catch B string during bend up
G♯5
8va
F♯5
BU
BD
grad.
[64]
C♯5
A5
D♯5
[67]
G♯5
F♯5
[69]
C♯5
E5
[71]

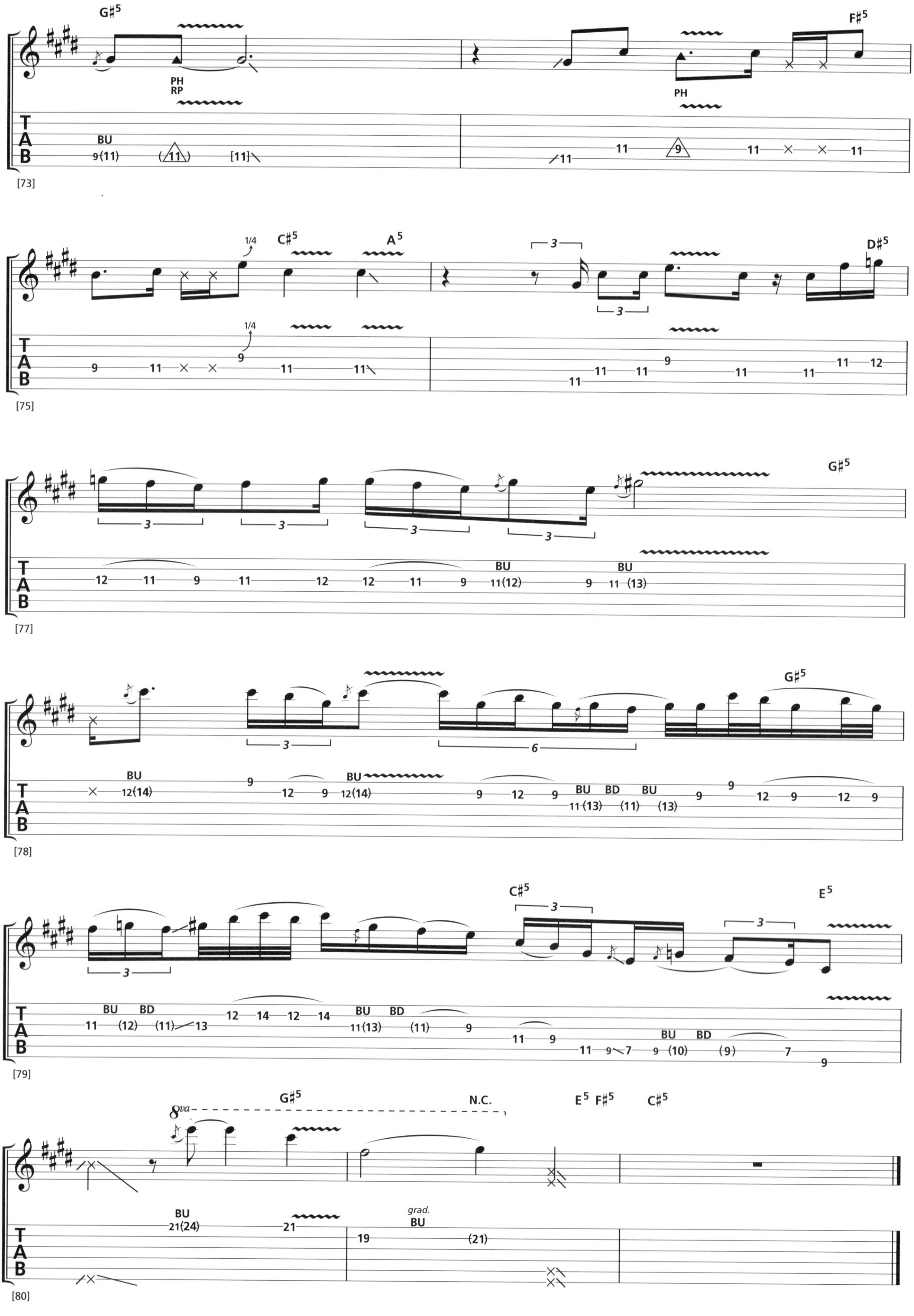
G♯5
PH
RP
F♯5
BU
[73]
1/4
C♯5
A5
D♯5
[75]
BU
G♯5
[77]
BU
BD
[78]
C♯5
E5
[79]
8va
G♯5
N.C.
E5 F♯5
C♯5
grad.
BU
[80]

Notes On The Full Transcription

Bar 7 | *Pinched harmonics*
If you haven't tried pinched harmonics before, select your bridge pickup and use a high distortion setting to help you. Place your thumb close to the edge of the pick and dig into the strings. Both the pick and your thumb should strike the string. Pinched harmonics will only sound at certain 'node' points along the strings, so you'll need to experiment with your picking hand position.

Bar 29 | *Applying vibrato to bends*
This advanced technique requires a lot of control to articulate. Focus first on getting the initial bend to sound in tune, then add your vibrato. Some players apply vibrato by releasing the bend by a *tiny* amount and then returning it to its 'in-tune' position. Others prefer to apply vibrato from the in-tune position in the same way you would to an unbent string. Experiment with both approaches and see which one you prefer.

Bars 34–41 | *Solo 1*
This solo changes key to E♭ minor and features one of Joe Satriani's most famous techniques: legato phrasing. The solo features long, flowing phrases that use slides, hammer-ons and pull-offs to create a seemingly endless flow of notes.

Bars 34–39 | *Legato phrasing*
These are very demanding phrases and you should break them down into chunks of one beat. Start slowly and make sure all of the notes sound clearly. As you increase the speed make sure all the notes continue to sound clearly because it's common for the notes in the middle of these types of phrases to become indistinct.

Bar 40 | *Pinched harmonic divebomb*
This wild technique is articulated by depressing the whammy bar with your *fretting* hand then performing a pinched harmonic on the open G string. This harmonic is preceded by a rake across the strings, so make sure you dig in to increase the chances of the pinched harmonic sounding strongly. Bring the bar up till it reaches its resting position and then pull it back down to execute the divebomb. This is an advanced technique that will take some time to master.

Bars 42–57 | *Solo 2*
This solo changes key to B minor and is more aggressive than the one that precedes it. It is based, initially at least, on the minor pentatonic scale and features more blues rock-inspired ideas than the first solo. The second half of the solo features another key change and some extreme whammy bar techniques.

Bars 44–45 | *Whammy bar vibrato*
The vibrato in these bars is articulated with the whammy bar. Bear in mind that even small whammy bar movements affect the pitch of a note quite drastically, so aim for small, fast and even movements to produce the correct sound.

Bars 50–53 | *Harmonics with fractions*
The most common harmonics are found at the 12th, 7th and 5th frets and you may also be aware of the less common ones found at the 3rd, 4th and 9th frets. There are also harmonics in many other locations on the guitar, but they are more difficult to play and require precise finger placement as they are not found directly over the frets. These harmonics are desirable for whammy bar work because they produce high-pitched notes. Use the TAB as a guide for the location and strike the strings very hard to help the note sound strongly (Fig. 1).

Bars 54–55 | *'Lizard down the throat'*
This signature technique is produced by gradually sliding your hand up the fretboard as you push the whammy bar down. Aim to keep the pitch of the note the same throughout the movement. Satriani named the sound this technique produces the 'lizard down the throat' (Fig. 2).

Bars 58–82 | *Outro*
This is a more conventional solo that uses blues rock phrases to complement the reprise of the earlier melody.

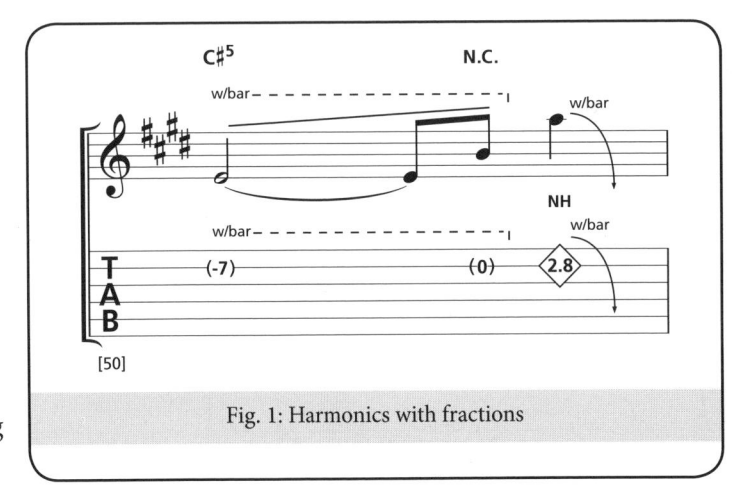

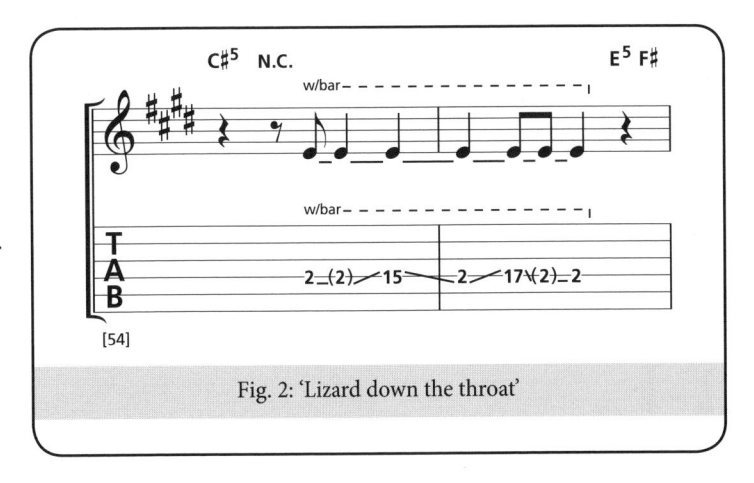

Fig. 1: Harmonics with fractions

Fig. 2: 'Lizard down the throat'

Iron Man

CD 2 Tracks 13 & 14

Black Sabbath
Words & Music by Frank Iommi, Terence Butler, William Ward & John Osbourne

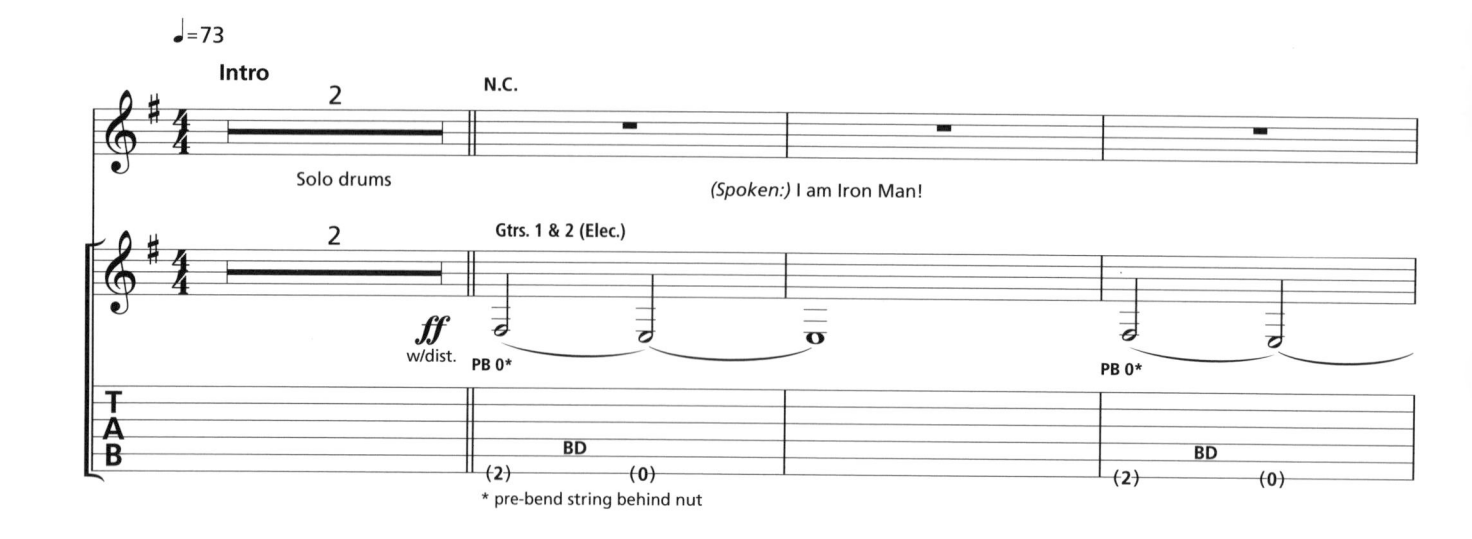

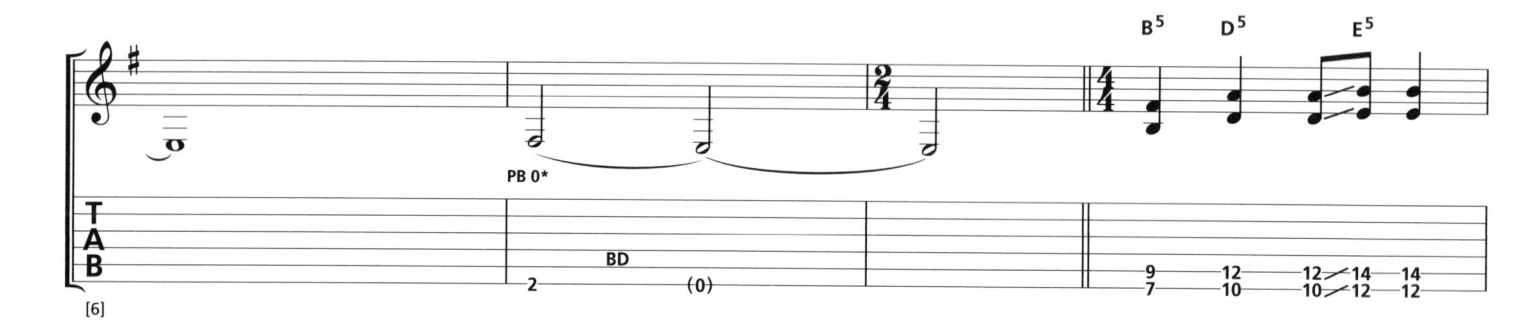

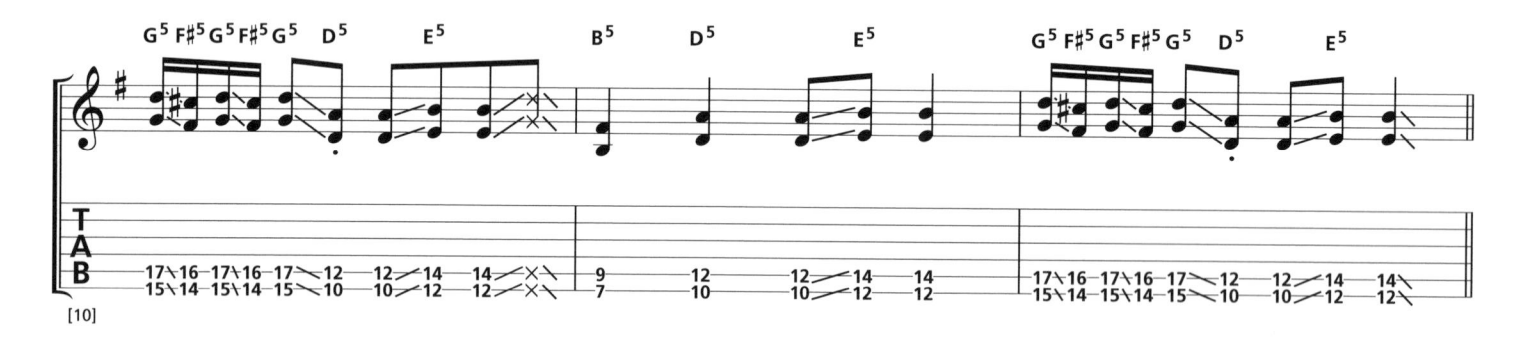

© Copyright 1971 Westminster Music Limited.
All Rights Reserved. International Copyright Secured.

1.
B5 D5 E5
G5 F♯5 G5 F♯5 G5 D5 E5
Or if he moves__ will he fall?
why should we___ ev - en care?
2.
N.C.
1/4
B5 D5 E5
N.C.
3. He was turned to steel in__ the__ great mag - ne - tic field,
4. Now the time is here for__ Ir - on Man to spread fear.
5. Hea - vy boots of lead fills__ his__ vic - tims full of dread,

To Coda
when he trav - elled time for the fu - ture of man - kind.
Ven - geance from the grave kills the peo - ple he once saved.
run - ning as fast as they can, Ir - on Man lives a - gain.
[31]
Chorus
E5
D5
B5
No-bo-dy wants him, he just stares at the world.
No-bo-dy wants him, they just turn their heads.
[33]
E5
D5
Plan-ning his ven - geance that he will soon un -
No - bo - dy helps him, now he has his re -
[36]
B5
- furl.
- venge.
[39]

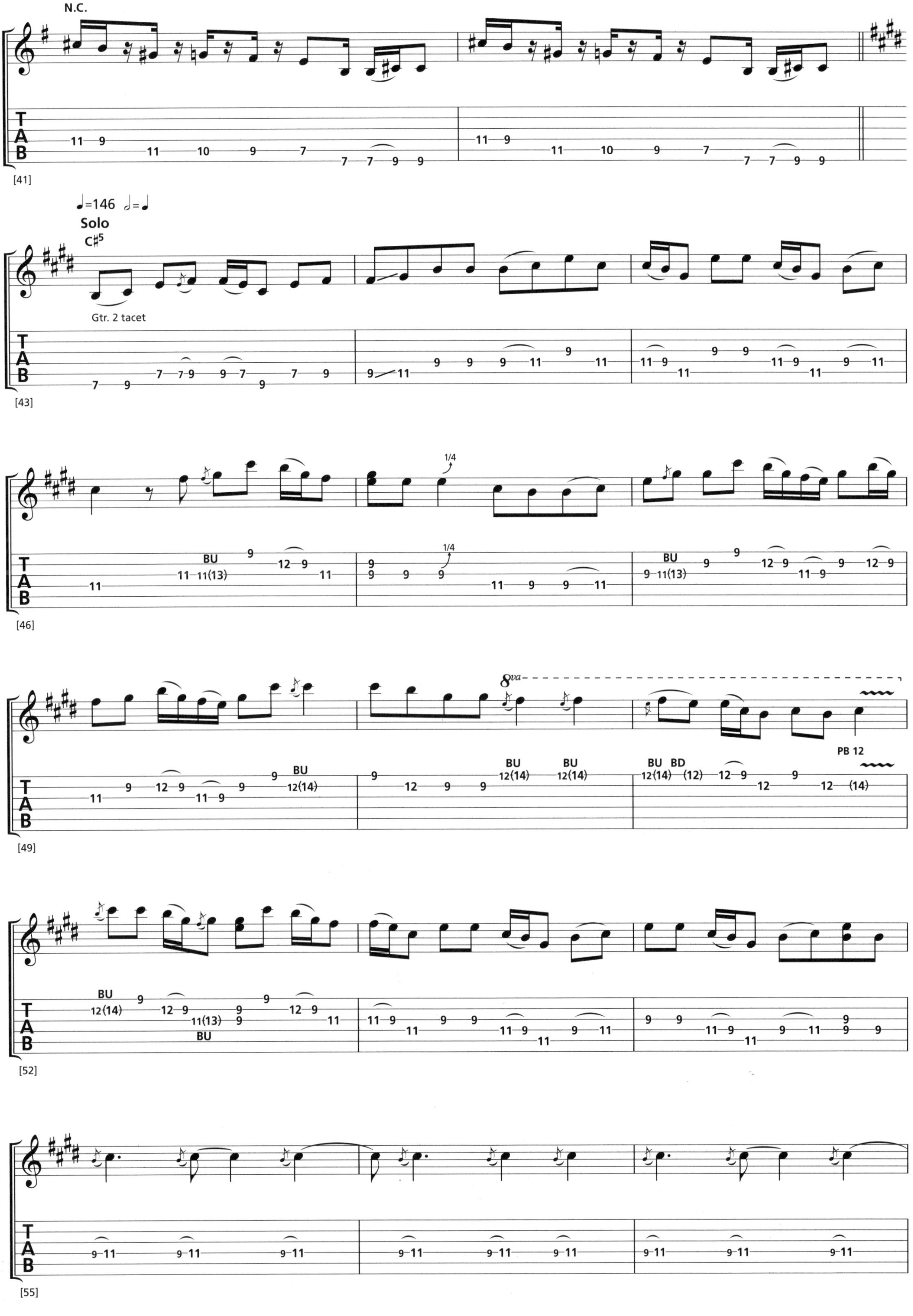
N.C.
[41]
♩=146 𝅗𝅥=♩
Solo
C♯5
Gtr. 2 tacet
[43]
[46]
1/4
[49]
8va
PB 12
[52]
[55]

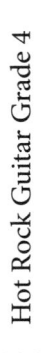

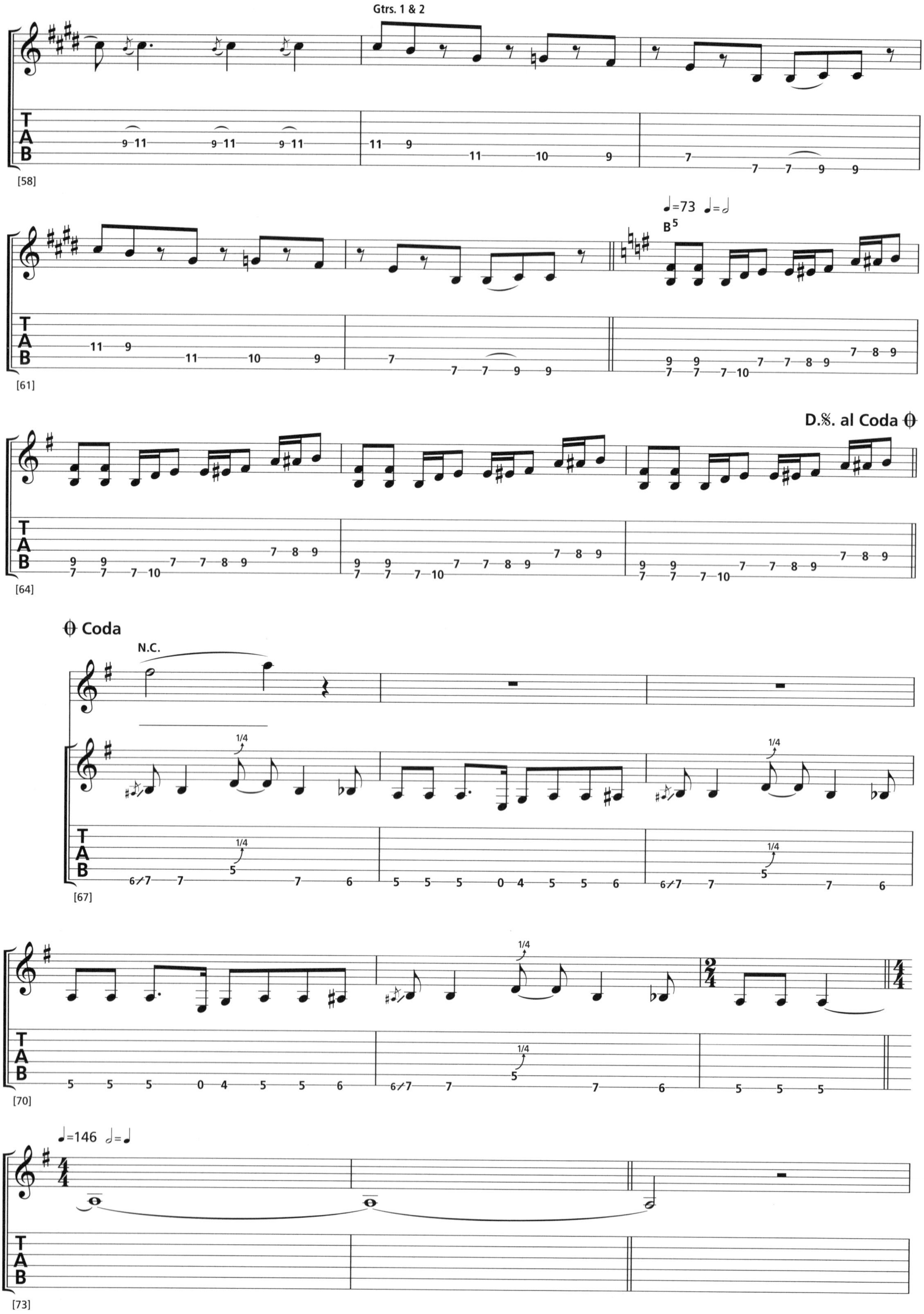
Gtrs. 1 & 2
[58]
[61]
♩=73 ♩=𝅗𝅥
B5
D.𝄋. al Coda 𝄌
[64]
𝄌 Coda
N.C.
1/4
[67]
[70]
♩=146 𝅗𝅥=♩
[73]

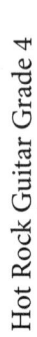

N.C.
(Drums & Bass)
[76]
BU
BD
† bend string behind nut
[80]
PB 0*
BD
* pre-bend string behind nut
[84]
E5
D5
C♯5
C5
[88]
Gtr. 1
PB 9
BD
Gtr. 2
[92]

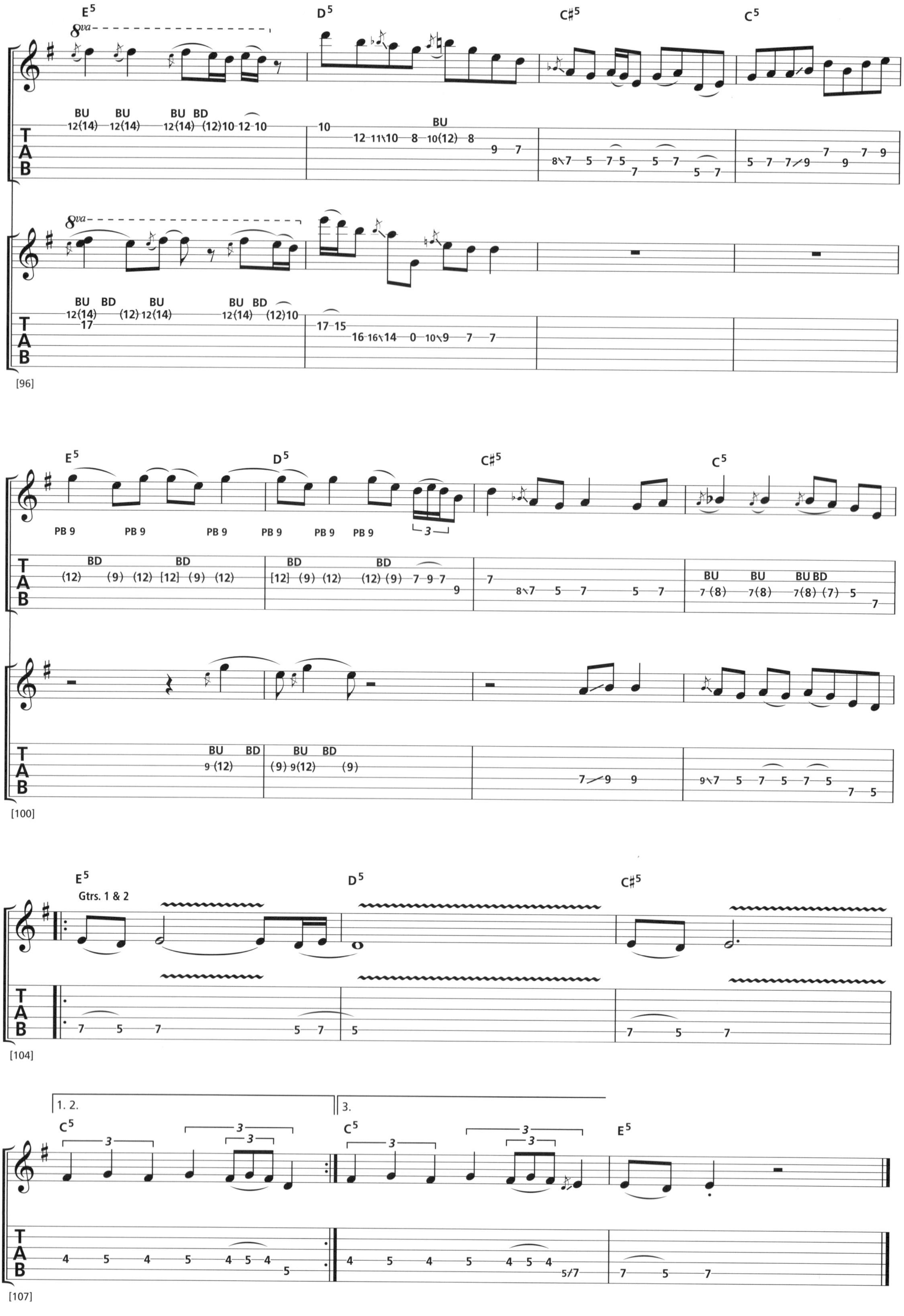
E5
D5
C#5
C5
8va
BU
BD
PB 9
[96]
[100]
Gtrs. 1 & 2
[104]
1. 2.
3.
[107]

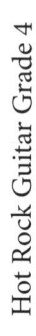

Notes On The Full Transcription

Bars 2–8 | *Bending behind the nut*
This unusual technique involves pushing down on the string *behind* the nut. Once bent, play the string then gradually release the pressure to create the falling sound heard on the original recording. You will have to push the string quite hard to reach the desired pitch. Make sure you release the bend slowly to get the correct sound. If you have a locking nut you can re-produce this sound by depressing the tremolo arm (whammy bar, wang bar) before striking the string and gradually allowing the string to return to its original pitch.

Bars 9–11 | *Moving powerchords*
Think of the powerchords in this riff as a single shape that is moved around the fretboard. Lock your hand into the powerchord shape when you play the B^5 chord then think of moving your whole hand rather than individual fingers.

Bars 9–11 | *Sliding powerchords*
Maintain pressure into the neck throughout each slide so that the strings ring out and there are no unwanted gaps. This is especially important when you play the 16th notes on the first beat of bar 2.

Bar 14 | *Slides*
The end of the single-note version of the riff features a slide up and down the fretboard. The TAB here should be treated only as a guide because, although a specific fret number is notated, these slides were likely placed in the riff to create an interesting sound effect rather than to hit a specific note.

Bars 43–58 | *Guitar solo*
This solo is a great example of Tony Iommi's lead style. It is based on the blues and uses the minor pentatonic scale throughout. Far from being a random collection of blues licks, this solo is strong rhythmically and based on driving eighth- and 16th-note rhythms that ensure the song doesn't lose its momentum. Repeated licks and rhythmic motifs give the solo its shape and musical identity.

Bars 43–58 | *Fast bends*
Fast bends are difficult to play accurately because your ear has less time to register the changes in pitch and recognise when the bend is in tune. Muscle memory plays a big part in fast bends. Play these types of bends slowly and repeatedly, paying close attention to the tuning. This will teach your fingers how far the string should be bent. Gradually increase the speed as you become more comfortable.

Bars 43–44 | *Extended scale position*
These two bars feature a device that's common in a lot of blues rock playing. The minor pentatonic scale is started from the ♭7 of the scale, in this case a B note at the 7th fret. This puts your hand in a position to play the scale as demonstrated in Fig. 1. This is a popular fingering because the notes in the lower octave fall under the stronger first and third fingers while avoiding the fourth finger, and allow licks to be easily transposed by an octave.

Bar 53 | *Rhythmic motif*
Two 16th notes played as either a hammer-on or pull-off followed by an eighth note is a rhythm that is played so often throughout this solo that it is worthy of study in isolation. Fig. 2 shows how bar 53 can be adapted to create a repeated exercise that will help to hone this particular rhythm/lick. Play to a metronome and start slowly, ensuring the hammer-ons are clean and precise.

Bar 100 | *Minor 3rd pre-bends*
This minor 3rd pre-bend lick will take a lot of strength and control to execute correctly. Bend the string using your third finger supported by your first and second. Play the target note before the pre-bend to check your tuning until you are sure you are pre-bending to the correct pitch.

Bar 107 | *Unusual triplet rhythm*
This triplet rhythm is unusual in that it contains an eighth-note triplet *within* a quarter-note triplet. Before attempting the eighth-note triplet make sure you can play the two quarter-note triplets correctly by counting "Ev-en-ly, ev-en-ly" across the bar. Once you feel comfortable with this try replacing the second note of the second triplet with an eighth-note triplet.

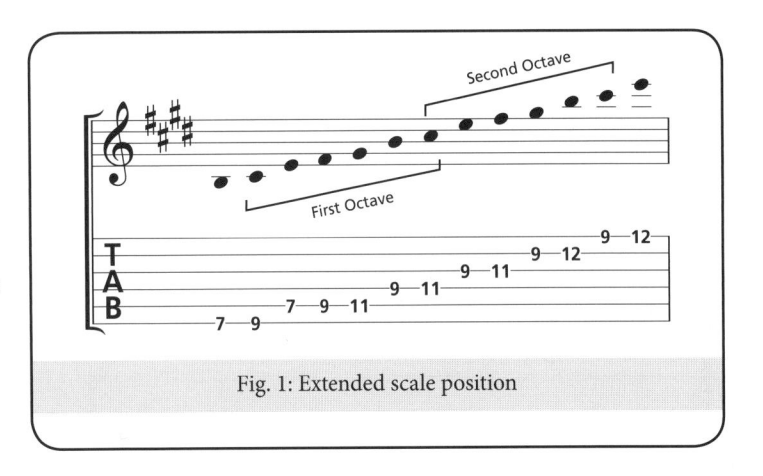

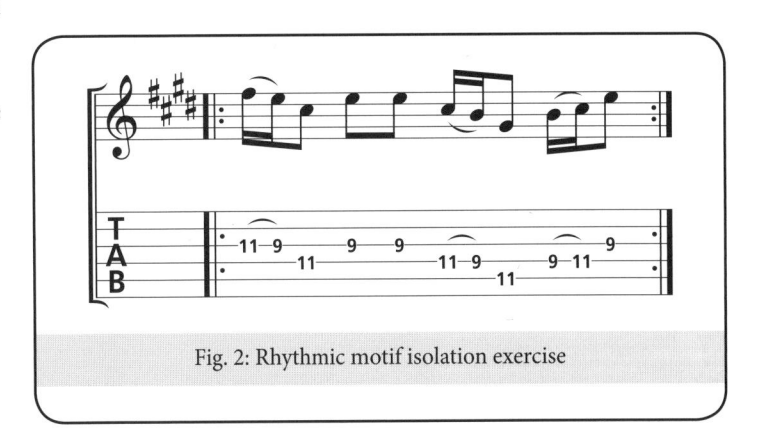

Fig. 1: Extended scale position

Fig. 2: Rhythmic motif isolation exercise

Whole Lotta Rosie

AC/DC

Words & Music by Angus Young, Malcolm Young & Bon Scott

N.C.
C5 D5 C5 A5 N.C.
She ain't ex - act - ly pret - ty,
ain't ex - act - ly small.
[14]
C5 D5 C5 A5 N.C.
Fort' - two, thirt' - nine, fif - ty six, you could say
[17]
C5 D5 A5
she's got it all.
[20]
N.C. A5 N.C. A5
Play 3 times
[23]

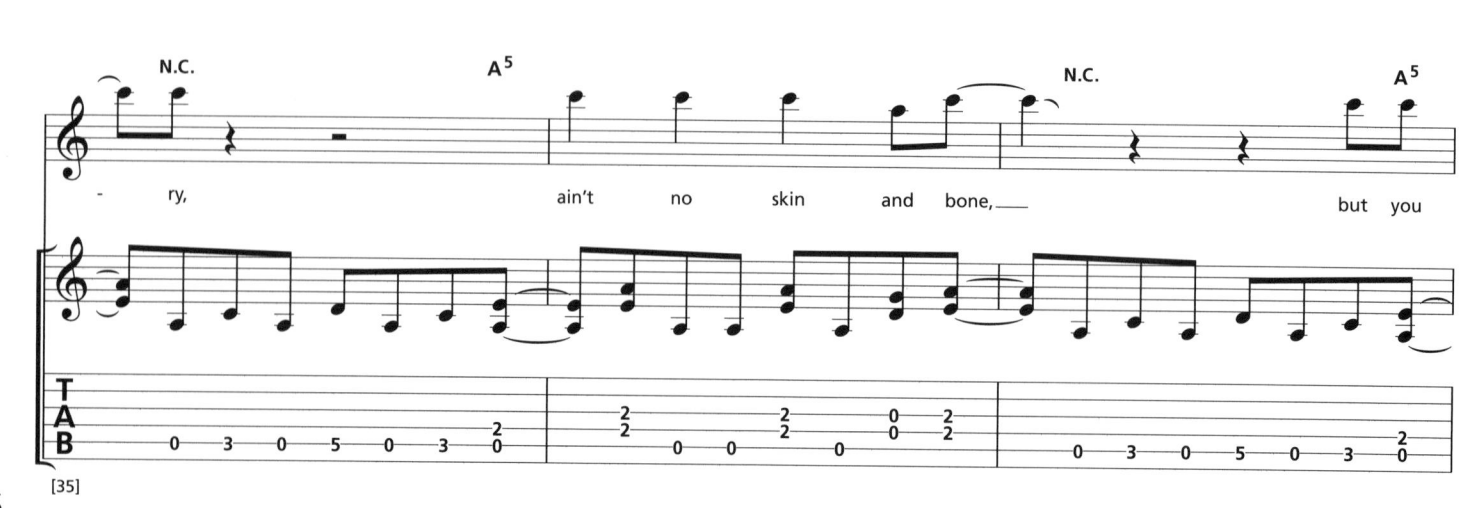

2. Never had a woman, never had a woman like you.
3. *See additional lyrics*

Do-in' all the things, do-in' all the things you do.

Ain't no fai-ry sto-ry, ain't no skin and bone, but you

N.C.
A5
give it all you got, weigh - in' in at nine - teen stone.
[38]
Chorus
F5
You're / She was a whole lot - ta wom - an,
a whole lot - ta
[41]
D5
wom - an,
whole lot - ta
A5
Ro - sie,
G5
[44]
whole lot - ta Ro - sie,
A5
G5
whole lot - ta
[47]

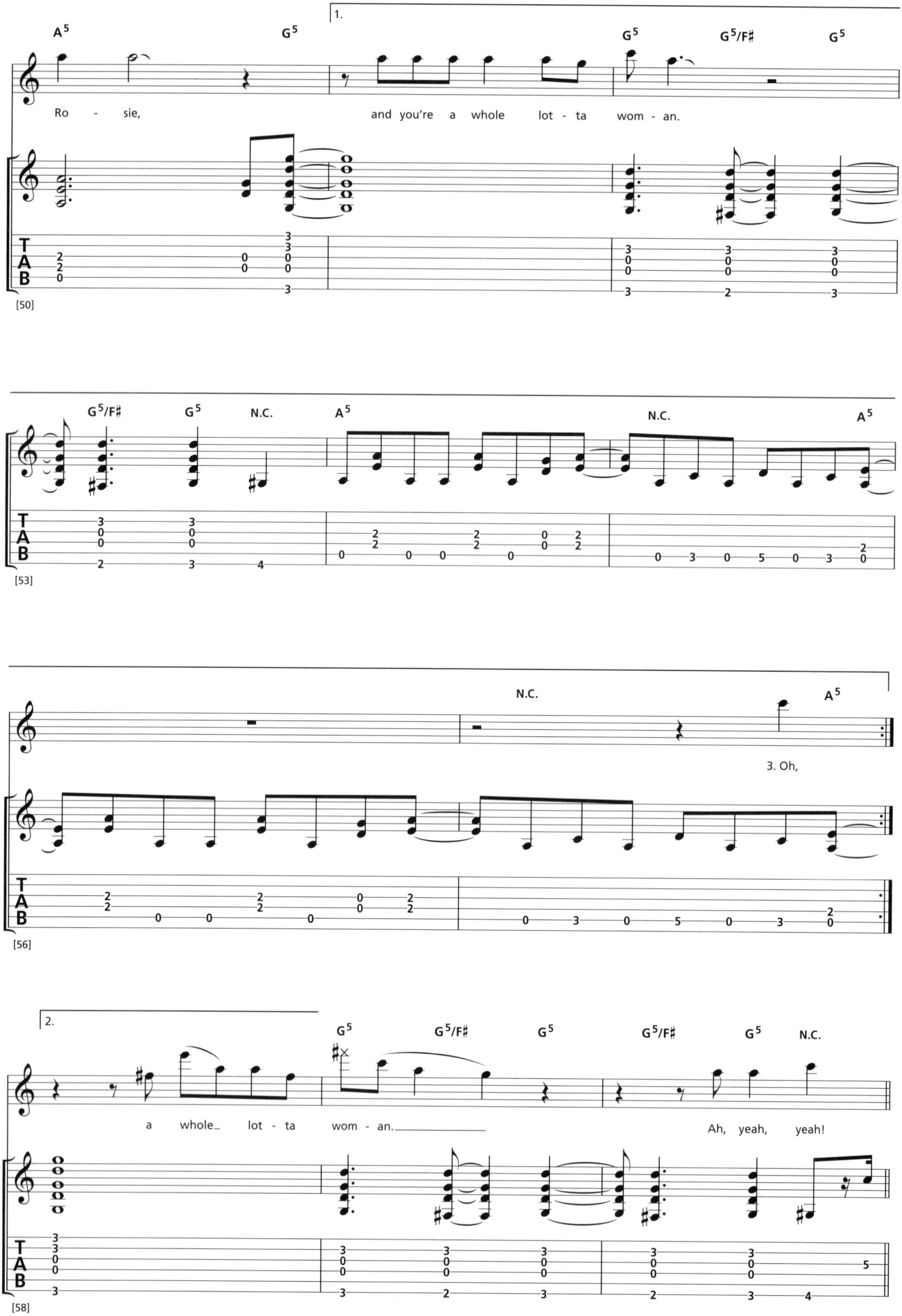
1.
A5
G5
G5
G5/F♯
G5
Ro - sie,
and you're a whole lot - ta wom - an.
[50]
G5/F♯
G5
N.C.
A5
N.C.
A5
[53]
N.C.
A5
3. Oh,
[56]
2.
G5
G5/F♯
G5
G5/F♯
G5
N.C.
a whole_ lot - ta wom - an._
Ah, yeah, yeah!
[58]

Guitar Solo

A5
N.C.
A5
[61]
N.C.
A5
N.C.
A5
[64]
N.C.
A5
BU
BD
BU
BD
[67]
N.C.
A5
RP
[70]
N.C.
A5
(RP)
[72]
N.C.
A5
[74]

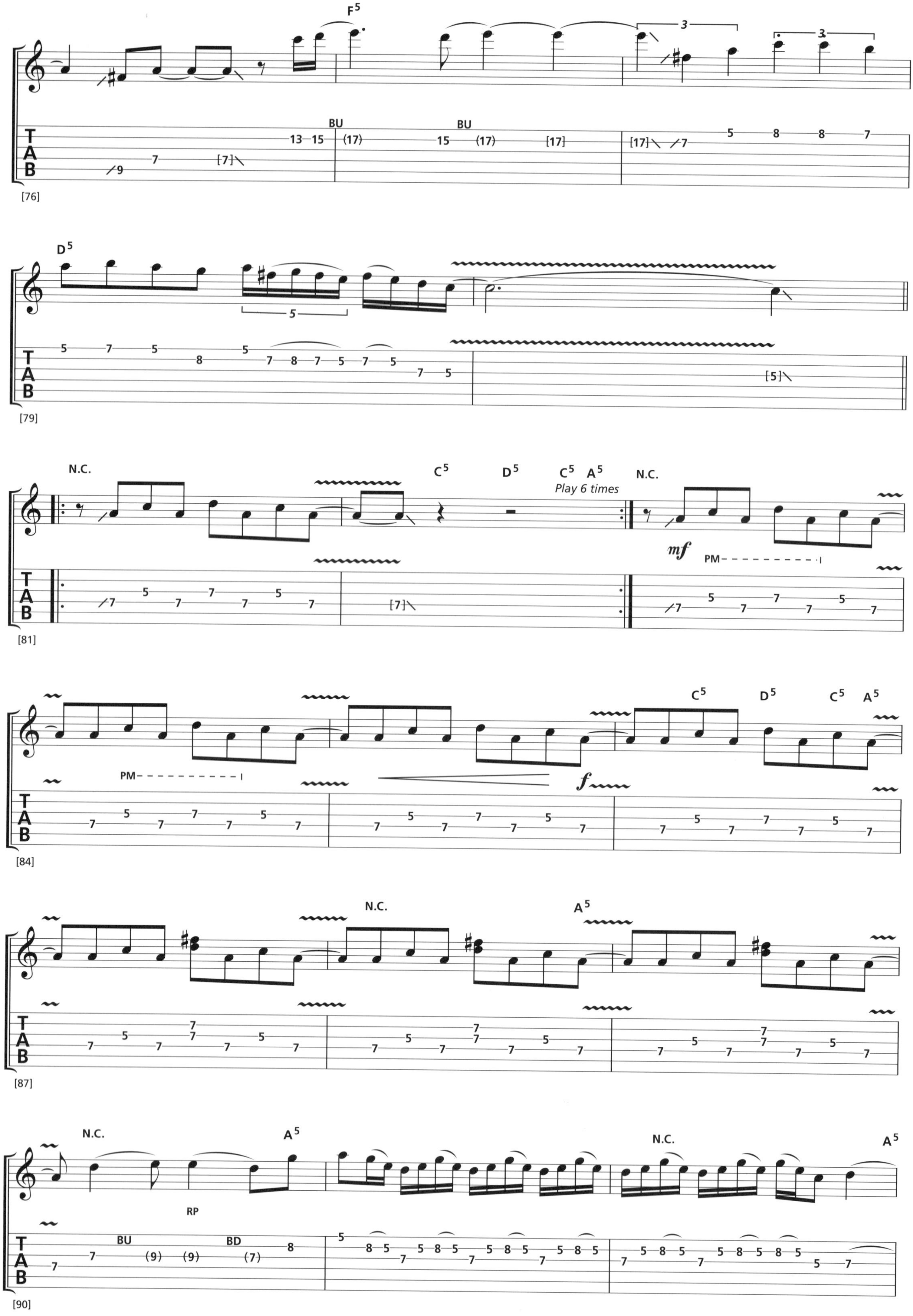
F5
BU
3
[76]
D5
5
[79]
N.C.
C5
D5
C5 A5
Play 6 times
mf
PM
[81]
PM
f
C5 D5 C5 A5
[84]
N.C.
A5
[87]
N.C.
A5
BU
RP
BD
N.C.
A5
[90]

N.C.
A5
[93]
N.C.
A5
[96]
N.C.
A5
[98]
N.C.
A5
Oh, a whole lot - ta
[100]
Chorus
F5
D5
wom - an, a whole lot - ta wom - an,
[103]

A5
G5
a whole lot - ta Ro - sie,
whole lot - ta
[106]
A5
G5
A5
G5
Ro - sie,
a whole lot - ta Ro - sie.
[109]
G5
G5/F♯
G5
G5/F♯
G5
N.C.
You're a whole lot - ta,
you're a whole lot - ta Ro - sie.
[112]
A
[115]

Notes On The Full Transcription

Bars 61–80 | *Solo 1*
This solo starts in the familiar 'box' position of the A minor pentatonic scale, using lots of string bends and Angus Young's signature fast and wide vibrato. The next section of the solo features fast picked lines that use the A natural minor scale and leads into the question/answer section of the song and then continues with more high-speed phrases that lead to the chorus.

Bars 61–66 | *Ghost picking*
Although this is technically a lead guitar lick it may be better to think of it as a rhythm part. Keeping your hand in a constant alternate picking motion between picked notes may help with this. When you don't want to strike the strings, move your pick a small distance away from them while maintaining the constant picking motion. This is called ghost picking and is similar to the ghost strumming method which you may be familiar with already. The song's high tempo means you will need to keep your 'strumming' action economical by avoiding moving too far past the string with each movement (Fig. 1).

Bar 62 | *Fast and wide vibrato*
Vibrato is one of the most instantly recognisable aspects of a guitarist's style. Angus Young's fast and wide vibrato is no exception. Whether you decide to imitate Young's vibrato style or not, you should ensure that your chosen vibrato is of consistent depth and speed, otherwise your playing will sound out of tune and lack the professional effect you are aspiring to.

Bar 72 | *Applying vibrato to bends*
This advanced technique requires a lot of control to execute correctly. Focus first on getting the initial bend to sound in tune, then add vibrato. Some players apply vibrato by releasing the bend by a *tiny* amount and returning it to its 'in tune' position. Others prefer to apply vibrato from the in-tune position in the same way you would an unbent string. Experiment with both approaches before deciding which you prefer.

Bars 72–75 | *Fast runs*
There are several fast runs in these bars and at 161 BPM, even the most experienced guitarists will find these phrases a challenge. Break each phrase down into small sections – work on a beat at a time if necessary. Pay close attention to accuracy and reducing excess picking motion (i.e. the pick moving too far from the string after it's picked). Don't increase the speed until you can play each phrase cleanly.

Bars 73–74 | *Licks as exercises*
Bar 73 is a perfect example of how part of a solo can be used to create an exercise to build your technique. It is a repeated four note pattern that is also used in the first 3 beats of the following bar. In isolation this is an excellent picking and coordination exercise. Set your metronome to a slow tempo of around 70BPM and use alternate picking. Focus on accuracy at all time and only increase the speed when you can play the exercise cleanly and without errors (Fig. 2).

Bars 90–102 | *Solo 2*
The second solo starts at the 5th fret and then moves to the 17th fret to play an octave higher. This creates a sense of excitement leading into the final chorus. It contains many classic pentatonic licks and while you may not wish to learn the original solo note for note there is a wealth of material here that would integrate into any guitarist's repertoire.

Bars 98–99 | *Picking options*
There are several ways to pick the phrase that starts on the last 16th note of bar 98. One is to move the pick across the strings in a single sweeping motion. This makes the lick easier to play, but the sweep will move the pick further away from the E string, which at 161 BPM can make repeating the lick a challenge. Another option is to play two upstrokes followed by a downstroke. Although the pick has to travel further to play the note on the G string, the downstroke moves the pick in the direction of the first note on the next beat. Try both methods and see which you prefer.

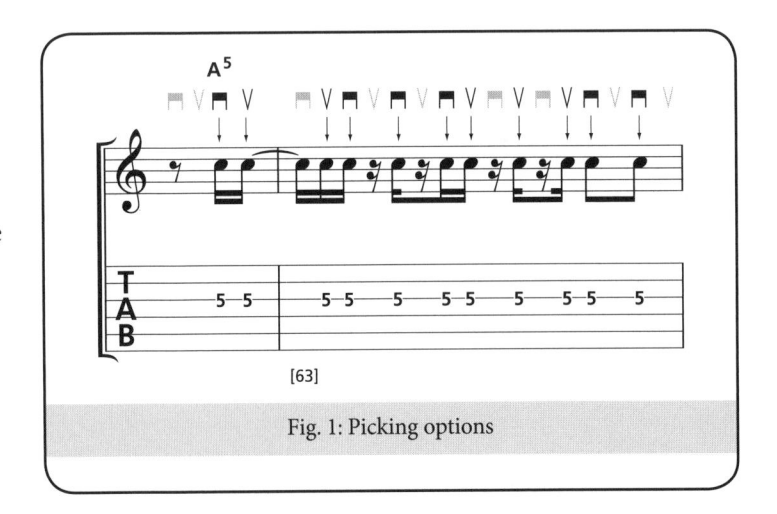

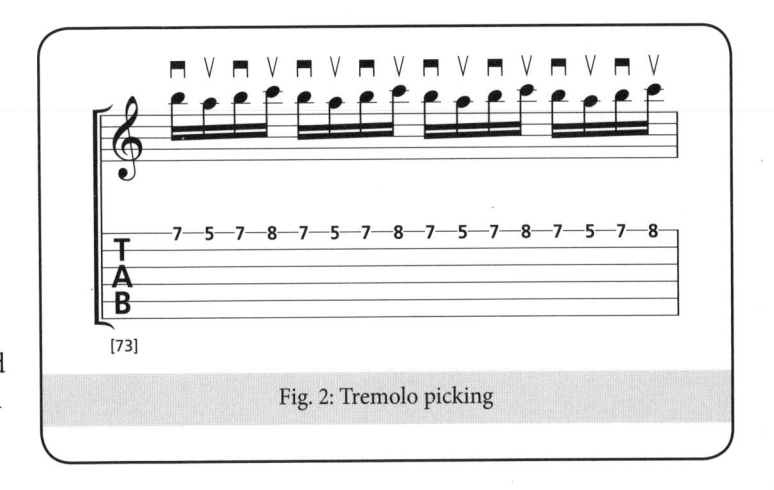

Fig. 1: Picking options

Fig. 2: Tremolo picking

CD TRACK COPYRIGHT INFORMATION

CD 1 & CD 2:

Before I Fall To Pieces
(Borrell/Burrows)
Sony/ATV Music Publishing

The Boys Are Back In Town
(Lynott)
Universal Music Publishing Limited

Don't Look Back In Anger
(Gallagher)
Sony/ATV Music Publishing

Edge Of Darkness
(Clapton/Kamen)
E.C. Music Limited/Intersong Music Ltd.

For Whom The Bell Tolls
(Hetfield/Ulrich/Burton)
Universal Music Publishing Limited

Ice 9
(Satriani)
Sony/ATV Music Publishing

Iron Man
(Iommi/Butler/Ward/Osbourne)
Westminster Music Limited

Whole Lotta Rosie
(Young/Young/Scott)
J. Albert & Son Pty. Limited

mcps